Writing

Related titles from Palgrave Macmillan

Julia Casterton, *Creative Writing: A Practical Approach Guide*, 3rd edition
Robert Graham, Helen Newall, Heather Leach, John Singleton (eds), *The Road to Somewhere: A Creative Writing Companion*
John Singleton and Mary Luckhurst (eds), *The Creative Writing Handbook: Techniques for New Writers*, 2nd edition

Writing

Self and Reflexivity

Celia Hunt and Fiona Sampson

palgrave

First edition published 2006 by
PALGRAVE MACMILLAN
Houndmills, Basingstoke, Hampshire RG21 6XS and
175 Fifth Avenue, New York, N. Y. 10010
Companies and representatives throughout the world

PALGRAVE MACMILLAN is the global academic imprint of the Palgrave Macmillan division of St. Martin's Press, LLC and of Palgrave Macmillan Ltd. Macmillan® is a registered trademark in the United States, United Kingdom and other countries. Palgrave is a registered trademark in the European Union and other countries.

ISBN-13: 978–1–4039–1876–5   hardback
ISBN-10: 1–4039–1876–7   hardback
ISBN-13: 978–1–4039–1877–2   paperback
ISBN-10: 1–4039–1877–5   paperback

This book is printed on paper suitable for recycling and made from fully managed and sustained forest sources.

A catalogue record for this book is available from the British Library.

Library of Congress Cataloging-in-Publication Data
Hunt, Celia.
    Writing : self and reflexivity / Celia Hunt and Fiona Sampson.
        p. cm.
    Includes bibliographical references and index.
    ISBN 1–4039–1876–7 (cloth) – ISBN 1–4039–1877–5 (pbk.)
        1. Authorship. 2. Creative writing. 3. Self in literature. I. Sampson, Fiona.
    II. Title.

PN145.H86 2005
808′.02–dc22   2005049317

10   9   8   7   6   5   4   3   2   1
15 14 13 12 11 10 09 08 07 06

Printed and bound in China

To our students

Contents

Preface and Acknowledgements

This book comes out of many years' experience in the field of teaching creative writing. Some of that experience even predates the rapid current expansion of creative writing as a subject specialism in Higher Education. This development has allowed students but also practising writers the space to think *about* their discipline; since writing is inherently a reflexive practice – or so we're arguing here – that space for reflection is good for our writing itself.

Many monographs and textbooks have looked at writing process: it is, after all, one of the most significant ways a culture makes for itself through the world. This book concentrates on the reflexive, self-aware writer who is at the heart of writing practice. It also reflects two different bodies of experience: we do not teach together on a single course in one institution, though we're long-term colleagues in the field of creative writing. The book reflects the kind of working dialogue we've had over a dozen years. We believe the greater range of experience and approaches such dialogue brings opens up this book in terms of the richness of its material; but that it will also allow it to be used in several ways, both supporting student processes and as a critical monograph. The book's starting points, the 'Introduction' and the chapter on 'The Self', are jointly written. Celia wrote the chapters which expand on these in the first half of the book – 'Voice', 'Authorship', 'Creativity', 'The Reader', 'Characters and Selves' – and Fiona those in the second half: 'Memory and History', 'Geography and Culture', 'Embodied Selves', 'An Essential Self?'.

We have dedicated this book to our students, whose learning and writing processes have so challenged and developed our own. We will also like to thank colleagues and friends who have read drafts of chapters in progress: Phyllis Creme, Patricia Duncker, Michael Moran, Amir Or, Alice Owens, Bernard Paris, Trevor Pateman, Rob Pope,

Robert Simpson. We are also grateful for permission to quote from published and unpublished works as follows:

Extract from *Lost in the Funhouse* by John Barth © 1968.

Extracts from *Roland Barthes* by Roland Barthes, translated by Richard Howard. Translation copyright © 1977 by Farrar, Straus and Giroux, Inc. Reproduced by permission of Hill and Wang, a division of Farrar, Straus and Giroux, LLC, and Palgrave Macmillan Ltd.

Extracts from *Brunizem* by Sujata Bhatt © 1988, reproduced by permission of the publishers Carcanet Press Limited.

Extracts from *Hallucinating Foucault* by Patricia Duncker © 1996 reproduced by permission of the publishers Serpents Tail Publishers.

Extract from *A Farewell to Arms* by Ernest Hemingway published by Jonathan Cape. Reproduced by permission of The Random House Group Ltd. Also with permission of Scribner, an imprint of Simon & Schuster Adult Publishing Group. Copyright 1929 by Charles Scribner's Sons. Copyright renewed © 1957 by Ernest Hemingway.

Extracts from *The Unbearable Lightness of Being* by Milan Kundera, English translation copyright © Harper and Row, Publishers, Inc. 1984. Used by permission of Faber and Faber Publishers.

Extracts from *Six Characters in Search of an Author and Other Plays* by Luigi Pirandello, translated by Mark Musa, copyright © 1995 by Mark Musa. Used by permission of Penguin, a division of Penguin Group (USA) Inc.

Extracts from *Words* by Jean-Paul Sartre, English translation by Irene Clephane, copyright © 1964 by George Braziller and Hamish Hamilton Ltd. Originally published in France as *Les Mots* 1964, copyright © Editions Gallimard, 1964; reprinted by permission of Georges Borchart Agency Inc., for Editions Gallimard, and Penguin Books, U.K.

Extract from Wallace Stevens' poem 'Credences of Summer' from *Selected Poems* reproduced by permission of Faber & Faber Ltd. and from *The Collected Poems of Wallace Stevens* by Wallace Stevens, © 1954 by Wallace Stevens and renewed 1982 by Holly Stevens. Used by permission of Alfred A. Knopf, a division of Random House, Inc.

'The Dress' by Mark Strand in *Selected Poems* 1995 reproduced by permission of the publishers Carcanet Press Limited. Also by permission of Alfred A. Knopf, a division of Random House, Inc. copyright © 1979, 1980 by Mark Strand.

Extract from *Collected Poems 1978–2003* by U.A. Fanthorpe © 2005, reproduced by permission of Peterloo Poets.

Introduction: Creative Writing as a Reflexive Practice

> My list of requirements for creativity begins with *motivation* and *courage*... My second requirement is *extensive experience* and *apprenticeship*... the next requirement [is] *insight into the workings of the self and into the workings of other minds*... Being able to know how your own mind works and how other minds work is an underlying prerequisite for creating great art.
>
> Antonio Damasio, 'Some Notes on Brain, Imagination and Creativity', 2001, p. 64.

It is commonly said that in order to be able to drive a car well we have to stop thinking about it. If we focus too much on the vehicle and how we're operating it – how the gears work or which pedal to press when – we're likely to end up in a ditch. The process has to become automatic. Somehow, and sooner rather than later, we have to reach the stage in which we're no longer consciously concerned about where we put our feet or how to manoeuvre a narrow gap. To drive smoothly and efficiently, we have to lose our self-consciousness and become one with the car. Writing, at its best, is like that too. If we focus too hard on what we want to say and how we want to say it, the page or the screen may remain stubbornly blank, or words may appear but refuse to come alive or convey what we want them to. Only when we stop trying and become absorbed in the work – when we *lose ourselves* in the writing – does the process begin in earnest.

T.S. Eliot thought of this 'loss' of self in the writing process as an 'escape from personality'. The writer, he believed, needs to be a vehicle, 'a finely perfected medium' through which feelings and emotions can 'enter into new combinations'; those feelings and emotions, however, not reflecting the writer's needs for self-expression but being the ones appropriate for the work of art (Eliot, 1953, pp. 26, 30). And some of the most influential thinkers on the relationship between creative writers and their writing, as we will see later, regard writing as a 'self-less' process.

But if we think about this carefully for a moment the idea that creative writing is a process of moving away from our own self seems insufficient to describe what is often an intensely personal experience: especially when we are drawing on our memories or trying to capture in words a particularly strong or painful experience. For many established writers writing isn't possible without a deep connection with the self. 'Writers who are not self-obsessed and wriggling through what they hope are their own labyrinthine psyches are very likely not writers at all', says novelist Jenni Diski (Diski, 1998, p. 45). And poet Ted Hughes, talking about Sylvia Plath's poetry, says: 'It's my suspicion that no poem can be a poem that is not a statement from the powers in control of our life, the ultimate suffering and decision in us' (Heaney, 1988, p. 161).

So we seem to have a contradiction: creative writing is deeply personal, deeply connected with the writer's self, but it also involves moving away from the self and becoming impersonal. How are we to understand this? The first thing to say is that impersonality doesn't need to imply an *escape* from the self. As David Lodge suggests, Eliot's 'cultivation of the idea of "impersonality" was in part a manoeuvre designed to conceal the very personal sources of his own poetry from inquisitive critics' (Lodge, 2002, p. 97). What Eliot calls impersonality is more usefully understood as *adopting a different stance towards* the personal. It involves relinquishing, even if only temporarily, the deep personal connection we have with our material; it requires a kind of internal distancing, allowing a space to open up between ourselves and our material, so that it can develop a life of its own in our imagination. This also makes it possible for us to bring our already-incorporated knowledge of the craft of writing to bear on this material, so that it can be transformed into art. Understanding Eliot's impersonality in this way means that there is, in fact, no contradiction between the personal and the impersonal in the writing process, for in order to develop as writers we need to be able both to plumb our own depths for the material for our writing and to set that material free so that it can be transformed into art; in other words we need to be able both to access and objectify our material.

But how can we do both of these things at the same time? This is a question that lies at the core of this book. Being able simultaneously to access and objectify our deeply felt material isn't easy; nor is it something that we just learn how to do once and for all and then it ceases to be a problem. In any writing process there is always going to be a tension between our own personal needs and the need of the writing to have a life of its own. Seamus Heaney is aware of this tension when he says that 'the poet need[s] to get beyond ego in order to become the voice of more than autobiography' (Heaney, 1988, p. 148). Many of us start to write out of autobiographical material: ourselves and our own experiences, things that preoccupy or perplex us. And that is perfectly legitimate; it is easier to start from the known than the unknown. But the danger of using autobiographical material is that, precisely because we know it so well, we may not be able to distance ourselves sufficiently from it to allow it to develop into art.

This is what Heaney suggests is the case with some of Sylvia Plath's poems, such as her famous 'Daddy' and 'Lady Lazarus'. In his view these poems are less successful than others because they are 'slighted in favour of the intense personal need of the poet'. A poem such as 'Edge', written in the last weeks before she died, does not fall into that category; it has achieved 'objectivity, a perfected economy of line, a swift surehanded marking of the time and space which had been in waiting for this poem'. It is 'a thing sufficient within itself' (Heaney, 1988, pp. 164–65, 168). But in the writing of 'Daddy' and 'Lady Lazarus', he implies, Plath has not been able to let go of the material sufficiently to allow it to become an object in its own right, separate from its author. Whether or not we agree with this rereading of Plath's late work, we might say that there can be too much closeness between the writer and her writing; and that it is possible to access deeply felt material without being able to objectify it sufficiently.

Conversely, the consequences of *not* accessing our felt material for our writing can be just as troublesome as failing to objectify it. It's not unusual to encounter people in creative writing classes – people who have in fact been writing for a long time – who have developed the craft of writing to a high degree but who have a sense that something is missing from the finished product, that the writing is 'dead' on the page. Their inability – or their unwillingness – to access their own deep personal material has prevented them from imbuing the writing with *felt* life.

What we are talking about here, then, is the need for *reflexivity*. Reflexivity is an important concept with a wide currency in contemporary thought, and it will help us to clarify it if, following Donna Qualley, we compare it with the closely related term 'reflection'.

When we reflect on something, we think about things that are in the main readily available to us. We 'take thought', as the saying goes, with its implication that those thoughts are there waiting to be taken. Reflection does not necessitate a change in the person reflecting (although the results of our reflections may lead to change), nor does it necessarily involve an engagement with another person (although we may reflect *with* others). Essentially, reflection is an individual activity that takes place independently of others (Qualley, 1997, p. 11).

Reflexivity is a different process and potentially a deeper one. At its heart is a particular kind of 'engagement with an "other"' (p. 11), whether another person or oneself as 'other'. Where reflection could be said to involve taking something into oneself – a topic, an event, a relationship – for the purpose of contemplation or examination, reflexivity involves putting something out in order that something new might come into being. It involves creating an internal space, distancing ourselves from ourselves, as it were, so that we are both 'inside' and 'outside' ourselves simultaneously and able to switch back and forth fluidly and playfully from one position to the other, giving ourselves up to the experience of 'self as other' whilst also retaining a grounding in our familiar sense of self.

In research in the social sciences, in anthropology for example, reflexivity is used to denote the ideal stance of researchers in relation to people they are working with, their so-called research 'subjects'. Contemporary anthropologists, instead of assuming that they are neutral observers, will be aware of the way they themselves influence the research process, and their reflections on their role will become an integral part of the written report. This approach involves suspending assumptions they've absorbed from their own culture and engaging with people from other cultures as far as possible on their own terms (Aull, 1999). Thus reflexivity involves not *getting rid* of the self, but *doubling* the self: distancing ourselves from ourselves to a greater or lesser extent, so that we have a sense of standing outside ourselves and observing what we are doing and thinking.

That there is a necessary reflexivity or doubling of self in the creative process has been recognised by a wide range of thinkers. For Sigmund Freud, the creative artist is blessed with 'a certain flexibility in the repressions' (Freud, 1949, p. 314), by which he means a greater ability than other people to suspend the potential criticism of his 'ego-self' and to listen to the unconscious. This, together with his highly developed techniques of writing, enables the creative writer to transform his (sexual) fantasies into art and to allow others to enjoy them without shame (Freud, 1908). Object-relations theorist Marion Milner also identifies a reflexive mechanism in the creative process, but sees it as universal rather than at work only in exceptional individuals. She posits two different 'modes of attention' in this process: the chaotic creative mode – what she thinks of as 'attending with the imaginative body', because of the accompanying sense of extension in space – which facilitates close contact with the inner life; and the more reasoned and orderly critical mode, which involves distancing and which facilitates the shaping or editing of the creative material. In Milner's view, the creative process involves not *expelling* the self but learning to switch back and forth smoothly between these two modes of attention or different senses of self, developing a 'dialogue relation' between them (Milner, 1971, p. 73).

How, then, can we learn both to access and objectify our personal material in order to develop reflexivity in our writing process? Many good and useful books are available now as guides. Some, such as Natalie Goldberg's *Writing Down the Bones* (1986) and Dorothea Brande's *Becoming a Writer* (1934), offer excellent suggestions for how to access our deep feelings and emotions for writing. Others, such as Peter Sansom's *Writing Poems* (1994) and Janet Burroway's *Writing Fiction: a guide to narrative craft* (2002) offer helpful suggestions for developing the craft of writing and thus being able to work on the material we have accessed. We can strengthen our ability to objectify our material by sharing our writing with other people on a regular basis, whether with individuals or in writing groups, and receiving critical feedback on it. This can help us to develop a more external view of our writing and learn how to become our own reader. These are important and useful ways of developing reflexivity for writing. The approach we adopt in this book is rather different, but – we suggest – complementary.

Underlying our approach is the assumption that engaging in creative writing is itself a reflexive practice. Some recent and contemporary analysts of the writing process, whom we will be discussing later, point out that writing, indeed all language, is intrinsically reflexive; that the moment we speak or commit words to the page we are doubling ourselves. For Jacques Derrida, there is an unbridgeable gap or *différence* between ourselves and our words (Derrida, 1976) and therefore the use of words in speech or writing always involves a doubling of the self, or 'being two-to-speak' (Derrida, 1992, p. 153; in

Royle, 2003, p. 127). Roland Barthes suggests a similar idea: the 'person' who speaks in the narrative is not identical with the 'real life' person who does the writing; so there are always at least two 'selves' in the writing process (Barthes, 1966, p. 261). Mikhail Bakhtin, whose term 'dialogic' carries a meaning similar to 'reflexive', suggests that creative writing is considerably more dialogic than everyday speech or writing. By this he means that creative writing – and he is talking about fiction rather than poetry – contains a high degree of 'double-voicing'. This is observable in literary styles such as irony and parody, where it is possible to 'hear' more than one point of view in the single voice of the narrator, but it is particularly noticeable in the 'free indirect style', used, for example, by Jane Austen and Virginia Woolf, which combines elements of first and third person in a single narrative voice (Bakhtin, 1981).

If creative writing is intrinsically double-voiced, as these thinkers suggest, then engaging in it offers us the opportunity of, as it were, practising reflexivity within the text, of experiencing the doubleness which reflexivity involves. But *understanding* how that reflexivity operates can, we suggest, be even more helpful to us in our develop-ment as writers. Standing back from the creative process and observ-ing the reflexivity going on within it gives us, in other words, a second degree of reflexivity, not simply a doubling of the self but a tripling. This book, itself 'double-voiced', works with that second degree of reflexivity in two ways: not only looking at theoretical understandings of what the writing process involves, but providing an opportunity to enter into a creative relationship with contemporary theory through writing exercises.

The benefits of this approach are several. Reflecting on the writing process from different points of view can put us in touch with unex-pected material for our writing. Moreover, understanding our own personal connection with the writing process can deepen and enrich our writing. Understanding ourselves in relation to the writing process can help us to develop a strong 'writing identity', a term we discuss in Chapters 2 and 3; and increasing our understanding of reflexivity in writing through a study of relevant theory can help us to work creatively with difficulties in accessing and objectifying personal material.

There is a further dimension to this approach, though it's not the main focus of this particular book. Exploring the relationship between ourselves and our writing process can lead to a changed sense of self.

This might happen through the writing process, through the closer connection with the inner life brought about as a result of thinking about topics such as voice and authorship, or through finding that the writing we have produced revealed things about ourselves of which we were not fully aware. For Donald Winnicott, as for many other psychoanalytic thinkers, the creative process is intrinsically self-developmental. Because both creativity and self-development, he suggests, take place in the 'potential space' between the person and the outside world – the 'intermediate area of experience' between inner and outer reality – in the creation of artwork the creative artist opens up the possibility of being transformed (Winnicott, 1971, pp. 13, 95–103).

Some literary critics also highlight the developmental or transformative potential of creative writing. For Bakhtin, the intrinsic 'heteroglossia' or 'multi-voicedness' of the novel allows the novelist to give space on the page to the many different voices of the self and to enter into a relationship with them on equal terms (Bakhtin, 1984). For Julia Kristeva, poetic language, because of its connection with the 'semiotic' – the pre-linguistic realm which manifests itself primarily through rhythm, sound and bodily feelings – has the potential for disrupting our tendency to become fixed in the 'symbolic', the realm of symbols, grammar and syntax (Kristeva, 1984b). In both these accounts, creative writing can help us to develop a more fluid and flexible relationship with ourselves, to become what Bakhtin calls 'polyphonic', able to give all the different voices of the self equal space; or what Kristeva calls a 'subject-in-process', whose identity isn't fixed but constantly developed and developing through experience (see Hunt, 2000, 2004a, 2004b; Sampson, 1998, 2004; and Hunt and Sampson, 1998).

To sum up, then, there is a creative tension, within the writing process, between action and reflection; between processes we understand and those of which we are less conscious. Yet, to return to our opening analogy of driving a car, once we've mastered the controls and have gained a degree of confidence in ourselves as drivers, the lessons we've learned should become part of the unconscious 'toolkit' in the background of our writing process.

Any discussion of creative writing as a reflexive practice must inevitably begin with a consideration of the concept of self. Thus the opening chapter sets out our thinking on this topic and provides a framework for the remaining chapters, which can be read in any order. These chapters unpack aspects of selfhood, both on and off the page, although our focus remains the many ways to think about selves engaged in the writing process. In the first three chapters – 'Voice', 'Authorship', 'Creativity'– we look at *writing process* as the envelope in which certain versions of ourselves may be at work. Next – in 'The Reader' and 'Characters and Selves' – we see how *selves on the page* are staged through writing. Three further chapters, 'Embodied Selves', 'Geography and Culture' and 'Memory and History' examine how *the located self* limits, and creates opportunities within, what we write. We return to questions about the identity of the self who writes in our final chapter, which rethinks the problems of *essentialism* for writing identity. Our thinking in each chapter ends with exercises that can be used for extending and deepening thinking and writing practice, either alone or in a group context.

1   The Self

> The house of fiction does not readily admit the self... Your relation-
> ship with it, as its creator, is tenuous, complex, subtle, utterly
> demanding. You are in it: you are absolutely stripped bare in front of
> it, exposed; yet somehow you are supposed to make sure that, at the
> end of the day when the lights are dimmed, the fire's blazing and
> everyone is sitting comfortably, it isn't *you* they see.
>
> Sue Roe, 'Shelving the Self', 1994, p. 51.

In her reflections on her experience of working on a novel Sue Roe
captures the paradox of the self in the writing process. The self is
deeply involved in the process – 'stripped bare', 'exposed' – but at the
same time it has to be 'shelved', removed from sight. How can we
understand the self as reflexive in the way Roe suggests? In this first
chapter we provide an overview of dominant trends in thinking about
the difficult and much-contested concept of self, in order to locate
our own approach and to provide a context for the remainder of the
book.

The humanist view of self

When we ask people, as we often do in our teaching, what they think
of as their 'self', we get a wide variety of answers. Yet one particular
idea looms large: the self as an entity existing somewhere inside us, a
single real or true self which we are constantly searching for and will
someday discover. This conception of self is part of what has been
called the 'grand narrative' of humanism and, by post-modernists, of
'modernism' (Lyotard, 2001). It assumes a rational order underlying
the natural world and an essential human nature underlying the
world of human beings; it privileges the mind with its powers of
reasoning over the body, experience and emotion.

The origins of humanist thinking can be traced as far back as ancient Greece, in the division of the human being into the body and the soul propounded by Plato (427–347 BC), for example in the simile of the cave, in which he argues that the 'real' world is more important and attractive than its mental 'reflection' (Plato, 1965, pp. 278–83). The soul is the incorporeal, ideal Form of the person, one of the many ideal Forms that lie behind the particular examples of things in the world. We know that the soul exists before we are born, Plato says, because knowledge is recollection, which implies that our souls must have been elsewhere before becoming trapped in the body. On the death of the body, the soul returns to reside again in the eternal realm of ideal Forms (Plato, 2002, pp. 47–53).

Christianity absorbs this split between the material body and the immortal soul. The soul is now seen as a spiritual essence derived from God and, whilst its sojourn in the body is problematical because of man's 'fall from grace' through 'original sin', there is salvation for the righteous on the death of the body when the soul returns to its origins in God's heaven. For Christian theologian Thomas Aquinas (1225–74), man's soul is not just immortal but rational, in that the faculty of reason is seen as having been given to man in order that he can access God's truth. Human knowledge is therefore always knowledge of God (Aquinas, 1952).

There is a similar privileging of the rational mind or soul in the philosophy of René Descartes (1596–1650), although his concerns are more scientific and mathematical than religious. In his quest to find a solid basis on which to develop scientific knowledge, Descartes subjected all his knowledge – all the opinions he had derived from study and all his observations of the world around him – to a strict process of doubt. As he did so, he observed that the only thing he could not doubt was that there was an 'I' doing the thinking and the doubting. This 'thinking thing' (*res cogitans*), the mind or the soul, thus became the first principle of his philosophy: 'Cogito ergo sum' or 'I think therefore I am', and was distinguished sharply from the body (*res extensa*): '…I recognised that I was a substance whose whole essence or nature is to be conscious and whose being requires no place and depends on no material thing. Thus this self, that is to say the soul, by which I am what I am, is entirely distinct from the body…' (Descartes, 1970, p. 32).[1]

Whilst, for Descartes, reliable thinking and reasoning presuppose the existence of God, for the eighteenth century 'enlightenment' thinkers reason did not need God for its operations. The seventeenth century discoveries of Galileo, Isaac Newton and others in the natural sciences had given rise to the view that Nature had its own mechanistic order, which only needed God's occasional small adjustments to keep it working properly. Enlightenment thinkers, such as David Hume, Adam Smith, Denis Diderot and F.M.A. Voltaire (Hume, 1989; Smith, 2003; Diderot, 2003; Voltaire, 1972) believed that there must be a similar order for the human world, which it was possible to discover through similar scientific methods of observation and experiment. All that was needed to determine what was 'true, or right, or good, or beautiful' for all men was the correct application of analytic reason (Berlin, 1997, pp. 1–24). These ideas, coupled with the rise of a new 'humanism' based on a reinterpretation of the Renaissance, enabled German-speaking historians and philosophers of the late eighteenth and early nineteenth centuries, such as Friedrich Schiller, J.W. von Goethe, Wilhelm von Humboldt and later Jacob Burckhardt, to develop the notion of a universal humanity or human-ness as the 'inseparable and central essence, the defining quality, of human beings' (Davies, 1997, p. 24).

The English Romantic poets of the early nineteenth century, such as William Blake, Samuel Taylor Coleridge, William Wordsworth, John Keats and Percy Bysshe Shelley, were strongly opposed to what they saw as the mechanistic nature of Enlightenment thought and its dehumanising social consequences in the Industrial Revolution of the late eighteenth century; and were not strictly speaking part of the humanist tradition. However, they also believed that human beings had a central essence. Their conception of the self was not so much Descartes' 'thinking substance' but more Plato's pure spirit whose imaginative powers put us in touch with an 'ultimate reality' beyond the everyday world. Nature, the innocence of childhood, dreams and reveries, and particularly poetry, were variously regarded as privileged points of entry into this transcendental realm. Abstract reason and the body were to a greater or lesser extent denigrated, and the poet cultivated the imaginative state in order to escape the body and gain insight, through his writing, into the realm of the spirit (Bowra, 1966, pp. 1–24).

With the increasing growth and sophistication of science and technology at the end of the nineteenth century, there was a return to the Enlightenment belief in the power of reason (see Chapter 7 below). Both the natural world and the social world of human beings came to be seen as underpinned by laws of nature that were essentially know-able through scientific methods of observation and interpretation. 'Man' was regarded as essentially 'perfectible' (Passmore, 1970), and it was held that social 'systems' could be instituted in order to make progress towards this ideal state. In the twentieth century the social sciences began this task in earnest, using the methods of the natural sciences. Second generation psychoanalytic thinkers, such as Donald Winnicott (1960), advocated psychotherapeutic methods as a means of accessing the 'real' or 'true' self of essential human nature, which had been obscured by the 'false self' formed in the personality by inadequate parenting.

Humanist thinking, and the modernism it led to, with its emphasis on fixed essences and particularly the idea of the self as an entity at the core of the individual, was dominant from the end of the nineteenth century until the middle of the twentieth. It continues to occupy a central place in the popular imagination, and to be a central tenet of Christianity; and other closely related religions, including Hasidic Judaism and Islam (Solomon, 2000; Arberry, 1964). But around the mid-twentieth century it came under serious attack from new thinking in the social sciences and the humanities. And indeed an essentialist view of self does not enable us to understand the self as reflexive or open to change and development, nor does it account adequately for the role of body, language, society or culture in the making of the person. But the abandonment of this view of self by the humanities and the social sciences has led to a rejection of the possibility that there is anything innate in the development of self or personal identity,[2] or indeed that there is anything we can call 'self' at all.

Poststructuralist or postmodern views of the self

In the second half of the twentieth century the humanist or modernist view of self was challenged from a number of different directions, particularly by what is known as poststructuralist thinking, but also by social constructionism and some strands of feminist thinking. Whilst these are quite different approaches, what they have in common is the idea that language, society and culture *create* the self or, as it tends to be called by proponents of this way of thinking, the 'subject', a term that is seen to embrace within it the first person subject of consciousness as well as its subjection to linguistic, social and cultural forces. As language is the most powerful tool of society and culture, the subject is sometimes regarded as a 'text' (see Chapter 3) 'written' by its immersion in language.

The dismantling or 'decentring' of the humanist view of self was already begun at the turn of the twentieth century by Sigmund Freud's division of the self into the 'ego', the main organising agency of consciousness, the 'superego' or internalised conscience, and the 'id' or the instincts, as well as by his positing of the 'unconscious' as a repository of repressed memories which tended to emerge involuntarily into consciousness through jokes, daydreams and slips of the tongue or pen (Freud, 1991). Not only did the idea of the self as tripartite run counter to a notion of the self as unitary, but the idea that there was an unknown and unpredictable unconscious underlying the conscious mind indicated that the self was not in control and therefore could not be the centre of meaning.

Freud was also the first to identify the important role which language played in the psyche, particularly in the separation and individuation of the infant. The French psychoanalyst Jacques Lacan took this idea further in his theory of the 'mirror stage' in human development. According to Lacan, before the child acquires language, it inhabits a realm called the 'imaginary' where it has no sense of itself as separate from the mother. At around the age of eighteen months it catches sight of itself in a mirror and identifies with the image it sees there, believing this to be its 'real' or 'true' self. This misidentification causes a split in the child's sense of identity because it is still deeply embedded in the imaginary and has not yet entered fully into the realm of language and separation, the 'symbolic', so that it hasn't had the opportunity to develop a sense of self that comes from using language and relating as a separate being. When the child does enter the symbolic, its psyche becomes intrinsically split between the spectral image formed of itself in the Mirror Stage and the sense of itself derived from language and relating to others. It is only when the child starts acquiring language, according to Lacan, that the unconscious begins to form. Therefore, there can be no real or true self before language (Lacan, 1977).

For French philosopher Jacques Derrida, the idea that there is a real or true self is one of the 'centralising agencies of meaning' in Western thought, which he seeks to 'deconstruct'. This, he says, is not to deny the self's existence, but to dismantle the idea of self as a 'meta-linguistic substance or identity, some pure *cogito* of self-presence' (Kearney, 1984, p. 125). Derrida's view of self becomes clear in his discussion of the relationship between speech and writing. While in the traditional view consciousness or subjectivity is accessed directly via spoken language, for Derrida speech is 'always already' inhabited by 'writing', by which he means not simply words on the page but the 'trace' of language permanently inscribed in the unconscious as a result of our immersion in the social world. Thus the self, if one can speak of it at all, is not a fixed presence accessible via speech, but an *absence* or a non-present trace of language laid down without a person's conscious awareness, although, in Derrida's notion of the 'supplement', the self is both present and absent simultaneously, there but not there, '*located...* in a *nonlocatable* experience of language' (Derrida, 1998, p. 29). In other words, self is a sort of fiction created by language, its meaning always deferred.

In Michel Foucault's thinking, the idea of any kind of internal self is rejected, in favour of a subject who is wholly created by linguistic, social and cultural forces. The very idea of the self, he argues, is the consequence of a powerful, primarily medical but later psychoanalytic, discourse of sex and sexuality, which arose in the eighteenth and nineteenth centuries. Sexuality progressively came to be seen as a fundamental but dangerous drive at the core of the self. This necessitated the invention of increasingly rigorous 'technologies of the self' (Foucault, 1988), such as confession or psychoanalysis, to 'police' it and to uncover its truth, the medical community becoming expert mediators between the self and the individual (Foucault, 1990). Thus the medical community first created the 'self', and then took control over the ways in which people related to it. This, for Foucault, is a good example of how elements within a society acquire and exercise power through the creation of discourses.

French psychoanalyst and critic Julia Kristeva, strongly influenced by Jacques Lacan, also believes that the 'subject' is an effect of language, and that we do not become fully conscious of ourselves until we acquire it. But unlike Lacan she posits a role for pre-linguistic feelings in our sense of self. Her idea of the 'semiotic' is not just a state of 'mergedness' with the mother, as in Lacan's 'imaginary', but a safe holding space provided by the mother which, drawing on Plato, she calls the 'chora'. It is in this imaginary space that subjectivity begins to find a form through bodily feelings, rhythms, gestures and sound. This pre-linguistic semiotic realm of experience is not lost when the subject moves into the realm of language, the 'symbolic'; it remains as an essential part of signification or meaning making. It is particularly present in poetic language, which, Kristeva maintains, has the power to disrupt our tendency to take on fixed identities in language and helps us to be 'subjects-in-process', constantly in flux between the given and created dimensions of ourselves (Kristeva, 1984b). The self on this view is certainly not 'essentialist', in the sense that it is a process rather than a fixed entity, but an element of 'given-ness', in this instance real bodily feelings, is allowed into the frame. This is useful, as we shall see later.

For the originators of what is known as 'social constructionism,'[3] social psychologists Charles Horton Cooley and George Herbert Mead, the 'I' is a kind of 'reflected or looking-glass self' (Cooley, 1902) created out of what we imagine we are like in the minds of other people in society, particularly our parents. This leads to a duality of the self of first and third person, or the 'I' and the 'me', in which the 'I' is the self that acts and the 'me' is the self that observes the 'I' acting (Mead, 1934). In Erving Goffman's theory, a third 'self' is posited: the self as character who wears the mask or *persona* necessary to conform to what is required to live in a particular society or culture (Goffman, 1957). Masks or personas tend to become the primary elements of self-identity, and in societies where people have a variety of roles, whether within the family or society, they will have multiple personas (McCall, 1977, pp. 277–80). Discussions of the socially constructed self see the possibility of both social conformity and individual trans-formation within this model; a person will, in his relations with others, become aware of 'what sort of person he really is' (p. 280). This implies that there is a real or spontaneous sense of self under-lying the role-identity brought about by social relations, but that this has somehow become subverted in the course of development (Turner, 1976). This idea has not, however, been pursued into con-temporary social constructionism. Kenneth Gergen sees Western culture, with its proliferation of communication technologies and global reach, giving rise to a 'social saturation [which] brings with it a general loss in our assumption of true and knowable selves. As we absorb multiple voices, we find that each "truth" is relativised by our simultaneous consciousness of compelling alternatives. We come to be aware that each truth about ourselves is a construction of the moment, true only for a given time and within certain relationships' (Gergen, 1991, p. 16, in Stevens, 1996). This, he believes, can have both positive and negative consequences: positive in that it liberates us to engage in a 'protean life-style' (p. 245), able to invent and reinvent ourselves for different contexts or relationships, negative in that it can lead to the superficial and relativistic putting on and off of fashion identities of the moment (pp. 248–9).

These various lines of thinking, generally subsumed under the headings of 'postmodernist' or 'poststructuralist', are reacting against the humanist and modernist idea of self with its focus on the mind soul or human nature as the fixed centre of the self which, as an 'essence', must pre-exist language and immersion in the social world. Postmodernist thinking emphasises 'the subject' as fluid and multiple rather than fixed and singular, and the important role of language and other people in self-identity. It also, in some versions, such as that of Kristeva, gives a role to the body in creating our sense of self. Postmodernist thinking on the self, however, is not without its problems. Whilst it acknowledges and indeed celebrates the fluid and changing nature of the self, this change is often seen as taking place wholly within language. This means that if the subject is 'written' by its immersion in a language-based society and fixed in particular ideological discourses, then the only way change can come about at the level of the individual is by choosing another story or discourse from those available. In this respect the postmodernist 'subject' sounds almost as fixed as the humanist or modernist self, consisting of different stories or discourses not of its own making and able only to move between them. This is reflexivity of a conforming kind (see Giddens, 1991), which serves the purpose of maintaining the status quo, not reflexivity as open to change and development.

The rejection of a possible dimension of self outside of or preceding language restricts the scope for real change to take place at the level of the individual. Kristeva's idea of the 'subject-in-process', which provides space in self-development for the pre-linguistic, is the most useful of the postmodern theories in this respect, although Kristeva thinks of the pre-linguistic as a *pre-personal* element in language: as the pre-constitution of the thinking autonomous subject. Derrida is also interested in the pre-linguistic, but sees it as a ghostly presence/absence in language, which is partly resolved and partly generated by the Mirror Stage, but which undermines any attempt we might make to pin ourselves down or to find a personal identity (Derrida, 1998, pp. 12–18). A further problem with the postmodern view of self is that it does not help us to account for the sense of stability that most people experience. If our identity is constantly in a process of linguistic flux – if we are constantly 'in process' – how do we manage to function so well? What is it that enables us to have a sense of continuity over time and of being an agent in the world? A model of the self that helps us to understand our ability to change whilst also having a sense of continuity needs to embrace both a linguistic and a pre-linguistic dimension of self, in other words a role for 'nature' or the body in addition to 'nurture' or language, society and culture. Because of past abuses of innate theories of self, such as eugenics,[4] postmodernist thinking has set its face against acknowledging a role for nature in the making of the self, and the nurture view has come to dominate the humanities and social sciences. There remains, however, a growing body of work which sees the self as a product of *both* innate and acquired elements, and which brings together insights from a range of disciplines, including philosophy, developmental psychology, psychoanalysis, and the cognitive and neurosciences. This approach is potentially extremely useful to the humanities and social sciences, in that it provides a broad framework within which the insights of postmodernism into the linguistic and socially constructed nature of the self can be brought together with a notion of a 'core self' or a 'core sense of self' pre-existing and underlying language and immersion in society and culture; a core self, however, which is not the fixed, unitary self of humanist thinking.

Developing the idea of the self-in-process

Over the past twenty or thirty years empirical work in developmental psychology has accumulated strong evidence that babies have senses of self before they acquire language. Cognitive psychologist Ulric Neisser identifies two very early kinds of self-knowledge: the 'ecological' and 'interpersonal' senses of self. The 'ecological' sense of self is 'the self as perceived with respect to the physical environment: "I" am the person here in this place, engaged in this particular activity' (Neisser 1988, p. 36). Countering the psychoanalytic view that the baby 'cannot tell the difference between itself and the environment, or between itself and its mother', Neisser maintains that the ability to perceive oneself in relation to the environment is present from birth (p. 40). This relationship is directly perceived via the senses, with sight playing a central role. Support for Neisser's view comes from experiments that demonstrate young babies' ability to reach for specific visual targets (Butterworth, 1998, p. 90).[5]

The 'interpersonal' sense of self, which also appears in earliest infancy, is an awareness of the self 'engaged in immediate unreflective social interaction with another person': 'I am the person who is engaged, here, in this particular human interchange' (Neisser, 1988, pp. 41, 36). Experimental psychology talks about this relationship, too, as directly perceived and based on emotional and other forms of communication specific to human beings. In the mother-child relationship, it manifests itself in various kinds of 'non-verbal communication', such as prolonged eye-contact, and babies' mimicking of the mother's facial movements, such as poking out the tongue, which has been observed in the earliest hours of a child's life (Butterworth, 1998, p. 96).

Both the ecological and interpersonal senses of self are assumed to be innate and crucially important for establishing a sense of bodily agency in relation to the outside world. They contribute significantly to what psychotherapist Daniel Stern calls the 'core sense of self' (Stern, 1998), which provides a framework for later senses of self developed through language and culture. This 'core self' is not the fixed, unitary entity or 'homunculus' of the old essentialist self – the little person who sits in the brain and observes what we are doing and thinking (see Damasio, 2000, pp. 189–92) – but an innate organising capacity.

There is no suggestion in these views that small babies have the sort of self-consciousness or the ability to reflect on themselves that adults possess; rather the 'core self' is seen as 'a form of unreflective consciousness' (Butterworth, 1998, p. 95). In this theory, as in those of Kristeva and Klein, self-consciousness – our sense of being an 'I' – starts developing through our engagement with other people, but is then hugely enhanced by the acquisition of language. Language gives us the means of conceptualising ourselves as an object (the self-concept); in other words, it enables us to develop a strong sense of 'standing outside' ourselves and of our engagement with the world, which is the essence of reflexivity.

The two-fold model of the self suggested by Antonio Damasio, which brings together a non-reflexive bodily self and a reflexive language-based self, provides a useful framework for understanding this reflexivity neurophysiologically. It also adds to Kristeva's notion of the 'subject-in-process' (see Nicholls, in preparation). Damasio suggests that there are two different levels of consciousness: 'core conscious-ness' and 'extended consciousness', each giving rise to a different sense of self, which he calls the 'core self' and the 'extended or auto-biographical self'. Damasio's 'core self' is not a fixed unitary entity, as it is constantly undergoing change as a result of encounters with the environment. Essentially it is a second-order, neural mechanism, a felt, bodily awareness of a ceaselessly generated 'narrative without words' (Damasio 2000, p. 168) taking place in the organism (the body and the nervous system) beneath the level of consciousness in the area Damasio calls the 'proto-self'. This non-verbal narrative occurs when the organism interacts with an 'object' – this might be a phys-ical object (a person) or a sense impression (a melody) or a memory – causing a change to take place in the organism. The interaction, together with its emotional concomitants, is experienced in the form of felt, bodily images, e.g. 'a sound image, a tactile image, the image of a state of well-being' (p. 9), and because it occurs continuously in pulse-like fashion it gives rise to 'an image of knowing centred on a self', or 'the sense of self in the act of knowing' (pp. 171–6), which Damasio calls the 'core self'. This, however, is not a reflexive consciousness.

Damasio's work here echoes that of the psychoanalyst Melanie Klein, for whom the infant's acquisition of language, and related development of a sense of individual self, is based on what we might call the pre-images or pre-processes of introjection and projec-tion. The infant ascribes qualities to significant objects in his experi-ence – such as his mother's breast – and, *because* there is not yet any separation between mother and child, nor any symbolisation, 'takes them on' as aspects of his self. This 'introjection' is what lays the groundwork for language acquisition (Klein, 1986, pp. 202–6).

For Damasio, reflexivity develops as autobiographical memories accumulate and the 'core self' becomes connected to a broader canvas, so that 'the sense of self in the act of knowing', Descartes's self-consciously 'thinking thing', is enriched by a growing knowledge of past events and the feelings and emotions associated with them. This 'extended consciousness' (pp. 195–233), with its ability to 'hold images active over time' (p. 198), makes the organism aware of its knowledge, thus facilitating planning, creativity and problem solving. It heralds the arrival of the 'autobiographical self' (p. 196). Language, which arrives in human evolution very late, enables us to translate felt knowledge into words, and contributes significantly to the further development of 'extended consciousness' and hence of reflexivity (p. 108). But extended consciousness is wholly dependent on core consciousness, which carries out the relentless work of neurally reactivating and enhancing autobiographical memories and making them explicit as *felt images*. This development, from the felt, core sense of self in the moment to the reflexivity of extended consciousness enhanced by language, is, in Damasio's view, a direct consequence of the evolutionary advantage to us of knowing about our emotions, which allows us 'to plan novel and customised forms of adaptive response' (p. 285).

Neither of Damasio's 'selves' are fixed, unitary entities in the essentialist sense. Both are constantly 'in process', yet both have the capacity to give us a degree of stability, the core self more so than the extended self. If memory, as is now generally assumed, is an interpretation of the past rather than accurate recall, then it cannot provide us with a stable identity over time as it is constantly changing. There are certain 'facts' of our existence, such as our name, our place of birth, significant people in our lives such as our parents, which are permanent and therefore more reliable, and our sense of identity in extended consciousness is largely anchored to them, as well as to regular and familiar routines in which we engage. However, it is the ceaseless and pulse-like mechanism that generates core consciousness through bodily feelings and emotions which provides us with a greater sense of stability over time, a tangible background sense of *what it feels like to be ourselves in the moment* beyond our dominant self-concepts or narratives of self that are the result of our immersion in language and the social world.

Damasio's model of the self, with its two levels of consciousness, helps to make sense of how nature and nurture work together in our make-up. The mechanism of core self, he suggests, is primarily innate and therefore part of nature; but it is also significantly affected and changed by experience, by nurture. Extended self, and particularly our sense of ourselves as being an 'I', is primarily the result of nurture, of the effects of language, society and culture; although it is underpinned by the bodily core self, or nature, which generates pulses of core consciousness every time we think, imagine or undergo an experience in the world.

This model also helps us to understand better the idea of reflexivity as a process of change and development. As we have seen, reflexivity is an effect of extended consciousness brought about by the acquisition of memory and language and the development of complex language-based societies. Language enables us to move beyond the *awareness* of feelings and emotions, which is the realm of core consciousness, to make our memories more *explicit* and to hold them over time; it enables us to have an extended sense of self in which we observe what we are doing and feeling, so that we can reflect on past experiences and plan how we are going to deal with things in the future. (We say 'a sense' here because it is Damasio's view that we do not *literally* 'stand outside ourselves'; rather our sense of being an observer of ourselves is part of the *process* of consciousness, constantly generated by the body's 'narrative' of feeling). But it is the 'core self', constantly monitoring and making us aware of our feelings, that provides the ground out of which this reflexivity takes place.

Indeed this pre-linguistic, bodily dimension of self turns out, in recent thinking in cognitive psychology and linguistics, to be crucially important in the development of our language-based culture. It has been suggested that 'oral culture' could not have evolved without the prior existence of a 'mimetic culture' (Donald, 1991), where thought was communicated primarily through bodily gesture and sound rather than words. Some of this gestural communication would have consisted simply of direct imitation, associated with the need to hunt or to fight, for example. Some of it, however, would have involved the use of bodily metaphor to communicate complex emotional states such as awe or grief, as evidenced by its continued presence in the dance rituals of aboriginal cultures at the end of the nineteenth century (Modell, 2003, pp. 187–192). As George Lakoff and Mark Johnson (1999) have extensively shown, metaphor is not simply an aspect of figurative language, but a primary form of cognition, which enables us to make meaning through translating abstract bodily feelings into words. Gestures – such as offensive and admiring ones – may be culturally specific, but they *are* part of communication and meaning-making in every culture.

A view of the self as in process, then – which embraces both the notion of a felt core self arising out of the body and the linguistic self of extended consciousness – may enable us to make sense of a self that is experienced as stable and continuous but is also constantly undergoing a process of change. It can help us understand the body's role in our sense of self, as well as that of language, culture and experience, as we will see in the chapters below. And a view of the self as in process also provides us with a basis for understanding our own reflexive self as it is engaged in the process of writing.

Recommended reading

Who Comes After the Subject? (eds Cadava, Connor and Nancy, 1991) is a collection of poststructuralist essays, primarily by French thinkers. *Models of the Self* (eds Gallagher and Shear, 1999) provides an overview of philosophical and neurobiological thinking on the self. Jerome Levin's *Theories of the Self* (1992) gives a broad, general overview, from a philosophical and psychodynamic point of view.

Constructions of the Self (ed. G. Levine, 1992) is an overview of constructionist and constructivist approaches. *Understanding the Self* (ed. R. Stevens, 1996) provides an overview of different approaches to the self from a social-psychological perspective. Charles Taylor's *Sources of the Self* (Cambridge: Cambridge University Press, 1992) argues for self as a moral basis.

Writing exercises

- Cognitive psychologist Ulric Neisser (1988) suggests that there are five main ways in which we know ourselves: through our sensed relationship with the physical world (our 'ecological self'), through our relations with other people ('interpersonal self'), through our memories of the past and anticipations of the future ('narrative' or 'extended self'), through our dreams and private thoughts ('private self'), and through our various socially and culturally constructed self-concepts, e.g. 'mother', 'writer', 'beautiful', 'intelligent' ('conceptual self'). Think yourself into each of these 'selves' or senses of self in turn and write a poem or short piece of fiction that captures them.
- Play with Kenneth Gergen's idea (1991) that we can invent and reinvent ourselves for different contexts or relationships, by creating a character out of yourself who changes identity every time he/she changes his/her outfit.
- Focus on your sense of yourself as 'the thing that thinks' (Descartes' *res cogitans*) and write from the inside about what it might be like to be a mind without a body (see Robert Murphy's autobiography *The Body Silent*, 1990, for an account of the gradual loss of bodily sensation which reduces him to a sense of being a disembodied mind).

- Take the nineteenth century idea of the homunculus – the little person who sits in the brain and observes what we are thinking and doing – and write in the first person about the relationship between him/her and the body he/she inhabits.
- Read Franz Kafka's short story 'Metamorphosis' (1916) in which the main protagonist, Gregor Samsa, wakes up one morning to discover that he has turned into a human-sized beetle. One interpretation of this story is that it is an extended metaphor for Kafka's discomfort with his physical body. In your own writing, create an extended metaphor for your own sense of body image or your sense of being a body in the world.
- Antonio Damasio (2000) identifies three categories of emotions: primary emotions – happiness, sadness, fear, anger and disgust; secondary (or social) emotions, such as embarrassment, jealousy, guilt, pride; and background emotions, such as well-being, malaise, calm, tension. Choose one or more of these emotional states and try to convey it through poetry or fiction without referring to it directly.

2   Voice

> We can learn…to move flexibly back and forth between using and celebrating something we feel as our own voice, and operating as though we are nothing but ventriloquists playfully using and adapting and working against an array of voices we find around us.
> Peter Elbow, *Everyone Can* Write, 2000, p. 218.

What does it mean when we say that we have 'found a voice' for our writing? The word 'voice' has a variety of meanings in common parlance. Most straightforwardly, it denotes the sound of the speaking or singing voice received by the ear: the opera singer, Placido Domingo, is said to have a powerfully resonant tenor voice. Metaphorically it is used to denote an empowering process: the introduction of universal suffrage in the early twentieth century is said to have 'given voice' to women. This is 'voice' conferred by an authority: the *right* to speak and to make one's voice heard. This sense of voice is also implicit in an individual's personal struggle to overcome the *fear* of speaking: we may say of a young man who has overcome his difficulty of speaking in front of his colleagues at work that he has managed to 'find his voice' and now has a greater confidence to express his opinions publicly. 'Voice' in these senses is a medium of oral expression of the individual or the group.

In a literary context the term 'voice' is used largely metaphorically and largely from the point of view of the reader of literary works. The reader 'hears' with the inner ear the 'voice' of a writer's writing when she reads a novel or a poem. If the reader is well read in the English literary tradition, she may, for example, be able to recognise unattributed extracts from the novels of Joseph Conrad or the poetry of Wordsworth simply 'by ear'. The choice and juxtaposition of words, the rhythms and the tone of the language, particular themes or characters, all combine to create a style that summons up in the imagination the familiar 'voice' of a 'Conrad novel' or a 'Wordsworth poem' (see Chapter 3 for Michel Foucault's notion of the name of the author as a 'function' within discourse).

Our reader may also, if she discusses literature with other people, talk about the particular voices of characters in a novel, which are recognisably different from each other, and also recognisably different from the voice of the narrator and from the voice of the author who has brought the novel into being. T.S. Eliot identified the different kinds of voice in poetry as 'the poet talking to the reader' and 'the voice of a dramatic character'. He also added a third: 'the poet talking to himself or to nobody', although this is also, in a sense, talking to the reader, where the writer is reader of himself (Eliot, 1957) (see Chapter 5 below). Voice here becomes a metaphor for a style of writing; it is linked to a particular writer by name but it also has a life in the text separate from the writer, particularly in the voices of the characters and other personae a writer creates (see Chapter 6 below).

All these different meanings of 'voice' are relevant to the idea of 'finding a voice' when we are speaking of our own writing process, for finding a voice involves not only getting our particular 'sound' or tone onto the page, which helps us to develop our own distinct style, but also asserting our right to speak, both in the sense of overcoming our own internal difficulties of speaking, and of creating a space to speak amongst the voices of others who speak through us and who potentially inhibit our speaking for ourselves.

Voice as the right to speak

Let's start by looking at this latter meaning of 'voice'. Theoretically, in a democratic society we all have the right to speak, the right to place our words on the page and to make them available to others in one form or another. But how do we know whether those words are really ours? Whose voice sounds when we start to speak or write?

In all likelihood the words we put on the page when we start to write will not be our own. They will belong to significant people in our life, and more generally to the society and the culture in which we were born and brought up. As the Russian philosopher and literary critic Mikhail Bakhtin says, the word, or rather the 'utterance',[1] is never simply our own; it is always half someone else's (Bakhtin, 1981, p. 345). If we were born in one culture and brought up in another, it may feel alien or uncomfortable to use the language of the host culture, even if we have been living in it for most of our lives. 'Which language has not been the oppressor's tongue?' asks Sujata Bhatt in her poem 'A Different History' (Bhatt, 1988, p. 37). And in a sense all language could be said to be 'the oppressor's tongue' in that we don't have a choice but to adopt it. We are born, as it were, into the middle of a conversation that was going on long before we arrived and that will continue long after we die. Somehow, in order to become writers, we have to make that language our own.

For Bhatt, making a language her own posed particular problems. Born in India into a Gujarati speaking home, she emigrated at age 12 with her family to the US where she started to write poetry in English. Not surprisingly, one of the dominant themes in her early poetry is her 'Search for My Tongue' (Bhatt, 1988, p. 63). There are days, she says, when her tongue eludes her. It's like the tail of a lizard, which she tries to grab, slippery, impossible to keep hold of. The problem is that she has two different tongues, a mother tongue which she has lost, and a foreign tongue which she doesn't know well enough to feel comfortable. When she speaks English, her mother tongue withers and dies, but during the night it starts to grow again, and in the morning there it is, interfering with her attempts to speak and write in English (p. 66). The poem mimics this process, Gujarati repeatedly intruding in between the English lines, subverting her attempts to think in English. Each of her languages brings with it a different experience of the world and of herself, the English and Gujarati words for 'sky', for example, capable of evoking entirely different visual images (p. 67).

Being 'between tongues' is complicated even further for Bhatt when she marries a German and goes to live in Germany. Now she has three languages, as she says in 'The Undertow' (pp. 89–90), all getting in each other's way. Only if she distances herself from them do they seem able to cohabit peacefully; she imagines them swimming together way out at sea 'like seals fat with fish and sun' (p. 89), their common sounds intermingling. She is jealous of their freedom but knows that she must not try to pin them down. All she can do is to go with the undertow, simultaneously embracing them and letting them go.

'Going with the undertow' evokes the idea of reflexivity, of relinquishing our control over what is fixed and singular, in this case a single language, in order to find a voice amongst the different languages that speak us. For Bakhtin, developing a reflexive relationship with the languages – or the discourses[2] – of others, is a central part of finding a voice. The discourse of others, whether those others are parents or teachers, or religious, social or political authorities, determines 'the very bases of our ideological[3] interrelations with the world, the very basis of our behaviour'. These are 'authoritative discourses' which, until we develop views of our own, are 'internally persuasive', determining how we think and speak.

An 'authoritative discourse' is a 'prior discourse'; it is 'fully complete' and has 'a single meaning'. It 'demands our unconditional allegiance...; one must either totally affirm it, or totally reject it'. It is not reflexive or 'double-voiced' (Bakhtin, 1981, pp. 342–44). An important part of individual development, in Bakhtin's view, involves becoming aware of the presence in our own consciousness of a variety of authoritative discourses, from which at first it is not possible to separate ourselves because they are 'internally persuasive'. Healthy development involves engagement in a struggle with these authoritative discourses and formulating our own internally persuasive word. This doesn't imply a complete rejection of the authoritative discourses; rather they become transformed, 're-written' or 're-told' in our own words. They change from being monologic to dialogic, and this opens up a creative potential:

> [The] creativity and productiveness [of the internally persuasive word] consist precisely in the fact that such a word awakens new and independent words, that it organizes masses of our words from within, and does not remain in an isolated and static condition. It is not so much interpreted by us as it is further, that is, freely, developed, applied to new material, new conditions; it enters into interanimating relationships with new contexts. More than that, it enters into an intense interaction, a *struggle* with other internally persuasive discourses (p. 346).

For Bhatt, this struggle becomes the subject matter of her early poetry as she develops her very particular voice. In her frustration at not having the right words to convey her experience, she creates new words that combine the sounds of her three different languages, words such as 'brunizem' and 'brummagem' (Bhatt, 1988, p. 105). These words don't have a literal meaning in any one of her languages, and that is precisely what she seeks to achieve by inventing them ('I've been meaning/ not to mean anything for once'), for when she gets beyond literal meaning, what remains in the words is her own *tone*, her own *feel* ('I just want to say, "brunizem!" / I feel brunizem/ when this man kisses me...') (p. 105).

Voice as tone

Tone is an important dimension of *voice* in both speaking and writing. We impart tone to everything we say and it has a crucial role in the meaning conveyed. The sentence 'It doesn't matter' can be uttered in an aggressive or exasperated tone, with the implication that it *does* in fact matter, and that the speaker will, sooner rather than later, return to the issue, probably with recriminations. It can also be said in a resigned tone, again with the implication that it *does* matter, but that the speaker is either too tired or not strong enough to pursue the issue further. In both of these instances, the tone conveys a value judge- ment; the speaker is evaluating the 'it' of the sentence and expressing his or her personal feeling about it. For Bakhtin and his colleague Voloshinov, all tone contains a value judgement and therefore carries 'an imprint of individuality' (Morson and Emerson, 1990, p. 134).

Tone can also be expressed without words. In the above example of a resigned intonation, an aspirated sigh or a shrug of the shoulders rather than the actual words would convey the same message. Here, tone becomes a bodily gesture with 'emotional-volitional' content (pp. 133–35), and if, as we said in Chapter 1, gesture was a form of metaphorical communication that preceded language (Modell, 2003, pp. 187–88), then tone can be seen as more closely connected with core consciousness or our felt bodily sense of self than extended consciousness or our linguistic self.

The idea of tone as a bodily gesture is an important part of Donald Wesling's and Tadeusz Slawek's notion of 'minimal voice' or 'minimal articulation', 'where sound has not come all the way over to concept, where the *vox confusa* of animals or the body has not reached *vox articulata* but still has human meanings' (Wesling and Slawek, 1995, p. 11; they draw on Kristeva's idea of the 'semiotic'). 'Maximal voice', by comparison, which they define as fully developed literary voice, 'has highly overdetermined meanings – meaning grafted onto meaning...' (p. 10). They suggest two different ways in which pre- conceptual 'minimal voice' expresses itself in literary writing: first, through *noise*, such as '...exclamation, birdsong, babble, phatic utter- ance,[4] phonic material that seems on the way to being articulate speech'; and, second, through *nonsense*, such as '...the deliberate minimal of the avant-garde where language is used to mime breakdown of language, so to force the reader to look at each word, syllable, stanza, sentence, paragraph, or other structural or semantic feature as itself in all its strangeness and materiality' (p. 10).

A good example of minimal voice as noise is Gerard Manley Hopkins' well-known poem 'The Windhover'. Here is the first stanza:

> I caught this morning morning's minion, king -dom of daylight's
>   dauphin, dapple-dawn-drawn Falcon, in his riding
> Of the rolling level underneath him steady air, and striding
> High there, how he rung upon the rein of a wimpling wing
> In his ecstasy! then off, off forth on swing,
>   As a skate's heel sweeps smooth on a bow-bend: the hurl and gliding
>   Rebuffed the big wind. My heart in hiding
> Stirred for a bird, – the achieve of, the mastery of the thing!
>
> (Hopkins, 1938, p. 29).

The poet seems to be using the phonic effects of language to capture the inward groan of ecstasy he experiences when he watches the falcon hovering and swooping in turn. From the outset the rhythmic repetition sets up a hum of feeling, particularly the alliteration of the m's and n's and ng's, with the assonance of the initial vowel sound in 'caught', 'morning', 'dawn', 'drawn', 'Falcon', echoing the exhalation of wonderment. The repetition of the present participle – 'rolling', 'striding', 'gliding' – accentuates this inner movement, this 'stirring of the heart'. The poet subverts normal word usage in his quest to capture the intensity of his experience, strengthening 'hurl' by changing it from a verb into a noun; creating word-combinations, such as 'dapple-dawn-drawn', that resonate with sound rather than literal meaning. 'Wimpling', an old English word derived from 'wimple', meaning an elaborately folded or pleated headdress, seems there as much for the 'rippling' sound the wing makes as the bird hovers as for its visual impact (Simpson, 2003). This use of language lifts words out of their usual meaning-making role, offering the reader an engagement with meaning at the level of feeling. Hopkins captures in the poem the 'sound' of his body, or the 'pitch of self', as he puts it (Hopkins, 1937, p. 309; in Hartman, 1966, p. 58), which he experiences in his encounters with the natural world and, through the natural world, with his God.[5]

The 'pitch of self' is captured in a rather different way in the outpourings of Samuel Beckett's character Lucky in *Waiting for Godot* (1956), which provides a good example of minimal voice as nonsense. Slave of the wealthy Pozzo, Lucky is no more than a beast of burden, kept on a long leash and forced to carry his master's luggage. Speechless and downtrodden, he seems to have no power to act on his own behalf, responding only to Pozzo's verbal commands and tugs on the leash. He doesn't even set down his burden until commanded to do so; and his only speech in the play happens, again, at Pozzo's command. But it would be misleading to say that Lucky speaks; rather he is spoken by a range of 'authoritative discourses' and clichés of Western culture. They tumble out, fragmented and disconnected, as if there was once a coherent speech here but the absence of an organising psyche has rendered it nonsensical. Lucky, it seems, has literally lost his reason. But as his outpouring proceeds, a tone begins to emerge. Individual words – 'alas', 'abandoned', 'unfinished' – are repeated more and more frequently and rhythmically. He makes strange bird-like sounds –'quaquaquaqua' (Beckett, 1970, pp. 42–5). It is as if the speaker, unable to order his thinking logically, resorts instead to trying to convey his own sound, his own anguished 'pitch of self'. And once begun, there is no natural end to it. Just as he had to be commanded to speak, so he has to be physically compelled to stop. As he is brought to the ground by his enraged listeners, he fittingly utters the word 'unfinished', and then reverts to his silent servitude. Whilst the clichés and fragments of 'authoritative discourse' littering Lucky's speech are devoid of feeling, the pattern and form of their utterance allow the minimal voice of bodily feeling to sound.

The tone of the voice, then, is closely bound up with the body. It is the indicator of a bodily self-presence underlying and informing the language we use. For Jacques Derrida, voice and tone are also connected with the body: '...what I like to do', he says, 'is... to let be heard in what I write a certain position of the voice, when the voice and the body can no longer be distinguished', which happens for him more in speaking than in writing (Derrida, 1995, p. 141). Yet there is no sense, in Derrida's thinking about voice, of the body's feelings and emotions as a source of *personal presence* in speaking or writing; rather, because the self, or 'the subject', is constituted by language, there cannot be anything of a pre-linguistic nature which constitutes a sense of self. Thus, the tone of the voice does not arise out of the emotions of an individuality, as Bakhtin suggested, but is a disembodied and impersonal 'ghostliness in the voice' (Royle, 2003, p. 37). In order for tone to 'sound' – and tone is what Derrida seeks 'to impart as if in spite of myself, to give or lend to others as well as to myself...', even though he often doesn't like the tone he imparts (Derrida, 1998, p. 48) – we have to get rid of self, to die to ourselves, as it were.

Voice as absence

Derrida's 'deconstruction'[6] or dismantling of the connection between voice and self-presence arises out of his considerations of the relationship between speech and writing. In the linguistic theory of Ferdinand de Saussure (1973), against which Derrida is working, speech was regarded as prior to writing, in the sense that the speaking voice was thought to give direct access to the self, so that the self said directly and spontaneously what it intended to say. Derrida calls this view 'phonocentrism' or 'logocentrism' (Derrida, 1976). By contrast, writing was seen as secondary, mediated by more deliberate and conscious thought processes, a 'supplement' to speech (ibid.). Derrida deconstructs this opposition between speech and writing by pointing out that speaking always contains writing, although he is using the term 'writing' in a broader sense than simply words on the page. 'Écriture' in Derrida's thinking means the whole system of signification in which we are immersed. Because we are born into a language-based society, language is constantly being 'written' and 're-written' in our unconscious, without our conscious awareness. To illustrate this idea Derrida borrows from Freud the metaphor of a 'mystic writing pad' for the psyche. The pad is described as consisting of a wax slab covered by a thin transparent sheet. Words are inscribed into the wax through the transparent sheet, and remain permanently, even after the transparent sheet is cleared by lifting it from the wax (Derrida, 1978, p. 223). In the psyche this permanent 'trace' informs our consciousness and our perception of the outside world, so that when we come to speak, our words arise out of what is 'always already' written in the unconscious. In this sense our speech is a sort of cliché, and the task of the creative writer is to raise words above their over-used and worn-out state, to give them new life and new meaning.

If, as Derrida suggests, the words we speak are always prior to our own speaking of them, then there is always a mismatch or a gap – Derrida calls it a 'différance', a term that conflates 'difference' and 'deferral' – between the words we utter and the meaning we are trying to convey, so that meaning is always at one remove, always deferred (Derrida, 1976). Rather than the speaking voice implying self-presence, then, for Derrida it implies the absence of self, or at least the absence of the kind of self-presence suggested by Saussure, or by the humanist or essentialist view of self. Nevertheless, he does not deny the presence of self altogether; rather, whatever self is – and Derrida prefers to deconstruct the concept rather than to speculate on what self might be – it is not graspable by language. It would be more correct to say that, for Derrida, self is absent *and* present in speaking and writing. Like tone, it is a spectre that haunts language. When we speak or write, it's quite normal to think that we are hearing the voice of ourselves, but this is 'the most impossible experience' (Derrida, 1982, p. 297; in Royle, 2003, p. 55).

Wesling and Slawek agree with Derrida that the assumption of a direct correspondence between the voice and the self in speaking and writing needs to be deconstructed, but they wish to retain a more defined role in the voice for the individual self or 'subject'. The subject, they suggest, *is* present in language, *does* have a voice – the 'minimal voice' we discussed earlier – but that voice can only 'sound' if the subject is *de-toned* of coherent language. *De-tonation*, an idea they derive from Derrida's early work, involves: '[the] overcoming of everyday logical discourse; of sentence-based progressive thought; of one primary tone ascribed to one person' (Wesling and Slawek, 1995, p. 151). Fully articulated speech, they suggest, results merely in a 'repetition of socially used and abused phrases'. We have to relinquish the safety and familiarity of self-identity that coherent language provides, so that the subject's voice can sound 'in the marginal and incomplete ruins of discourse' (pp. 150–151). Yet the voice that sounds once we relinquish our language-based identity is, for Wesling and Slawek, not a personal voice; it is a 'human but *impersonal* voice', the pre-linguistic sounding of the body which we share with animals and which signals the expression of 'desire' (pp. 167–68).

This is a strange conclusion to an argument that locates the tone of the voice squarely in the body, although 'desire' here is being used in the Freudian sense of 'libido', which is seen as an impersonal universal instinct pervading the body. Nevertheless the idea that finding a voice involves a 'de-toning' of the self, in the sense of distancing ourselves from fixity in language, is useful, and it also helps to make a link with Bakhtin's ideas discussed above. From the perspective of the two-tier model of consciousness we discussed in Chapter 1, when we 'de-tone' ourselves of – or, better, distance ourselves from – rigid self-concepts or narratives of self which are part of the 'authoritative discourses' of extended consciousness, we create space for the tone of our bodily felt sense of self, or core consciousness, to 'sound', and this enables us to reformulate authoritative discourses into our own internally persuasive word.

Voice as presence and absence

The emergence into creative writing of a bodily felt sense of self is central to Seamus Heaney's understanding of what it means to find a writing voice. 'Finding a voice means that you can get your own feeling into your own words and that your words have the feel of you about them', he says, and he describes how he experienced this for the first time in the writing of his celebrated poem 'Digging' (Heaney, 1980, p. 43). In this poem Heaney compares and contrasts his difficult calling as a writer with the no less difficult calling of his forebears as farmers. He celebrates the rhythm and precision of his father's and grandfather's cutting of the earth with their spades; he conveys the sense of awe he experienced as a young boy watching his grandfather at work on the turf, and there is a hint of pain and guilt that he is not following in the family tradition, but in the final stanza he finds a meaningful connection between his own vocation and theirs. Like them, he is deeply committed to his calling; like them, he digs deeply and cleanly, but the instrument he uses for digging is the pen, not the spade (Heaney, 1966, pp. 10–11).

It was in the writing of this poem, Heaney says, that 'I thought my *feel* had got into words'. It was 'the first place where I felt I had done more than make an arrangement of words: I felt that I had let down a shaft into real life. The facts and surfaces of the thing were true, but more important, the excitement that came from naming them gave me a kind of insouciance and a kind of confidence'; this was 'poetry as revelation of the self to the self' (p. 41). By the time Heaney composed this poem, he had been writing for a while and knew about craft and the sound of words on the page. Some of his poems had been published in the literary magazine at the university where he was studying. But they were written, as it were, from the surface of himself: '...nothing happened inside me. No experience. No epiphany. All craft…' (pp. 46–7). Not that craft wasn't important; it was an essential part of the process, but something else needed to happen:

> Learning the craft is learning to turn the windlass at the well of poetry. Usually you begin by dropping the bucket halfway down the shaft and winding up a taking of air. You are miming the real thing until one day the chain draws unexpectedly tight and you have dipped into waters that will continue to entice you back. You'll have broken the skin on the pool of yourself (p. 47).

Heaney creates a powerful metaphor here for the writing process: the deep cylindrical shaft of the well and the bucket being lowered into the darkness conjure up the plunge into the unknown which writing involves, the relinquishing of safety and familiarity. If we are serious about our writing we do this day in, day out, especially in the early days, never quite knowing whether anything worth committing to the page will result. It is a chore, all this winding out and winding back. But we are learning to flex our literary muscles, gaining familiarity with the mechanisms, and sometimes we produce something that is pleasing. Then one day something else happens; a connection is made deep down. We have made contact with *what it feels like to be ourselves*, and something of that gets dragged up in the bucket. Our *feel* gets into our words.

In an essay on the development of his writing, Philip Lyons describes a similar moment of getting his 'feel' into his words, which occurred as a result of several different but related experiences. He had been working in a prison running writing workshops for the prisoners, which he found challenging, unnerving; it made him feel impotent, powerless. The poetry he was writing at the time reflected those feelings and, in spite of the fact that he tended to keep himself at a safe distance in his poems, occupying the role of the 'observing I', the language of incarceration he was using – 'locked up', 'walls are walls' – started to sound like metaphors for his own state of mind (Lyons, 1999, p. 78). A similar thing happened when he started attending a creative writing group that took place in a former psychiatric day hospital where he had previously worked. Writing a poem about the former patients of the hospital who, he imagined, still occupied the building as ghosts, he found himself portraying them as unloved, needing to be loved, waiting for someone to love them. Again, he recognised something personal hovering on the periphery of what the poem was saying, but it was still tightly controlled, 'metre and rhyme... techniques I have used to contain what otherwise threatens to overwhelm me' (p. 79).

Soon afterwards, he met a woman with whom he fell in love, an event that caused him to leave his partner of fourteen years, completely disrupting his life. At the time of writing his essay, it didn't look as if the new relationship was viable, but the experience, which in retrospect seemed to have been foreshadowed in his writing, shifted him into a different relationship with his poetry. Now, not only was he able to let go of the fixed and containing structure of metre and rhyme, and write open-ended free verse, but where previously his own presence in the poems had been a distanced 'observing I', now he was the main protagonist. He describes this poetry as written 'directly from the heart, or the gut even, taking a risk with my own vulnerability, my own humanity'. It is 'an expression of who I am; it reflects the development of a *voice...*' (p. 80). In fact the poem 'Lunch', which Lyons includes as an example, contains several different voices or several different layers of voice: the voice of himself as first person narrator describing himself eating lunch at his home and the remembered voices of himself and his lover in mostly inconsequential dialogue the day before, with the voice of his vulnerable 'feeling self', like Sujata Bhatt's 'mother tongue', repeatedly intruding in between the other voices in order to declare itself. These different voices jostle with each other for a place on the page, for the right to speak, but it is the presence of the vulnerable feeling self which ultimately determines the fragmented shape of the poem and which has the final say, in the last truncated line: 'I love you. I love you. I...'. Here the 'minimal voice' of feeling rises up out of the 'incomplete ruins of discourse', not a 'human but impersonal voice' but the *emotional tone* of the suffering that love has caused this particular writer.

David Applebaum suggests that 'voice minus suffering equals speech. Speech is a negative whose subtraction is a plus' (Applebaum, 1990, p. 134; in Wesling and Slawek, 1995, p. 29), speech here meaning coherent, articulated language. In Lyons' account, it was only when suffering broke through his defences that he was able to relinquish coherent, articulated speech in his writing and find his voice. In Heaney's account, too, there is a hint of pain and suffering in his recognition of the need to leave behind his forefathers in his calling to be a poet. And certainly many writers write out of their own anguished states. Yet suffering is insufficient to constitute the only ingredient of voice; it leaves out of account a wide range of felt experience. It would be more useful to amend Applebaum's equation to *speech plus feeling equals voice*, where feeling implies a deep connection with 'core consciousness' or our bodily, felt sense of self (Damasio, 2000).

In the experience of Heaney and Lyons, then, finding a writing voice involves a certain kind of self-presence (presence of a bodily, felt sense of self) and a certain kind of self-absence (the suspension of a familiar identity in language). Or, to put it another way, finding a voice involves tolerating absence and presence simultaneously, being able to be a self-in-process between language and the body. What these two examples indicate is that it is not unusual for our bodily felt sense of self to be more absent than present in the early stages of our development as writers, and for linguistic form or structure to constitute a barrier to a greater self-presence. Lyons in particular was using 'the orderliness of the form' as a buffer, to keep at bay painful areas of felt experience threatening to overwhelm him. Their emergence into consciousness caused a breakdown in the coherent, articulated language he was accustomed to use in his writing and gave rise to a much 'freer and looser' style, which was nevertheless 'still crafted' – the removal of the constraint did not lead to total incoherence (Lyons, 1999, p. 77). Rather what it did was to enable him to write with a number of different voices, his own as well as those of others. This might suggest that 'finding a voice' should be re-phrased as 'finding *voices*'. In fact 'finding a voice' precedes 'finding voices', for, as Peter Elbow says in the epigraph to this chapter, it involves developing a more fluid and flexible relationship with ourselves, so that we are not only able to imbue our writing with our own particular tone but also able to *ventriloquise* the voices of others. And indeed ventriloquism is an apt metaphor here; it implies not simply a parroting of others' voices but speaking simultaneously in one's own voice and the voices of others who speak in and through us. (It also makes an apt connection with the body. The OED's second meaning of 'ventriloquism' is: 'The fact or practice of speaking or appearing to speak from the abdomen'.) Mikhail Bakhtin calls this a *dialogic* relationship with self, in which we move from a sense of ourselves as singular to a sense of ourselves as multi-voiced or 'polyphonic' (Bakhtin, 1981).

Writing voice and writing identity

Finding a voice is, for Heaney, one of the two main tasks we have to master in order to become writers; the other is learning the craft of writing. When a writer has both, he says, he then has at his disposal *technique*. This involves:

> not only a poet's way with words, his management of metre, rhythm and verbal texture; it involves also a definition of his stance towards life, a definition of his own reality. It involves the discovery of ways to go out of his normal cognitive bounds and raid the inarticulate: a dynamic alertness that mediates between the origins of feeling in memory and experience and the formal ploys that express these in a work of art... It is that whole creative effort of the mind's and body's resources to bring the meaning of experience within the jurisdiction of form (Heaney, 1980, p. 47).

What he is talking about here is the development of a *writing identity*, a firmly based yet flexible grounding in ourselves and in the craft of our particular genre of writing which 'allows that first stirring of the mind round a word or an image or a memory to grow towards articulation', and he uses the image of a water diviner intuitively able to make 'contact with what lies hidden' (Heaney, 1980, p. 48). As Heaney says, once we have developed that grounding, we can move out of our everyday way of thinking and plumb even greater depths within ourselves, such as the culture and history that lie, like archaeological layers, in our psyche (as Heaney himself does in his poems 'Bogland' and 'Toome' in *Wintering Out*). We can get beyond ego and become the voice of more than autobiography. We can experiment with forms of writing that go beyond personal tone, seeking, for example, to develop a 'textual voice', where 'any identifiable speaker' is absent (Wesling and Slawek, 1995, p. 181), so that we can play at being Eliot's impersonal vehicle for the intermingling of many different texts. We pursue this theme further in the following two chapters.

Recommended reading

Part III of Peter Elbow's *Everyone Can Write* (2000) includes several thoughtful pieces on the concept of voice from the writer's point of view. Mikhail Bakhtin's 'Discourse in the Novel' in *The Dialogic Imagination* (1981) is a good starting point for getting to grips with his thinking about voice and voices, and authoritative and internally persuasive discourses. Nicholas Royle's *Derrida* (2003) is a stimulating and lucid introduction to Derrida's thinking about voice, tone and self, from the perspective of the practising writer. Wesling and Slawek's *Literary Voice* (1995) is a thought-provoking but challenging exploration of the role of 'the subject' in the voice. Geoffrey Hartman's *Saving the Text* (1981) similarly argues for retaining a role for 'the subject' in our understanding of voice. David Applebaum's *Voice* (1990) offers a fascinating discussion of bodily dimensions of voice, such as the cough, the laugh, the breath, babble and song. A very recent book on voice is Al Alvarez' *The Writer's Voice* (2005).

Writing exercises

- Read a poem or section of a novel or short story, then put it aside and try to 'hear' the sound of the 'voice' in which it is written; then write your own poem or short piece of prose using that voice.
- Identify an 'authoritative discourse' from your childhood which continues to play a role in your life (for example: 'Always be nice to people and they will be nice to you'). Imagine yourself into this discourse and write a short prose piece in which a character plays it out. Then write another piece, in which the discourse is subverted.
- Using Sujata Bhatt's idea of creating her own words to convey feelings beyond meaning, identify one or more of your own 'feeling states' – your own 'pitch of self' at different times and in different circumstances – and create your own made-up words to convey them.
- Taking Hopkins as a model, closely observe a phenomenon in the natural world, such as an animal or a bird in motion, or a particular kind of weather, and try to capture it by using unusual or made-up verbs of motion.
- Use a dictionary to find some words whose sound you like, irrespective of their meaning. Use them to create a nonsense poem that conveys feeling.
- Identify a rhythm which appeals to you – this may come from everyday life, such as the rhythm of the train in which you travel to work, or from a poem you particularly like, such as a standard

5-foot line (iambic pentameter), or from a remembered activity in childhood, such as swinging on a swing, a clapping game or skipping rope. Live with it for a day simply as a rhythm, playing it in your head from time to time, moving your body in time with it; only when you are fully familiar with it – when you have felt your way into it – start to add some words to the rhythm and develop it into a poem (this exercise was devised by Cheryl Moskowitz).

- Write a poem or short prose piece using the idea of 'voice' as a ghost.
- If you are bi-lingual or reasonably fluent in more than one language, use your knowledge of those other languages to import foreign words into a poem, with the emphasis more on the sound of language than the meanings of individual words.

3   Authorship

The most essential stage of the writing process, it is often argued, is the process whereby the writer comes to stand outside the experience he intends to mirror in his book. The chief element of this 'alienation' is the conscious desire to examine oneself and the experience from 'without', from a standpoint at which both the writer himself and his surroundings lose their concrete features, and separate themselves from everyday reality after a long period of struggle and uncertainty to enter a fluid and less rigidly limited dimension. This new dimension exists only in the writer's consciousness; within it the elements of reality no longer obey the earthbound laws of gravitation; the minutiae of time and place cease to be important.

> Jerzy Kosinski, 'Notes of the Author on *The Painted Bird*',
> 1965, p. 201.

The idea of a writing identity brings us to the concept of authorship and what it means to be an author. Over the past thirty years or so discussions of authorship in literary theory have focused very largely on the place of the author in the finished product of writing – or, to be more precise, on the *absence* of the author from the finished product. In this chapter we will be looking at the main elements of this theory from the perspective of the creative work in progress, to see what it has to offer to us as practising writers seeking to deepen and extend our sense of authorship.

The author as name

If you ask people outside of the academic world 'what is an author?', in all likelihood they will name a particular person, someone like J.K. Rowling, author of the Harry Potter novels. They might be able to tell you how she wrote her first book whilst a single mother living on social security; how she wrote by hand in a café whilst her daughter was at school, her flat being too claustrophobic to work in. They might say something about how she drew on various aspects of her own experience and people she knew for the material for her novel. They might marvel at the huge readership she has acquired and the vast amount of money she has earned, and admit to a degree of envy at the comfortable life she is now able to lead. In the public mind, authors are living beings intimately connected with the books they have written.

For French philosopher Michel Foucault an author's name is also the main focus for thinking about the question 'What is an author?' but he is more concerned with how that name functions in society than with the connection between the name and the person who bears it. The name of the author, he says, indicates not so much a particular person as a particular body of writing. It is a 'means of classification' which groups together 'a number of texts and thus dif-ferentiate[s] them from others' (Foucault, 1977, p. 123). From this perspective 'Virginia Woolf' designates a body of prose fiction written in a heavily poeticised style, with a focus on the moment-by-moment inner consciousness of largely upper middle class characters living in England in the period between the two World Wars. Using Woolf's name in this way enables us to distinguish this particular style of writing from another, such as that of 'Jane Austen', a name which des-ignates a body of prose fiction written in an ironic style, with a focus on the consciousness of bourgeois, upper middle class and aristo-cratic characters living in England in the early part of the eighteenth century.

An author's name, for Foucault, may also designate a 'discursive practice', a broad field of thinking, which allows other writers to develop, extend or amend the author's original ideas, whilst still retaining them within the field (p. 132). Freud's discourse of the self is one such example, the term 'Freudian' no longer simply indicating the originating author and his ideas, but a field of developing practice and theory, key concepts of which, such as 'libido' and 'ego', have become part of everyday parlance. The author in Foucault's thinking is not an individual who seeks expression or meaning through writing, but an impersonal organising principle which engages with prevailing discourses at a particular time and place, sometimes redi-recting them into new discourses. Ultimately, what matters is not *who* is speaking but the effect a particular discourse has on people in a society (p. 138).

The author and the text

Foucault's essay 'What is an Author?' was an attempt to explore what he saw as the gap in thinking about the author opened up by Roland Barthes' celebrated essay 'Death of the Author', published in 1968. For Barthes, strongly influenced by Saussurean linguistics as well as the work of Julia Kristeva and other French poststructuralists, it is not the author who speaks in a literary work but the *text* or rather the *intertext*. Before Barthes and Kristeva, the word 'text' commonly denoted any line of words on a page or a complete book, such as a standard textbook. Whilst the term *intertextuality* was not used in literary criticism – it was coined by Kristeva (1984a) who was drawing on Bakhtin's ideas – there was a general assumption that any one text drew on, or was influenced by, other texts. In the work of Barthes and Kristeva, the meaning of the word 'text' is extended to embrace any use of language, written or spoken, as well as the language of visual images and sounds. The text saturates the environment in which we live and think; it is 'a tissue of quotations drawn from the innumerable centres of culture', although we are not aware of them as quotations. When we come to write, we enter 'a multi-dimensional space in which a variety of writings, none of them original, blend and clash' (Barthes, 1977, p. 146). This has radical consequences for the role of the author.

Like T.S. Eliot, Barthes maintains that the writer needs to develop impersonality in the writing process, so that the text can 'act' or 'perform' through him (p. 143). Writing necessitates a fundamental loss of identity, an emptying out of 'passions, humours, feelings, impressions'; in fact a kind of death of the self: 'writing is the destruction of every voice, of every point of origin...the negative where all identity is lost, starting with the very identity of the body writing' (p. 142). Only by evacuating the self can the writer draw on the 'immense dictionary' in the 'neutral, composite, oblique space' of writing (pp. 142, 147). Even the term 'author' has to be jettisoned, as it carries too many associations with the personal, and reeks of closure and control. In the author's stead, Barthes instates the 'scriptor', a detached, selfless and historically neutral organiser of discourses 'born simultaneously with the text', who allows it free play without feeling the need to fix meaning (p. 147). Only the reader brings meaning to the text, and as each reader reads differently, there are as many meanings to a text as there are readers (p. 148).

At first sight these views, which have been, and continue to be, highly influential, might appear bleak and unhelpful for anyone trying to develop as a writer. How can we develop a sense of authorship if we have to remove ourselves from the writing process? As we said in our introduction, focusing solely on the impersonal dimension of writing leaves out of account the important personal dimension, and in a moment we will be looking at Barthes' views to see what has happened to the personal in his thinking. And yet the idea of the text, or the intertext, can be potentially liberating for thinking about the writing process in the sense that it opens up the traditional borders of writing (Furness and Bath, 1996, pp. 325–26). Rather than seeing creative writing as a domain open only to those who are steeped in the literary tradition and have managed to master literary language, it gives all of us, whatever our background, permission to bring into our writing practice our own particular ways of speaking and writing. The appeal of James Berry's poetry, for example, lies partly in his imaginative incorporation into the English literary frame of the rhythms and sounds of his native Caribbean language. In *Lucy's Letters* (1982) his fictional female narrator writes letters from England to her cousin in Jamaica using colloquial Jamaican patois. In a similar way, Scottish writer Irvin Welsh makes extensive use of colloquial Scottish dialect in his novels *Trainspotting* (1999) and *Filth* (1998). Intertextuality in this sense becomes a means of subverting and expanding dominant literary discourses, making space for non-traditional voices. It also makes space for the intermingling of so-called 'high' and 'low' cultures. In his novel *White Noise* (1984) American novelist Don DeLillo incorporates random phrases from supermarket advertising and television programmes in amongst the 'high culture' narratives of his various academic characters to create an intertextual hubbub – or 'white noise' of his title – which captures the interpenetration in the modern world of strikingly disparate discourses.

Authorship and the self

The idea of intertextuality, then, as propounded by Barthes and others makes us aware of the rich space of the text and our potential within it. But what about the impersonality of authorship which engaging with the text apparently necessitates? It helps to understand Barthes' radical shift to impersonality if we see his essay on 'The Death of the

Author' as in part a reaction to the biographical approach to literary criticism dominant in the 1960s, which sought the explanation or meaning of a literary work solely in the biography of the author (Barthes brilliantly satirises this approach in 'The Writer on Holiday', 1981). However, there is also reason to suggest, as we will see below, that Barthes had strong personal reasons for killing off the person of the author. Indeed, Sean Burke argues that he had to exaggerate the dominance of author-centred criticism in order to create an 'Author-God' suitable for execution (Burke, 1998, p. 26). Unfortunately for literary theory, as well as for thinking about the role of the author's self in the writing process, the majority of critics since Barthes have either adopted or rejected his theory of impersonality without unpacking it or exploring it in the context of his other writings (p. 17). In fact, when looked at from the perspective of the self-in-process, Barthes' ideas turn out to be quite helpful for understanding and developing our own sense of authorship.

A close examination of Barthes' own autobiography reveals that what his theory of impersonality tries to achieve is not to kill off the self as author altogether but to do away with one particular dimension of it, the 'autobiographical self' in Damasio's terms (see Chapter 1). *Roland Barthes by Roland Barthes*, published just six years after 'Death of the Author', seeks to put into practice the message of that essay, and it is paradoxical that Barthes chooses autobiography – that most author-centred genre of writing – for his practical exercise in killing off the author. The main body of the autobiography consists of numerous fragments of prose arranged more or less alphabetically but written at different times in response to random ideas, single words or phrases, or quotations from the writings of others. In the main Barthes writes about himself in the third person, although first person and second person intrude not infrequently, and at the outset he instructs readers that they should consider everything 'as if spoken by a character in a novel'. Anything substantively biographical is omitted from this main text or, when it is included, rendered bland and impersonal; rather he seeks to work with ideas that come into his head at the moment of writing, following one of the main principles of his theory, that: 'Linguistically, the author is never more than the instance writing, just as I is nothing other than the instance saying I' (Barthes, 1977, p. 145; he is drawing here on Benveniste, 1971). As far as he is able, he adopts the stance of the scriptor he has posited, operating, as he puts it elsewhere, like a 'guest' (Barthes, 1986, p. 61) amongst the many different texts that flow through his free-floating consciousness.

A number of themes emerge out of this difficult but fascinating piece of writing. One which recurs repeatedly is the writer's dislike of being fixed in any identity, whether by photos or by belonging to a particular stratum of society, or a profession such as teaching or writing, or even by the tendency of individual words to acquire consistency or accepted meanings (Barthes, 1994, pp. 49, 62, 70, 143, 166, 168). He longs for dissolution, multiplicity, fragmentation, a drifting mode of existence not constrained by language or images (pp. 87–8, 102, 106, 118, 132; Barthes may have been influenced in this by Charles Baudelaire's idea of the 'flâneur' or 'stroller', the detached observer or spectator of urban life, although his obsession with it indicates that it is more than a consciously adopted stance towards life). By writing in this mode, he succeeds in killing off the biographical part of himself that belongs to the 'symbolic' (in Lacan's sense; see Chapter 1), and becomes a 'subject without referent' in the 'imaginary': 'I myself am my own symbol, I am the story which happens to me: freewheeling in language, I have nothing to compare myself to; and in this movement, the pronoun of the imaginary, "I", is *impertinent*; the symbolic becomes literally *immediate*: essential danger for the life of the subject: to write on oneself may seem a pretentious idea; but it is also a simple idea: simple as the idea of suicide' (p. 56).

Yet Barthes' autobiographical suicide does not, as he seems to imagine, leave him without a referent. The body, which he refers to repeatedly in different and contradictory ways, stubbornly refuses to disappear. Musing about 'His Voice', he discovers, when he stops trying to describe it literally, a 'voice *without rhetoric* (though not without tenderness)'. Belonging more to feelings (tenderness) than to words (rhetoric), this voice is not possible to capture in language, '...so great is the gap between the words which come to me from the culture and this strange being (can it be no more than a matter of sounds?) which I fleetingly recall at my ear' (pp. 67–8). The removal or, better, suspension, of the constraining 'autobiographical self' rooted in language and history makes space not only for the intertext to speak, but also for the felt, bodily self – 'this strange being' – to sound in the gaps between the texts. And indeed, Barthes' autobiography can be seen primarily as an attempt to write the felt, bodily sense of self beyond language, even though his theory of authorship denies the relevance of a personal self outside of the text.

Paradoxically, having worked hard to exclude his autobiographical self, Barthes retrospectively indulges himself ('the author's treat to himself') by including in the published work a series of photos of himself at different stages in his life from childhood to adulthood, as well as of his mother and other significant people in his life, and of his home town Bayonne; in fact an extensive autobiographical narrative with a commentary full of the sights and sounds and smells connected with being the living person Roland Barthes. Situated at the beginning of the 'authorless' text that forms the main part of the work, this biographical section contextualises the rather abstract alphabetically arranged material to come, softens its hard edges, indeed personalises it to a high degree. It is as if, in the writing of his authorless text, he repressed the personal as long as he could, but the need to express it could not be contained.

In Barthes' own practice, then, the death of the author turns out not to mean the complete banishment of the author's self from the writing process, but the suspension of the 'autobiographical self' created by language and history, in order to make space not only for the intertext to sound, but for the felt, bodily sense of self as well. (It might well be that Barthes suffered from an inordinately oppressive and controlling autobiographical self, which made the expression of feeling and thus the writing process difficult. Getting rid of his autobiographical self thus frees him to express himself more spontaneously. Indeed, he refers explicitly to this in his autobiography, in the section 'My head is confused', pp. 176–7). This is in fact very similar to the ideas we discussed in Chapter 2, where finding a writing voice was seen to involve suspending or getting beyond, but not killing off, our linguistically 'extended' sense of self, in order to connect with our 'core consciousness' or bodily, felt sense of self.

Authorship and identity

For French feminist, Hélène Cixous, being an author does not *remove* identity; rather it *confers* it. In the early stages of a writing apprenticeship, writing is a means of constructing ourselves out of the past that lives in the unconscious, 'this primitive primordial chaos that is ours, these darknesses in which we struggle when we are young' (Cixous, 1989, pp. 6–7). Writing enables us to 'emerge from this hell in the direction of the hidden day...the present' (p. 7). But having established a stronger sense of identity through exploring the unconscious, we need to move on to a second phase, which involves relinquishing this identity and allowing others to speak through us. Cixous sees this shift from writing the self to writing the other as a necessary part of a writing apprenticeship:

> It seems to me that there is an entire span of time, the time of the ego,[1] through which one must pass. One must become acquainted with this self, make a descent into the agitated secret of this self, into its tempests, one must cover this complex route with its meanderings into the chambers of the unconscious, in order to then emerge from me towards the other. The ideal: less and less of me and more and more of you (p. 9).

The fulfilment of the apprenticeship is to reach the point 'where the ego will hold fast, will consent to erase itself and to make room, to become, not the hero of the scene, but the scene itself: the site, the occasion of the other' (p. 9). This is no less than a 'state of "*démoïsa-tion*" [de-egoization], [a] state of without me, a depossession of the self, that will make possible the *possession* of the author by the characters' (p. 13).

Cixous is clearly advocating a version of Barthes' 'death of the author', the death of the autobiographical self, but there are important differences. First, a writing identity has to be created, and Cixous is aware of the importance of getting in touch with the felt, bodily self for this purpose. Second, the 'writing I', once created, is not killed off completely; rather it retracts and transforms itself into the space or site or scene where the voices of others will be heard. It provides a frame, but doesn't interfere, doesn't censor or edit, or even structure whatever emerges into the space. Indeed, for Cixous, along with some other feminist writers, the point is not to kill off the author *per se*, but rather to get beyond the *male* author, which they associate with singularity, linearity, control and reason, and to open up a space for a different conceptualisation of authorship more appropriate to women and minority groups and their need for agency (Miller, 1993). Writing as a woman – 'écriture feminine' – involves, for Cixous, relinquishing these male attributes and embracing what she sees as the essential chaos of woman's nature: it involves 'leaving oneself go, leaving oneself sink to the bottom of the now' and opening oneself up to 'a force and a materiality that will come, manifest itself, an ocean, a current that is always there, that will rise and carry me' (Cixous and Calle-Gruber, 1997, p. 41). She both argues for and demonstrates this 'leaving oneself go' in her celebrated essay 'The Laugh of the Medusa', a roller coaster of raw feeling, which subverts the linear form of the typically male, or 'patriarchal', academic essay. It is written, she says, in blood and 'white ink', alluding to the milk of motherhood (Cixous, 1981; cf. Jones, 1981, for a critique of Cixous's essentialising of women's nature).

In Cixous's later writings the relinquishing of control by the 'auto-biographical self' leads to a proliferation of voices in the text. *The Book of Promethea* is 'dictated' by two 'others': Promethea, about whom it is never clear whether she is a real 'other' or the self-other in Cixous's psyche, the ungraspable self in its entirety; and H, presumably standing for 'Hélène' and closely identified with the pre-linguistic bodily self: 'singing, burning, abolishing, liquidating, flowing, gushing' (Cixous, 1991, p. 6). The 'writing I' is a 'minor character', a scriptor in Barthes' sense, who merely receives the material dictated to her by the 'real makers' (p. 5), although she is the only one of the three who has language (p. 10), the only one who is capable of 'putting life into words' (p. 21). Cixous confesses, in the epigraph, to a certain fear of the book she is writing, because she doesn't know what will happen; she just has to plunge in and be in the 'burning bush'. It is an act of love.

For Cixous, then, removing the author does not amount to 'anonymous textuality' in Barthes' and Foucault's sense, but to a loving clearing of a space where the voices of the self and the voices of others can be heard; not 'the destruction of every voice' but a 'proliferation of the possibilities of hearing' (Walker, 1990, p. 568).

Authorship and agency

Cixous' attempt to do away with the singular author in favour of a plurality of authors is in some respects an advance on Barthes' thesis, but demoting the 'writing I' to a minor character who merely records the many different voices of the self and others in the writing space may simply result in DeLillo's hubbub of 'white noise' rather than a work that is readable by others. If the 'writing I' is disempowered, who or what in us has the agency or authority to edit and shape the work, to bring form to bear on our raw material, or indeed to declare the work finished (see Wollheim, 1974, on the painter's signature as determining what counts as a completed artwork)? This is a question that concerns novelist and critic David Lodge. Responding to Barthes' rejection of the idea that the author 'nourish[es] the book... exists before it, thinks, suffers, lives for it, is in the same relation of antecedence to his work as a father to his child', Lodge says that 'I *do* feel a kind of parental responsibility for the novels I write, that the composition of them *is*, in an important sense, my past, that I do think, suffer, live for a book while it is in progress' (Lodge, 1990, p. 15).

The analogy of the author involved in a work in progress with a benevolent parent bringing up a child is, in fact, a useful one and, as Lodge points out, 'truer to experience... than the [model] [Barthes] offers in its place' (p. 159). Good parents do not force their child to become what *they* want it to be, but try to provide a caring and guiding framework within which it can develop its potential. So, too, the working writer provides a framework within which the text will develop its own spontaneous life. In both of these scenarios there is an element of both freedom and control. Barthes and Cixous, in their different ways, want to abolish any element of control and allow the writing complete freedom. Within our analogy, they might be seen as bad parents, at best over-indulgent to their offspring, at worst neglectful and irresponsible. Indeed, whilst they argue for absolute freedom for the text, there is clear evidence in their own writings, as we will see in a moment, of a mind at work that structures and holds the work together.

Wayne Booth refers to the mind at work in literature as the *implied author*. As a writer writes, he says, 'he creates not simply an ideal, impersonal "man in general", but an implied version of "himself" that is different from the implied authors we meet in other men's works' (Booth, 1991, pp. 70–71; we will assume that Booth includes women here). The implied author is different from the narrator, 'the speaker in the work' (p. 73); it is the author's 'second self', although different works by the same author may contain quite different implied authors. It cannot therefore be thought of as identical with the real author, but elements of the real author's facts and values are likely to find their way into this textual 'self'. The implied author is the presence in the work of the person 'who has chosen, consciously or unconsciously... every detail, every quality, that is found in the work or implied by its silences' (p. 429); the person 'who apprehends the work intuitively as a completed artistic whole'

(p. 73). Shlomith Rimmon-Kenan agrees that the implied author acts as the 'governing consciousness' of the text, but prefers to think of it as 'de-personified', 'a set of implicit norms' which govern the text, rather than 'a speaker or a voice, i.e. a subject' (Rimmon-Kenan, 1996, pp. 88). Nevertheless, the 'implicit norms' could only have got into the work via the author's consciousness or unconscious and therefore imply a degree of personal presence. Mikhail Bakhtin's notion of the 'posited author' supports this view. The author is present in the text:

> ...as a point of view that differs from the point of view of the narrator. Behind the narrator's story we read a second story, the author's story; he is the one who tells us how the narrator tells stories, and also about the narrator himself. We acutely sense two levels at each moment in the story; one, the level of the narrator... and the other, the level of the author, who speaks (...in a refracted way) by means of this story and through this story... If one fails to sense this second level, the intentions and accents of the author himself, then one has failed to understand the work (Bakhtin, 1981, p. 314).

Even in Barthes' autobiography, which purposely sets out to remove the author, there is clearly discernible the presence of someone who determines the shape of the work as a whole, chooses to place one fragment next to another. Barthes calls his fragments 'so many stones on the perimeter of a circle: I spread myself around: my whole little universe in crumbs...' (Barthes, 1994, pp. 92–3). Note that it is *his* universe, that of his 'writing self', rather than the universe of impersonal language. Elsewhere he explains that whilst he has arranged the fragments in alphabetical order, where meaning threatened to arise spontaneously from the alphabetical arrangement, he has purposefully disrupted that potential by inserting other fragments into the sequence non-alphabetically (p. 148). He is also clearly present in the biographical section of photos and commentary at the beginning of the book, the person who determined retrospectively that they should be there, the person 'indulging' himself, as he puts it.

   If a work is to be more than a random, and potentially unreadable (to anyone other than the author), collection of words on the page, there has to be a governing consciousness who sets the voices and discourses in motion, makes choices about the form and structure of the work and holds the whole thing together whilst it is in progress. As Lodge says:

> Works of literature – in our era of civilization, at least – do not come into being by accident. They are intentional acts, produced by individual writers employing shared codes of signification according to a certain design, weighing and measuring the interrelation of part to part and parts to the developing whole, projecting the work against the antici-pated response of a hypothetical reader. Without such control and design there would be no reason to write one sentence rather than another, or to arrange one's sentences in any particular order (Lodge, 1990, p. 158).

Authorship and intention

Lodge highlights here the important question of intention in the writing process, which has been implicit in much of what we have said so far in this chapter. As with critical discussions of the role of the author in the work, discussions of the author's intentions have, over the past thirty years or so, focused primarily on the finished work rather than the work in progress, and have been polarised between those who see the author's intentions as the primary source of meaning in a work (e.g. Hirsch, 1967) and those who deny them a role altogether (e.g. Wimsatt and Beardsley, 1954). Neither of these is the most helpful in understanding the role of the author's intentions in the writing process. Clearly each of us who writes has different levels of intention when we conceive of, or start work on, a writing project. Some of us will be quite clear what we intend to say; others will begin with a blank sheet and wait for material to emerge spontaneously. Even if we adopt the latter approach, as soon as material starts to emerge, intentions will emerge with it, influencing the way we shape and develop the material. It seems highly unlikely that we can write creatively without having any intentions at all, although our inten-tions may be predominantly unconscious, and what we intend to say may be quite different from what we end up saying. But having too many *conscious* intentions at the outset, or at least intentions that cannot be modified as the writing proceeds, is likely to inhibit the spontaneous life of the text and impair the end product. Of course it may be the case, as we discuss in Chapter 6, that there is an inevitable tension between our intentions for our writing and the spontaneous life of the text, but ideally we need to develop *a stance* towards the work in progress that allows our material as much freedom as possible whilst also taking into account the need to hold and shape the material as it develops. As the Polish-American novelist Jerzy Kosinski says in the epigraph to this chapter, an essential stage in the writing process is the point at which we learn to stand outside the material we want to write about, and this requires learning to stand outside of ourselves and our everyday reality as well, thus entering 'into a fluid and less rigidly limited dimension' of consciousness (Kosinski, 1992, p. 201). This is not a complete 'de-egoization', in Cixous's sense, but a reflexive relationship with ourselves in which our writing identity – our 'writing I' – instead of being rigid and controlling, becomes fluid and flexible. To put it another way, it is *a metaphorical relationship with self,* which enables us to entertain, in the 'space of composition' (Clark, 1997), more than one aspect of ourselves simultaneously. Philip Lyons, whom we discussed in the last chapter, calls his sense of a writing identity 'a fictional I which is both me and not me' (Lyons, 1999, p. 77).

The Argentine writer Jorge Luis Borges demonstrates very well this 'me and not me' relationship with the self-in-the-writing-process in his short prose piece 'Borges and I' (Borges, 1981a, pp. 282–3). Borges, the first person narrator, is walking through the streets of Buenos Aires musing about Borges the author, his writing-self. This other Borges is the one written about in biographical dictionaries, the one who receives letters in the mail. Whilst it is the narrator who comes up with the ideas, it is this other Borges who takes them over, often subverting them in the process. As time goes by the narrator recognises himself less in the books of Borges the author than in the books of others or in the occasional phrase of music. There is sadness for him in all this, and yet he is not hostile towards his writing-self. Whilst his physical body will eventually die, he has a sort of permanence in the words of Borges the author, so the writing somehow justifies his existence.

The narrator here could be said to be a 'guest' in Borges' text, but rather than a 'paper author' created at the moment of writing (Barthes, 1986, p. 61), he is a privileged guest, the person who gives life to the ideas, and who holds and shapes the material whilst it is in progress. At another level of the text, one senses in Borges' story an implied or posited author who benevolently and ironically allows his narrator to amuse himself with his thoughts. He is a 'governing consciousness' who creates a space for the text to *play* (p. 62). Thus there are no fewer than three different textual 'selves' in this short piece of writing.

The idea of the author as a benevolent governing consciousness is central to Bakhtin's view of authorship in the novel, although at times he seems also to want to deny the author such a role (see Bakhtin, 1984). The author's stance, he suggests, is both inside and outside of the work in progress: inside it to the extent that he has managed to communicate aspects of himself in the work in the guise of a narrator or the consciousness of a character, but outside it, in that he cannot speak directly in his work: 'The writer is a person who is able to work in language whilst standing outside language; who has the gift of indirect speaking' (Bakhtin, 1986, p. 110). This objectifying of the self or 'outsideness' does not imply indifference; the author's relationship to what he creates is 'indirect empathy' (Palmieri, 1998, p. 51). In order to achieve such a relationship, the author has to relinquish his fixed and singular identity and to become an 'unfinalizable' or open-ended self-in-process. Indeed, Bakhtin sees human beings as intrinsically 'unfinalizable', although with a tendency to become fixed in singular, monologic identities. Our awareness of our unfinalisability is greater, he suggests, when we are in the process of creation than in everyday life, hence the potential of creativity for personal development: 'By objectifying myself... I gain the opportunity to have an authentically dialogic relation with myself' (Bakhtin, 1986, p. 122).

Authorship and responsibility

If it is the case that the self of the author is an important presence both inside and outside of the text, it follows that authorship entails a considerable degree of responsibility for what is written. This might sound commonsensical, but as Barthes says in his autobiography, if the scriptor is created in the moment of writing and has no life beyond the text, he cannot be held responsible, to others or to himself, for the words he places on the page (Barthes, 1994, p. 153). Such a view provides an easy alibi for writers wishing not to be associated with their ideas. Ironically, this was a focus of considerable debate around the poststructuralist critic Paul de Man who, with Barthes and others, was highly influential in establishing the cult of impersonality in writing, but who, after his death, was identified as the author of some 170 anti-Semitic and pro-Nazi articles published in a Belgian collaborationist newspaper in the early 1940s (Burke, 1998, pp. 1–7).

For Bakhtin, personal responsibility is a central feature of art making. The author is a 'chronotope', a prism of time and space through which his words are projected (Bakhtin, 1981, pp. 84, 254–7). Every chronotope is individual, in that no-one else can have the same experience as us, even though we may occupy a similar time-space location. Writing is an 'act' in which we express our unique perspective on the world. The most important thing about an act is that it is *signed* or *signed off* by the person acting, that the writer takes responsibility for his particular location in time-space. In this sense, as authors, we are under an ethical obligation to express our chronotope through our writing, for 'no-one else can do what we can do, ever' (Bakhtin, 1993; translation in Morson and Emerson, 1990, p. 179). This is a very different perspective on the writing process from that put forward by poststructuralist critics. Where, for Foucault, it doesn't matter who is speaking in a piece of writing, for Bakhtin the author's signature indicates that it is the work of a unique, unrepeatable individual located at a particular time and place, with a personal responsibility for that work and for deciding when it is finished. This doesn't mean that authors cannot subsequently change their views. As we have said above, the human being, for Bakhtin, is intrinsically unfinalisable, open-ended, constantly subject to change. The artwork, too, is unfinalisable in the sense that it is always open to new interpretations, new readings, by ourselves and others. It is the *act* of writing itself that is a finalisation, and taking responsibility for the act is what Bakhtin is concerned with. In his later writings his notion of responsibility developed more of a connotation of 'answerability', increasing the emphasis on the ethics of the creative act. On this view authorship is seen as an ethical responsibility to say what we have to say because we occupy a unique niche in history. This is potentially a very powerful motivation for writers in the process of writing, although – as the experience of Salman Rushdie demonstrates (see Ruthven, 1991) – the writer's responsibility may be accompanied by considerable personal risks.

Authorship and literary tradition

Taking responsibility for the time and place we occupy is part of the challenge we take up when we choose to become writers. Another is to develop a relationship with the literary traditions out of which we write. For T.S. Eliot it was the poet's responsibility to contribute to the 'ideal order' of the 'existing monuments' of the literary tradition, by simultaneously working within that order and modifying it by the creation of new work. 'What is to be insisted upon is that the poet must develop or procure the consciousness of the past and that he should continue to develop this consciousness throughout his career'. This involved 'a continual surrender of himself as he is at the moment' – the state of impersonality we talked about earlier – 'to something which is more valuable' (Eliot, 1953, pp. 23–6). This characterises the English literary tradition as oppressive, in the same way that in Borges' day there was an expectation on Argentine writers to embody within their work national traits and local colour, to help their nation to develop a cultural tradition (Borges, 1981b, pp. 214–5). Needless to say, Borges argues strongly against such expectations: 'We cannot limit ourselves to purely Argentine subjects in order to be Argentine' (p. 219).

For literary critic Harold Bloom, the writer's relationship with literary tradition is oppressive in a different way, fraught with what he calls the 'anxiety of influence'. The writer (whom he conceives of as male) is in Freud's Oedipal relationship with his literary forebears, the son who must supercede or symbolically kill the father in order to possess the mother, the text (Bloom, 1973). In Bloom's view it is only 'strong' poets who can successfully break out of their forefathers' influence to become original in their own right; 'weak' poets, by contrast, never manage to do this and continue to work within the tradition. The process by which 'strong' poets achieve originality is by misreading their forefathers' writings, or indeed *not* reading them, as the important works of a literary tradition – say those of Shakespeare in the English literary tradition – may be known to an apprentice writer without him having read them closely. Indeed he may not be fully aware of the extent to which he is writing out of or against a particular precursor and may defend himself against the knowledge that this is what he is doing (Bloom, 1975).

Whether or not we see this in Oedipal terms, there can certainly be an element of competitiveness in our relation with the work of other writers, a tendency whenever we read a published novel or a poem to compare it favourably or unfavourably with our own work. Sandra Gilbert and Susan Gubar focus on the damaging aspect of such comparisons when they suggest that writers (here specifically women writers) suffer not so much from an 'anxiety of influence', as an 'anxiety of authorship'. They draw attention to 'the tensions and anxieties, hostilities and inadequacies writers feel when they confront not only the achievements of their predecessors but the traditions of genre, style, and metaphor that they inherit from [their] "forefathers"' (Gilbert and Gubar, 1979, pp. 48–51). Women, they suggest, need to find their 'foremothers' in the literary tradition in order to gain confidence in their own writing and to develop a style and genre of their own. Henry Louis Gates Jr. makes a similar point about the need for African-American writers to find their own 'canon' of precursors, in order to provide a nourishing context for writing (Gates, 1992).

As both male and female writers attest in letters, diaries and essays, identifying the work of others writers with whom they feel a rapport can sustain them in the 'essential solitude' (Blanchot, 1982) of the writing life. Franz Kafka, for example, noted how important it was for him to discover the writings of Søren Kierkegaard, whose state of mind he saw as very similar to his own: 'He bears me out like a friend' (Kafka, 1978, p. 230). In turn, Kafka was one of the writers with whom Hélène Cixous felt a deep affinity. But this was a purely textual relationship, and she was still 'feeling a little lonely in literature'. Then she discovered the work of a living novelist, Clarice Lispector, who was 'the equivalent for me of Kafka', and it became possible to make a real, sustaining relationship with this 'unhoped for other' (Cixous, 1989, p. 10; see Conley, 1992, p. 128, for a critique of Cixous' idealisation of writers as 'a special group of the *Happy Few*', amongst whom she implicitly includes herself).

Wide reading across cultures and literary traditions, and across critical and creative boundaries, can help us to find points of contact with other writers whose style or themes resonate with us and help us to develop our own. We may consciously or unconsciously make use of these styles or themes intertextually, as Graham Swift does by using the narrative technique of William Faulkner's *As I Lay Dying* (1929) in his novel *Last Orders* (1997); or we may consciously use others' writing as a basis for our own, as Jacqueline Rose does by basing her novel *Albertine* (2002) on a character from Marcel Proust's *In Search of Lost Time* (1913–27). These borrowings imply a nourishing and dialogic relationship between writers working within literary traditions. They return us to our theme of reflexivity, this time a simultaneous closeness and distance in our relationship with the works of others.

Recommended reading

Sean Burke's excellent anthology *Authorship from Plato to the Postmodern* (1995) contains many extracts from key texts, including those of Eliot, Barthes, Foucault and Cixous. Burke's *The Death and Return of the Author* (2nd ed. 1998) is also essential reading. Mikhail Bakhtin's early work on authorship 'Author and Hero in Aesthetic Activity' in *Art and Answerability* (1990) is important but quite difficult to come by. Morson and Emerson's *Mikhail Bakhtin: Creation of a Prosaics* (1990) is a fine, detailed companion to the reading of any of Bakhtin's works. David Lodge's *After Bakhtin* (1990) contains thoughtful chapters on authorship from the author's point of view, in the light of Bakhtin's work. Graham Allen's *Intertextuality* (2000) provides a clear and wide-ranging introduction to the main theoreticians of intertextuality and authorship.

Writing exercises

- Think of the way members of your family speak; perhaps you come from a family which speaks (or whose forebears used to speak) with a particular accent or dialect, but which you yourself have lost; write a poem or prose piece in that dialect in the voice of a family member.
- Write a poem or piece of fiction under the title 'The Death of the Author'.
- Imagine yourself into Roland Barthes' 'guest in the text' and write a piece from the guest's point of view.
- Taking 'Borges and I' as a model, write about your relationship with your writing self, your 'self-on-the-page'. You might, for example, like to arrange a meeting between the two (or more!) of you.
- Look at a novel or short story and try to distinguish between the narrator who speaks in the work and the implied author. Write a commentary on the novel or story in the first person from the point of view of the implied author.
- Make a list of ten books or writers who have influenced your own writing; try to rank them in order of importance. If you are working in a group, explain in what way these books or writers have influenced you.
- Write a letter to one of the writers who have influenced you, telling him or her about the nature of their influence. Write a letter back from the writer.

4   Creativity

Lie down on the bright hill
with the moon's hand on your cheek,
your flesh deep in the white folds of your dress,
and you will not hear the passionate mole
extending the length of his darkness,
or the owl arranging all of the night,
which is his wisdom, or the poem
filling your pillow with its blue feathers.
But if you step out of your dress and move into the shade,
the mole will find you, so will the owl, and so will the poem,
and you will fall into another darkness, one you will find
yourself making and remaking until it is perfect.

Mark Strand, 'The Dress', 1995.

In the above poem Mark Strand uses the metaphor of a dress to explore the self in the writing process. The dress, with its white folds, conjures up reason and orderliness, correct comportment in the world. As such, it is an impediment to the creative process; it interferes with the poet's necessary contact with the more unruly unconscious, here represented by the night and the creatures intensely going about their business in the darkness. Sloughing off the dress removes the impediment, frees the body-self, thus making possible a deeper engagement with the unconscious. Only then can the real creative work begin in earnest.

Strand's metaphor evokes again the idea of 'shelving the self' or reflexivity in the writing process, which has been the central concern of the last few chapters. But how do creative writers actually do this 'shelving'? How do they manage not only to suspend their reason in order to gain access to their deeper selves, but also to objectify their material so that it can be developed into art?

Creative writers and daydreaming

This, from the psychoanalyst's perspective rather than the writer's, is the problem Freud considers in his essay 'Creative Writers and Daydreaming' (1908): how do creative writers create, where do they derive their material from, and 'how do they manage to make such an impression on us with it and to arouse in us emotions of which, perhaps, we had not even thought ourselves capable?' (Freud, 1985, p. 131). In attempting to answer these questions, Freud looks for an everyday activity with which to compare the writing process. His first thought is that it is similar to childhood play. Both the child and the creative writer create a world of their own, a fantasy world that they take very seriously, investing it with a great deal of emotion, but which they are also able to distinguish clearly from reality (p. 132).

This similarity is, however, paradoxical. Most adults, as they mature, relinquish childhood play in favour of the world of career, moneymaking and responsibility. Where the adult is unable to do so, play becomes transposed into daydreaming which, because in Freud's thinking it is largely of a sexual nature, has to be hidden from others and is usually accompanied by feelings of shame; often it is repressed altogether into the unconscious, which Freud sees as the repository of unwanted or forbidden thoughts and feelings. Fantasy life for Freud is essentially unhealthy: 'a happy person never fantasises', he says (p. 134), and if fantasy becomes overwhelming, it can constitute an illness. Only two categories of people are accustomed to revealing their fantasies: those suffering from nervous illnesses who tell their fantasies to doctors in hope of a cure, and creative writers. These latter are able to suspend their critical intelligence and, like children, allow their fantasies free play without being overwhelmed by them or feeling ashamed. Unlike children, however, they have the ability to disguise their fantasies through fictionalising, and bring form and structure to bear, allowing others to derive pleasure from them without self-reproach (p. 141).

Creative writers, then, for Freud, are sick because they cannot relinquish their fantasies, but specially gifted because they have a more flexible, or reflexive, relationship with their inner life and the ability to transpose their fantasies into art. He never resolved this unhelpful conundrum, and his thinking about creativity was always negative in that he saw it as an aberration, a diversion of sexual energy from its natural object, the opposite sex. Nevertheless there is much in Freud's thinking here that is useful. His comparison of creative writing with childhood play captures very well the self-absorption and spontaneity of the creative process. His understanding also of the reflexivity of the creative process – the writer's ability both to suspend his critical intelligence in order to gain access to his fantasies, and to distance himself from them and reshape them into a form that others can enjoy – is an important contribution.

Freud believed that these abilities were innate and that creativity was therefore a special biological endowment. Recent thinking in the neurosciences suggests that, whilst we all have the *potential* to be creative, the way the brain is 'wired' has an important role to play in the degree of creativity we experience. But encounters with the physical and social environment play a crucial role in shaping and developing that 'wiring' and, of course, the production of creative artefacts requires a cultural context (Damasio, 2001, p. 59). However nature and nurture work together in creating the conditions for creativity, it is possible to *develop* our creativity, and an important starting point, as Strand's poem makes clear, is understanding that the creative process cannot be forced to happen. The poem will not come into being through the use of reason and intention alone; rather the writer has to wait and let the poem come to him. In the first instance at least, creativity is very much a 'hands-off' process, not so much a 'doing' as a 'being'.

Writing with the imaginative body

This is indeed what Marion Milner, one of the most eloquent explorers of the creative process, discovered in her attempts to draw. When she drew deliberately, copying the object, the results were lifeless and unsatisfying (Milner, 1971, p. 35). In order to animate her drawings she had to develop a different way of relating to objects, to attend not so much in 'thinking mode', the sharp-pointed focusing with the mind, but in 'feeling mode', the broad, hovering attention with the body, what she called her 'imaginative body' because it felt like an extension of her bodily self into space (p. 36). She had already identified this 'feeling mode' in her earlier attempts to find out, through journal writing, what her unconscious mind liked, as opposed to the things she tended consciously to impose on herself

(Milner, 1952). It involved what she referred to as an 'internal gesture' (p. 70), whereby her everyday 'I' relinquished its usual control and took, as it were, a step back, allowing an inner space, a womb-like inner realm, to open up inside her, so that she was simultaneously inside and outside of herself, both the observer and the observed. She describes this 'internal gesture' more precisely as 'simply to press my awareness out against the limits of my body till there was vitality in all my limbs and I felt smooth and rounded'. It was very much a physical feeling, a sense of becoming 'fatter', even though it was a gesture of the mind (p. 74).

Drawing with the 'imaginative body', Milner found, changed her relationship to her chosen object. Instead of experiencing it as separate, somewhere 'out there', it became a part of herself, so that instead of trying to draw, say, a chair 'as it really was' in the outside world, she was able to allow her unconscious spontaneously to imbue the object with her own felt, imaginative life. She had learned to inhabit what Donald Winnicott called the 'potential space', the imaginative space where inner psychic reality and the external world meet. Winnicott believed that this first comes into being between the mother and the baby during what he called the 'transitional stage', when the child is learning to be on its own. As the baby becomes aware of its mother as a separate being, it learns to tolerate her absence by adopting as substitutes objects that are associated with her. Whilst these objects come from the outside world, they are imbued with the child's emotional life through the connection with the mother; therefore they are 'transitional' between inner and outer. Winnicott sees the creating of the 'transitional object' as the child's first creative act, which sets the stage for all subsequent creativity (Winnicott, 1971, pp. 95–103).

For Milner, what emerged spontaneously into the 'potential space' wasn't always benign. In practising her 'free drawing', she had to contend with the emergence of aspects of herself that she didn't particularly like or want to see, her own particular 'monsters' (Milner, 1971, pp. 35–44). Giving free reign to unconscious forces, she found, could be an unpredictable and potentially dangerous business. Strand's poem also characterises the creative process as a risky undertaking. Taking off the dress involves exposure and vulnerability. His use of the term 'shade' evokes a connection with the underworld – 'the shades' of Greek mythology – a darkness deeper than night and fraught with unknown dangers. In order to hold open the space for the imagination, then, we have to be able to tolerate the chaos and discomfort of our inner lives, the uncertainty of what may emerge and the possibility that, like Milner and Strand, we may encounter 'monsters' in the process. Somehow, in spite of the dangers, we have to find a way of keeping the 'potential space' open, so that our raw material can emerge spontaneously and become available for transforming into art. This has strong similarities with what John Keats called 'negative capability', a state in which the writer 'is capable of being in uncertainty, mysteries, doubts, without any irritable reaching after fact and reason' (Keats, 1947, p. 72).

Developing negative capability in the creative process

Many creative artists have experimented with ways of attaining 'negative capability' in the creative process. Some, like the nineteenth century writer Thomas de Quincey, advocated drugs as a means of bypassing the critical faculty and giving rise to spontaneous mental imagery (De Quincey, 1821), and writers such as Aldous Huxley and William Burroughs continued this line of experimentation into recent times. A less hazardous approach is Carl Jung's method of 'active imagination', devised for the therapeutic purpose of achieving a healthy balance between the conscious and the unconscious, but which has an obvious application to developing artistic creativity. Jung believed that it was possible to train ourselves to produce 'free fantasies' through 'systematic exercises for eliminating critical attention, thus producing a vacuum in consciousness', an inner space not intruded upon by the 'inner critic or judge who immediately comments on everything' we say or do (Jung, 1916, in Chodorow 1997, pp. 50, 54). Active imagination can be practised through any of the arts; it involves turning the attention inwards and focusing on a feeling, however vague, and allowing it to emerge into a visual image, idea or shape, which is then given form. For the writer this might be done through automatic writing.

Writers from André Breton and the Dadaists to Allen Ginsberg and the Beat poets have used automatic writing as the basis of their creative process. More recently the American educationist, Peter Elbow, has done much to develop it as a technique for training people to write. His method of 'freewriting' advocates dividing the creative process into two distinct stages: the chaotic creating stage where the critical faculty is suspended, and thoughts and feelings emerge freely and spontaneously; and the more leisurely and considered editing stage, where the critical faculty is employed to craft and edit the material into its final form. This, in his view, enables writers to avoid the premature censorship of the critical faculty and to overcome the fear of the blank page (Elbow, 1973). Others, such as Natalie Goldberg (1986), suggest a similar approach.

The way the freewriting exercise is constructed (full details are given at the end of this chapter) makes it an ideal tool for developing 'negative capability' in writing: rather than simply advocating free association onto the page, with all the uncertainty and anxiety that involves, it provides a frame within which unconscious thoughts and feelings can emerge freely. The fixed time slots, the rules and, in the second and subsequent free-writes, the focus on the chosen word or phrase, create a 'holding environment' (Winnicott, 1971) or 'framed gap' (Milner, 1987), a background role, in fact, for the retracted critical faculty, which helps to keep open the space for the imagination and to render it, if not entirely safe, then at least manageable for short periods.

A fine literary representation of a 'framed gap' that provides space for the emergence, through free association, of unconscious thoughts and feelings is Virginia Woolf's short story, 'The Mark on the Wall' (Woolf, 1993). The story's first person narrator is recounting a recent experience. She was sitting reading in front of the fire after tea on a winter's afternoon, when she looked up and noticed a small, round, black mark on the wall just above the fireplace. This aroused her interest, but feeling lazy she didn't get up to look at it, rather she started musing about what it was and how it might have got there. Perhaps the previous owners of the house had made a hole to hang a small picture. This immediately led to wondering who the previous owners were, and before she knew it her thoughts had veered off in another direction altogether, and she had consciously to rein them in to focus again on the mark on the wall. And so it went repeatedly, the narrator trying to find an explanation for the mark, but each time she let her mind run free over the possibilities, her thoughts headed off in other and sometimes uncomfortable directions, to things she didn't really want to think about – thoughts of the war, the instability and unknowability of life, and the horrors that inhabited her dreams. She tried to keep the dark thoughts at bay by conjuring up pastoral idylls or things that made her feel good about herself, but slowly and surely the thoughts and feelings that really bothered her came to the surface. Like the chosen word or phrase in Elbow's exercise, the mark on the wall and the desire to make sense of it acted as a long but finite leash for the unconscious; it allowed the narrator to encounter unconscious thoughts and feelings through free association but to rein them in when they became too threatening.

At one level the story is a literary representation of the mind's natural tendency to free associate, a version of the 'stream of consciousness' technique beloved of the Modernist[1] writers. At another level it captures effectively the inevitable tension in the creative process between order and chaos, the necessary 'rhythmic interchange of the two kinds of attention' that Milner observes between the critical faculty with its tendency to organise and order everything into hierarchies, and the more relaxed watching mode of the 'imaginative body' that allows access to spontaneous material, but which also runs the risk of uncovering dangers that lie in the unconscious (Milner, 1971, p. 84). The precariousness of this 'negative capability' is underlined by the ending of Woolf's story, where the narrator's companion both identifies the mark on the wall and gives voice to the dangers in the narrator's mind, thus on the one hand destroying her creative reverie but on the other rescuing her from the discomforts associated with it.

Free associative writing on Peter Elbow's model can be an effective technique for developing the kind of reflexivity in writing that Freud identifies as the special mark of the writer, and particularly for gaining access to raw material in the unconscious that may be repressed or not easily available. It can also be seen as a means of *developing* the unconscious itself and hence, enhancing creativity in a different way. Psychoanalyst Christopher Bollas regards the unconscious in a much more positive light than Freud. He sees it not simply as Freud's repository of banished, unwanted material, but as a receptacle where 'ideas or feelings and words...[are]...given a mental space for development which is not possible in consciousness' (Bollas, 1993, p. 74). He describes the unconscious as a network or 'meshwork' of interconnecting thoughts and feelings (Bollas, 2002, p. 38) within which there are areas of the self's psychic life that constantly gather impressions. These Bollas calls 'psychic genera' (p. 45). Forming initially 'through the associations of thoughts during the day' in response to lived experience, these psychic genera progressively gather to themselves further thoughts and impressions (p. 48). These 'gathering points'

press for representation in one form or another, sometimes expressing themselves in dreams, sometimes in works of art. The work of free
association, whether within a psychoanalysis or outside of it, extends
the reach of the unconscious, developing and flexing the networks
and connections that make it up (pp. 39–40). For the creative writer,
this kind of 'combinatory play' of the unconscious (Bollas, 1993,
pp. 75–7) is an essential characteristic of the process of moving from
the formation of an initial idea, which may be wholly vague and
unformed, through the gathering of associated material, to the point
where the artwork begins to take shape on the page.[2]

Thus, engaging on a regular basis in a free associative activity such
as freewriting not only gives us access to unconscious material, but
can also help us to develop the reach of the unconscious and to facilitate the unconscious work of the creative process.

Creativity as intrinsically reflexive

The view of creativity we are pursuing here – a free-associative,
reflexive model involving collaboration between the critical faculty
and the unconscious – characterises it as a dynamic process in which
writers abandon their need for certainty and security, and find out
what they have to say in the course of the writing itself. Gary Morson
calls this 'creation by potential' (Morson, 1987, pp. 173–89). People
new to writing are often accustomed to think of the creative process
on the model of the 'classical' view, according to which writing
involves first finding ideas, and only when they are clear and thor-
oughly worked out, committing them to the page. This emphasis on
craft and intellectual control rather than on intuition and spontaneity
privileges the role of the critical faculty. Edgar Allen Poe's comments
on the writing of his story 'The Raven' are representative of this
approach:

> It is my design to render it manifest that no one point in its composition
> is referrible either to accident or intuition – that the work proceeded,
> step by step, to its completion with the precision and rigid consequence
> of a mathematical problem (Poe, 1967, p. 482; in Morson, 1987, p. 178).

An equally popular but opposite view, which places the emphasis on
the spontaneous, intuitive dimension of the creative process, is that

the writer's material emerges ready-made and in its final form directly from the unconscious, obviating the need to work on it. This view was particularly prevalent amongst the nineteenth century 'romantic' poets. Here is Percy Bysshe Shelley's celebrated 'A Defence of Poetry' (1840):

> Poetry is not like reasoning, a power to be exerted according to the determination of the will. A man cannot say, 'I will compose poetry'. The greatest poet cannot even say it; for the mind in creation is as a fading coal, which some invisible influence, like an inconstant wind, awakens to transitory brightness; this power arises from within, like the colour of a flower which fades and changes as it is developed, and the conscious portions of our natures are unprophetic either of its approach or its departure... I appeal to the greatest poets of the present day, whether it is not an error to assert that the finest passages of poetry are produced by labour and study' (Shelley, 2003, pp. 696–97).

'Creation by potential' brings into play simultaneously the two dimensions of the creative process represented by the classical and romantic views, and is particularly well described by Mikhail Bakhtin in his discussion of Dostoevsky's writing method (Bakhtin, 1984). For Bakhtin, when Dostoevsky enters the fictional space of a novel he does so not in the spirit of control or superiority to his characters and narrators. Of necessity he brings them into being and establishes the scenario in which they find themselves, but once this is done, he relinquishes his privileged status as author – the 'surplus' of knowledge he has of his characters and narrators by virtue of having created them – gives them freedom to speak in their own voices and to act in their own right, and enters into a dialogue with them on equal terms (pp. 47–77) (for a fuller discussion see Chapter 6). As we have said in the last chapter, the author – or rather the 'implied' or 'posited' author – holds the work together as the governing consciousness of the whole and thus has a significant role in providing shape and structure, but within that 'framed gap' he allows the story to develop a life of its own without undue interference. It is out of the *potential* contained in this 'polyphony' of voices (Morson would argue also for a 'polyphony of incident') that the finished work emerges. The American writer, Robert Coover, plays with this approach to the creative process in his short story, 'The Magic Poker' (Coover, 1973).

The main events of Coover's story might be summarised as follows: two city girls make a visit by motor boat to an island on a hot summer's day, where they explore the vandalised remains of a mansion and its outbuildings, encounter two men and find a poker lying in the grass, which they take with them when they return to the mainland. This unpromising outline is, however, misleading, as events in this story are neither linear nor straightforward.

The story is told by a first person narrator who, at the outset, is still in the process of creating the island, the mansion and the area immediately surrounding it. Whilst he does this light-heartedly, there is something malicious and wilful about him. He is not a benign creator god conjuring something beautiful out of nothing; his creation certainly has the potential for beauty, but before anyone has had a chance to enjoy the mansion, he makes a point of wrecking it. Nor is he an omnipotent creator god, in full control of his creation. 'Anything can happen', he tells us ominously (p. 14), and indeed things do happen, some of which the narrator has obviously not planned. A boat arrives carrying two women. A wild, naked, Caliban[3] figure crouches in the woods watching them, the caretaker's son, we are told, who got left behind as a child, when the island was abandoned. And then, incongruously, an elegant, pipe-smoking man appears on the verandah of the dilapidated mansion. It is as if the author-narrator has conjured up a scene and then sits back to watch what will happen. The result is partly willed and partly spontaneous. Like Plato's artisan-god or demiurge, he creates the world out of whatever material comes to hand and once it is in existence he cannot ensure that it will behave in the way he expects. Thus odd things occur: contradictory moments of action, magical comings and goings that defy reason.

There is a strong atmosphere of menace in the unpredictability of this chaotic world as well as in the potential violence and sexuality of the characters' freedom. Indeed, the narrator himself becomes alarmed at the way the fantasy world he has set in motion is developing when, for example, the pipe-smoking man entertains thoughts of removing the tight, gold trousers of one of the girls. Before long, the narrator realises that the scenario is acquiring a life of its own and doesn't need him any more. He observes a history of the mansion and its inhabitants beginning to take shape, the emergence of two young children at the piano, and an older woman who turns out to be the children's grandmother. Once established, these characters become an integral part of the story, present and past intermingling in a confused mélanges that the narrator is powerless to control.

Towards the end of the story the narrator tries to impose order by constructing a retrospective plotline on the material that has emerged. He toys with various possibilities, which progressively become more and more fanciful and tend increasingly to fairytale. By the end, the narrator has effectively relinquished his attempts to contain what he has set in motion and has handed over responsibility to the original owners of the house, who are now seen as having created it in the first place. As in Woolf's story, when fantasy life gets too difficult to handle, someone else has to be brought in to deal with it.

Clearly, Coover's story takes Bakhtin's ideal relationship between author-narrator and characters to its logical extreme and makes ironic play of it, but in so doing he captures, as Woolf does in a different way, the tension in the creative process between freedom and control, and the chaotic, unpredictable and potentially dangerous nature of creativity. The author creates an outline scenario, a 'framed gap', which in the guise of narrator he settles down to observe. Material emerges spontaneously into the gap and the narrator does his best to find a place for it even when it doesn't make obvious sense or when it upsets or shocks him. He neither censors the material, nor does he (at least at the outset) try to impose a single narrative shape on it. Rather he revels in the play the material offers. Paradoxically, it is his relaxed attitude and ability to let the material develop a life of its own that lead to problems. Rather than achieving a workable balance between the spontaneous creative forces and the critical faculty, he lets the creative forces get out of hand; as demonstrated by his frantic and belated attempts to draw the material together into a linear whole, his 'gap' has been too loosely framed. The dangers of allowing fantasy too much freedom are underlined in the final paragraph of the story where we learn that the feral man has, without the narrator's knowledge, been killed.

Of course in this metafictional[4] world, one detects behind the inept creator god who narrates the story an implied author whose implicit intention is to experiment with ideas and who can intervene to order the chaos if he wants. But there is a strong sense in this story that he is purposefully suspending his natural tendency to order and control his fantasy world and is prepared to allow it free reign, with all the uncertainty and potential dangers that entails.

Here, the writer with his fantasy world certainly fulfils Freud's comparison with the child at play and, as for Freud's writer, there is no shame or guilt about his fantasies, surprise and alarm certainly, but for the most part he tolerates both the chaos and the unpredictability of his unconscious. Indeed, the initial threat of violence and sexuality is dissipated in the lightheartedness and pleasure of play, and by using a first-person narrator who talks directly to the reader, the author encourages the reader to participate in this risky and tantalising game, to delight in the forbidden. It is only at the end that we are reminded of the double-edgedness and danger of the game. Fantasy, even childhood play, can sometimes get seriously nasty.

Creativity and trust

In order then to transpose our fantasies into art, we have to learn to operate on a precarious borderline. We have to be prepared to give up our familiar, everyday sense of ourselves, to relinquish, even if only temporarily, our reason and to tolerate a state that may seem like a kind of madness or a kind of dreaming whilst awake, with all the potential hazards that involves. In other words, we have to rediscover in ourselves our childhood capacity for spontaneous play and become a self-in-process. But we also have to find a way of holding that creative state, to give it a frame, in order that whatever emerges may be shaped and transformed into an end-product which, as Freud says, creates an impression on others and arouses in them emotions of which they have not thought themselves capable. Keats' 'negative capability' is an apt description of this state in that, although 'negative' here seems primarily to imply 'absence' rather than 'disagreeableness', it also evokes 'presence' – the presence of the dark side of creativity and the difficulties and dangers inherent in it. As Gabriel Josipovici suggests, the mark of those writers whom we regard as 'great' is that they manage to *trust* the negative in themselves long enough to allow them to transpose their difficult material into art (Josipovici, 1999). This is true of a writer like Franz Kafka who, as his letters and diaries attest, was an excruciatingly self-tormented individual, and yet who managed in his short life to produce novels that transposed his painful 'feeling states' into powerful images: in *The Trial* (1925) an all-pervasive sense of guilt for which there is no obvious reason, and in *The Castle* (1926) an endless striving after something that is forever tantalisingly out of reach. What enabled Kafka to stay with the negative in himself was, at least during his most productive phase, the balance between closeness and distance which he managed to establish through his epistolary connection with his long-suffering fiancée, Felice Bauer (Canetti, 1982). With her unwitting help he achieved, if only temporarily, the kind of 'holding environment' that Winnicott believed was necessary for creativity to occur.

We too have to find our own particular ways of holding the space for the imagination, of rendering it 'safe enough' for creativity to take place. Mentors and writing groups can be effective in providing environments where our work can be nurtured and held. Reading widely and studying the craft of writing help us develop an intuitive understanding of the conceptual spaces (Boden, 2004) within which we work as writers. Ultimately though we have to find the motivation and the *courage* to create, and learning to work with and trust the unconscious is a central part of that process.

Recommended reading

Arthur Koestler's *The Act of Creation* (1977) is a classic text. Margaret Boden's *The Creative Mind* (2nd ed. 2004) explores the idea of conceptual space in creativity. For recent neurophysiological thinking and its resonance with creative artists, see Karl H. Pfenninger and Valerie R. Shubik (eds), *The Origins of Creativity* (2001). Daniel Nettle's *Strong Imagination: Madness, Creativity and Human Nature* (2001) offers an interesting if controversial view of the relationship between madness and creativity. M.H. Abrams' *The Mirror and the Lamp* (1953) continues to be a useful introduction to the 'romantic' view of creativity, but see Marilyn Butler's critique in *Romantics, Rebels and Reactionaries* (1981). Timothy Clark's *The Theory of Inspiration* (1997) is a scholarly account of composition and subjectivity in Romantic and post-Romantic writers. Rob Pope's *Creativity: History, Theory, Practice* (2005) is a creative synthesis of history of thought about creativity and contemporary science. For writers' reflections on their own creative processes, see the *Paris Review* interviews.

Freewriting exercise (following Peter Elbow, 1973)

1. Set yourself a period of, say, three minutes and just start to write whatever comes to mind. Don't stop to reflect; don't go back and correct spelling, grammar or punctuation. If you get stuck, just repeat the last word you have written until the flow starts again. The object of the exercise is to write continuously without stopping, although you do not need to write any faster than normal.
2. Read through what you have written and underline any words or phrases that strike you as interesting or significant. Choose one of these words or phrases and write it at the head of a clean sheet. Then do another three minutes of continuous writing, starting from the chosen word or phrase. This time, if you get stuck or the flow dries up, you can re-focus on your chosen word or phrase.
3. (*Optional*) Read through and underline, as before. Is there a theme emerging in the writing or an interesting topic or feeling? If so, write this at the top of another clean sheet (if not, you might simply select another word or phrase from the piece that strikes you as interesting). Then do another three minutes of continuous writing.

At this stage you might wish to put the material away without reading it through and come back to it at a later date, to see if anything has emerged for working up into prose or poetic form. Alternatively, proceed to the next stage.

4. Now, in more leisurely mode, read through and reflect on the writing you have done. Is there something interesting or significant emerging from the pieces overall? Or perhaps the first free-write was the most productive for you, whilst the other more focused stages felt restrictive? Try and pull something out of the writing, a theme, a strong idea, an image or set of images. Arrange your words in a pleasing order, adding or removing words as appropriate. Can you give them a shape? Is there the beginning of a poem or a piece of prose fiction here? Spend 15–30 minutes working on your material until you have produced a piece of writing that pleases you. If you are working in a group, the results can be shared with others.

If you find freewriting useful, the time you spend on the continuous writing slots can be gradually increased to ten minutes; you may find that a smaller or larger number of slots are best for you.

Freewriting can be used in conjunction with Dorothea Brande's idea (1934) of early morning writing, which involves waking up half an hour earlier than usual and, before doing anything else, starting to write whatever comes into your mind: thoughts of the day, snippets of dreams, spontaneous imagery. Alternatively, you might like to start a freewriting diary, which you could use, for example, at the end of the day, to reflect on the day's happenings, or significant thoughts or ideas for writing.

Bear in mind that freewriting doesn't work for everyone, but many people find it a very valuable tool for getting in touch with material for writing and for finding out what one has to say in the process of the writing itself.

5   The Reader

'The writer's audience is always a fiction'.

Walter Ong, *Interfaces of the* Word, 1977, p. 53.

What role does the reader play in our writing? This is unlikely to be the first thing we think about when we start putting pen to paper; we are more likely to be concerned with getting words onto the page. And yet, as we will discover in this chapter, the question as to whom we are addressing in our writing is just as important as what we have to say.

The reader in the writing process

For Mikhail Bakhtin, speaking and writing are always acts of communication. Our words are never simply ours; they are always seeking a response. The reader or audience is always present in the utterance and contributes to its shaping (Bakhtin, 1986, pp. 126–29). Bakhtin's colleague Voloshinov shares this view:

> ...the word is a two-sided act. It is determined equally by whose word it is and for whom it is meant. As word, it is precisely the product of the reciprocal relationship between speaker and listener, addresser and addressee... I give myself verbal shape from another's point of view (Voloshinov, 1973, p. 86).

When we sit down to write, then, we are not simply finding the best words to express what we want to say, but finding the best words to express what we want to say *to someone*. And whom we are addressing makes us into a particular kind of author and indeed a particular kind of self. When we write a letter to a close friend or lover, for example, we will have a different sense of ourselves as authors than when we are writing to a bank manager. We may feel that we can be 'more ourselves' in the former than in the latter, although it is more likely that different dimensions of ourselves come to the fore in each case. When we write an autobiography, we are likely to feel under an obligation to give as true an account of our lives and ourselves as we can, because of the 'autobiographical pact' between author and reader implicit in this genre of writing (see Lejeune, 1989, pp. 119–37). Of course we may be deceiving ourselves that we are telling the truth, but the obligation to do so provides us with a particular sense of ourselves as writers and a particular stance in relation to our story, both of which will strongly influence what we tell and how we tell it.

When we write a diary, we may imagine that we are not writing for or to anyone and that therefore, this is the place where we can be totally ourselves. In fact, in a diary we are usually addressing ourselves in some guise or another; or perhaps an internalised image of a significant person in our lives who is absent at the time of writing, a spouse or parent or child; or even, if there is a chance that the diary may one day be published or read by family members, a future reader or audience. Our sense of ourselves in the writing process and of what we want to say is always subtly influenced by who is 'listening' or likely to be reading our writing in the future, and by how we want to be perceived by those readers or listeners.

Reader and audience

Our relationship with the reader or audience when we are engaged in creative writing is complex and multi-layered. As Walter Ong says, when stories were told orally, the audience was more straightforward; it was literally the people gathered around the storyteller, and the storyteller would tailor the telling of his tale to the nature of that audience (Ong, 1977, p. 56). The Greek poet Homer, for example, would undoubtedly have told the story of the *Iliad* differently to a group of children than to a group of old soldiers who had experienced the events. When we write, of course, the audience is not literally present and indeed should not be, for writing is, generally speaking, a solitary activity that can be interfered with by an audience (p. 57). This means that we have to imagine our audience, and we do this in different ways. For example, when we start writing, we may think about the market we are aiming at: teenagers, say, if we are writing fiction, or other poets, if we are writing poetry. This may take the form of a generalised, rather abstract sense of a particular group of real readers 'out there' who are likely to read our writing. Peter Rabinowitz calls this the 'authorial audience' (Rabinowitz, 1977).

Another way we imagine our audience is to borrow the sense of audience other writers have written into their work (Ong, 1977, p. 57). Rabinowitz refers to this as the 'narrative audience', because it is part of the created world of the narrative (Rabinowitz, 1977; see below for the related concept of the 'narratee'). Having read, say, J.D. Salinger's *Catcher in the Rye* (1951), in which the first person narrator, Holden Caulfield, speaks directly and colloquially to his narrative audience (Bakhtin calls this 'skaz', a form of double-voiced discourse; 1984, p. 192), we may 'hear' and 'feel' so clearly the tone of 'voice' he uses to do this that we can proceed to write in that voice and to that audience, but with our own particular subject matter:

> If the writer succeeds in writing, it is generally because he can fictionalise in his imagination an audience he has learned to know not from daily life but from earlier writers who were fictionalising in their imagination audiences they had learned to know in still earlier writers, and so on back to the dawn of written narrative (Ong, 1977, p. 60).

At least that is often how writers start out, but becoming an 'original writer', finding one's own voice, involves not just 'project[ing] the earlier audience', but altering it (p. 60), transforming the authoritative discourse of literary tradition into an internally persuasive one (see Chapter 2).

Ong also suggests that it is not correct simply to say that writers write for *an audience*, at least when we are talking about what 'fires the writer's imagination' (Ong, 1977, p. 57). When we are actually engaged in writing, we write for 'readers' (p. 58). But again we are unlikely to have in mind an individual member of the public reading the book on the London underground or on a beach in Tenerife. So who are these readers for whom we write? Reflecting on this question, the Canadian novelist Margaret Atwood tells a story of how the adult leader, the 'Brown Owl', of the Brownies troop she joined when she was nine years old became her first reader. She didn't know the woman's name but she was 'wise and fair, and as I needed someone like that in my life at the time, I adored this Brown Owl' (Atwood, 2002, p. 150). As part of the 'various badge-collecting projects',

Atwood made some little books containing words and pictures, which she sewed together with darning wool. She gave these to 'Brown Owl', who appreciated them, thus establishing her 'first writer-reader relationship'. Much later, Atwood made 'Brown Owl' into a character in her novel *Cat's Eye* (1989), thinking that by then she would be long dead. But then, towards the end of the 90s, a friend told her that 'Brown Owl' was her aunt and was still alive. A meeting was arranged, at which 'Brown Owl' returned to Atwood the little books she had made all those years earlier. Thinking about this episode from her childhood helps Atwood to answer the question for whom she writes: 'the writer writes for Brown Owl, or for whoever the equivalent of Brown Owl may be in his or her life at the time. A real person... singular, specific... the Dear Reader... the ideal reader...' (p. 151).

When she writes, then, Atwood – whatever authorial and narrative audiences may be operating at other levels of the writing process – has a sense of writing for a specific, real person who will receive and accept what she is writing in the way she most wants and needs it to be accepted: an ideal reader. But literary critic Wolfgang Iser rules out the possibility that the ideal reader can be a real person:

> An ideal reader would have to have an identical code [i.e. attitudes and norms] to that of the author; authors, however, generally recodify prevailing codes in their texts, and so the ideal reader would also have to share the intentions underlying this process. And if this were possible, communication would then be quite superfluous, for one only communicates that which is *not* already shared by sender and receiver (Iser, 1978, pp. 28–9).

Ong supports this view: the reader-in-the-writing-process cannot be a real person because he or she is not literally present. Even if we are writing a poem for or to a particular person we know well, we have to *fictionalise* him or her in the same way that we create characters out of real people (Ong, 1977, pp. 55). Indeed, Atwood acknowledges the fictional nature of the ideal reader when she says that it 'exists on a continuum somewhere between Brown Owl and God' (Atwood, 2002, p. 151), the 'somewhere between' inevitably turning 'Brown Owl' and God into imagined beings. So on this view, we write primarily for an ideal imagined reader, in all likelihood based on someone we know personally, someone, in fact, who may never read our writing and, if they did, whose *real* views we probably wouldn't want to hear.

The ideal imagined reader

The idea of the ideal reader as an imagined real person whose views of our writing we never hear but who nevertheless motivates us to write is a dominant theme of Patricia Duncker's novel *Hallucinating Foucault* (1997). One of the main protagonists, the writer Paul Michel, is sustained in his writing by what he imagines to be an intimate relationship with the philosopher Michel Foucault. Even though the two have never spoken, Michel believes that they write for each other, their books answering the deepest thoughts and feelings of the other. This imaginary relationship enables the isolated and painfully tormented Michel to write. As he says in one of his letters to Foucault which, in all likelihood, are never sent: 'You are my reader, my beloved reader, I know of no other person who has more absolute a power to constrain me, or to set me free' (Duncker, 1997, p. 62).

One of the characters in the novel explains Michel's need for an ideal reader in terms of the writer's need for a Muse:

> Every writer has a Muse…, no matter how anti-Romantic they are. For the irredeemably boring, the Muse is a woman they've cooked up in their heads, propped up like a voodoo doll on a pedestal and then persecuted with illusions, obsessions and fantasies. Paul Michel wasn't like that. He wanted someone real; someone who challenged him, but whose passions were the same. He fell in love with Foucault. It is absolutely essential to fall in love with your Muse. For most writers the beloved reader and the Muse are the same person. They should be (pp. 36–7).

Michel elaborates on this idea further in his letters to Foucault. He seeks:

> a democratic version of the Muse, a comrade, a friend, a travelling companion, shoulder to shoulder, someone to share the cost of this long, painful journey. Thus the Muse functions as collaborator, sometimes as antagonist, the one who is like you, the other over against you… (p. 61).

The main role of the ideal reader here is to keep the writer company during the rigours of writing, to be there in the thick of it, as it were, a benevolent sparring partner in the dialogue of writing. But it goes beyond that:

> For me the Muse is the other voice. Through the clamouring voices every writer is forced to endure there is always a final resolution into

> two voices; the passionate cry laden with the hopeless force of its own
> idealism – that is the voice of fire, air – and the other voice. This is the
> voice that is written down with the left hand – earth, water, realism,
> sense, practicality. So that there are always two voices, the safe voice
> and the dangerous one. The one that takes the risks and the one that
> counts the cost. The believer talking to the atheist, cynicism addressing
> love. But the writer and the Muse should be able to change places,
> speak in both voices so that the text shifts, melts, changes hands. The
> voices are not owned. They are indifferent to who speaks. They are
> the source of writing (p. 61).

Here the ideal reader or Muse is an internalised image of a powerful
real person who protects the writer against 'the monsters of the mind'
(p. 63) and enables him to write what is most difficult. The reader
strengthens the inner voice of reason and stability, thus helping to
keep the balance in Michel's dangerously unstable psychic world.
Without this presence, he is alone and powerless in the face of the
difficult material he feels he needs to write. The image of the ideal
reader is a crucial element in the 'frame' we talked about in the last
chapter, which holds open the space for the imagination.

Michel's description of the Muse or ideal reader evokes Bakhtin's
concept of the 'superaddressee'. As we have noted above: 'Any utterance always has an addressee... whose responsive understanding the
author of the speech work seeks and surpasses', the necessary
'second party' of the utterance with whom the speaker or writer is in
dialogue (Bakhtin, 1986, p. 126). And the imaginary Foucault certainly
seems to fulfil that role for Michel. But he is not only *present in* the
dialogue, he also *transcends* it, holds it, provides a context for it: in
Bakhtin's terms he is also the invisible third person of the utterance,
the 'superaddressee', who stands above all the participants in the dialogue, and 'whose absolutely just responsive understanding is presumed, either in some metaphysical distance or in distant historical
time' (p. 126). Thus Foucault, as Michel's internalised ideal reader,
functions at two different levels of the writing process, not only
engaging in the dialogue of the work in progress but also holding and
rendering safe the 'space for the imagination'. And this works, as long
as the real Foucault – the external referent for Michel's fantasy – is
alive, but when Foucault dies, Michel can no longer write, and quickly
succumbs to the 'darkness' that has been progressively gaining
ground on him (Duncker, 1997, p. 64).

Undoubtedly this is an extreme example of the sustaining role of an ideal imagined reader, but it highlights a phenomenon which is crucial for many of us who write: the sense of a benign inner presence which helps to render the writing space 'safe enough' for creativity to take place. Psychotherapist Donald Winnicott was of the view that in order to be able to use our aloneness effectively, we first have to learn how to be alone in the presence of someone (Winnicott, 1958). In favourable circumstances this happens in the normal course of childhood when the mother first introduces the child to toys with which they play together, and then gradually allows the child to play on its own in her quietly observing presence. Gradually the child internalises into the unconscious the image of the mother as a benign accompanying presence, and learns to use its aloneness effectively. Without that benign inner presence, Winnicott believed, the child was likely to experience its inner world as too chaotic and frightening for 'play' to take place, and creativity might consequently be impaired.

The imagined reader as critic

Apart from the imaginary people who keep us company in the writing process and whom we would *like* to read our writing, there are also the imaginary people we *fear* will read it and who may well be hostile to what we have to say. If, as Voloshinov suggests, we give ourselves verbal shape from another's point of view, what happens when the space for the imagination is inhabited by potentially hostile critics? This dilemma forms the subject matter of the following poem:

Pagefright[1]

Something is stopping me
from writing this poem
about myself.

It's my mother
watching the page
judging my self-indulgence
or not wanting to see
sadness blotting
the smooth surface.

It's feeling that
Me and I
are such big words
to commit myself to
in proud print.

It's thinking
those words
aren't really
me.

So I'm not going out there
on the page
alone.

I'll just stay here instead.

Just as the ideal reader in the examples discussed above is an imagined version of a real person, here the imagined critic also derives from a real person, the writer's mother, who is perceived as standing in judgement on the writer's arrogance and self-indulgence for elevating herself into a 'first person' on the page, or for revealing her sadness, which the writer presumably keeps hidden from her mother in everyday life. This potentially hostile critic looms over the writing process, making it difficult for the writer to place herself and her real feelings on the page. The mother is, as it were, a 'negative superaddressee' whose 'responsive understanding' cannot at all be presumed. And yet, paradoxically, by virtue of having completed the poem, the writer manages to counter the inhibiting presence. She defuses the imagined critic's potentially negative response by anticipating it and building it into the structure of the poem.

Bakhtin calls this style of writing 'the word with a sideways glance' (Bakhtin, 1984, p. 196). Rather than simply writing a poem in the first person about her sadness, the writer 'squints [her] eyes to the side, towards the listener, the witness, the judge' (p. 237), which leads her to write a very different poem, one that incorporates and reacts to the implied words of the judge she senses on the periphery of consciousness when she writes. This is done at two different levels and through two different authorial agents in the text: the narrator and the implied author. By refusing, in the terms set out in the poem itself, to go out onto the blank page, the narrator – the speaking voice in the poem – protects herself from the anticipated criticism. She says: 'I'm not going to write about me and my sadness, because you'll only say it's arrogant and self-indulgent, and I don't want to be defined as such'. But by actually writing the poem about not going out onto the page, the implied author (see Chapter 3) confronts the imagined critic. She says: 'Okay, I know it's arrogant and self-indulgent to write about me and my sadness, but I'm going to do it anyway, and I dare you to criticise me!' The result of this 'internally polemical discourse' (p. 196) with the imagined critic is that the implied author calls the critic's bluff, pre-emptying her attack. She creates for herself a 'loophole', as Bakhtin calls it, retaining for herself 'the possibility for altering the ultimate, final meaning of [her] own words' (p. 233). Thus she successfully defends herself against being given verbal shape from the other's point of view, against having her identity 'finalized' by the imagined reader.

The imagined reader as guarantor of the writer's self-image

The young Jean-Paul Sartre, by comparison, is only too happy, as he tells us in his autobiography, *Words* (1967), to be given verbal shape by the imagined reader. Indeed, he desperately needs the imagined reader in order to keep in place his identity as a 'great writer'.

Sartre began writing at an early age, against a background of having been an avid reader, not only of the classics, which he read primarily to please his grandfather, but also of comics and cheap adventure novels. The latter appealed to him particularly because they enabled him to indulge in fantasies about being a knight-errant who saves maidens in distress. Brought up and educated at the home of his maternal grandparents (his father died when he was a baby), he quickly learns that being loved and approved of involves pandering to his scholar-grandfather's need to create him in his own image, and he consequently fails to develop an authentic sense of identity.

Writing is a great discovery, because it helps to consolidate and extend the fantasy self he has created through reading. Strongly influenced by one of the books in his grandfather's library, *The Childhood of Famous Men*, he imagines himself into the role of the great writer who writes for an admiring readership. Where, as a reader, he was a fictional heroic character in an adventure novel, as a writer he becomes a 'real knight errant whose exploits would be real books. I was sought after! People were waiting for my works...'

(p. 107). Later, when he realises that there is no apparent need for a writer-knight in the political environment of his childhood, he becomes a 'writer-martyr' who, working in isolation, saves the world by the mere fact of writing (pp. 112–13). It never occurs to him 'that a man might write in order to be read' (p. 113). He has no need for real readers or indeed for an ideal imagined reader to keep him company in the difficult space for the imagination; the imagined admiring readership is ever present, confirming his identity as the great writer and protecting him from self-doubt. Sometimes it takes the form of particular people, such as the kind of men who visit his grandfather; at other times it is a generalised sense of admiring others: 'Other consciousnesses have taken charge of me. They read *me* and I leap to their eyes; they talk about *me* and I am on everyone's lips, a universal and singular language; I have made myself a prospective interest for millions of glances' (p. 122).

It is the identity as writer, which this admiring readership confers on him, that is most important: 'Now and then, I used to stop writing and pretend to hesitate so that I could feel I was, with my furrowed brow and far-away look, *a writer*' (p. 91). The quality of the writing is of little consequence. Rejecting his grandfather's scholarly world, he churns out the same slight adventure novels he had previously loved to read, or rather parts of novels: '...my pen moved so rapidly that, often, my wrist ached: I would sling the filled exercise books to the floor. In the end I forgot them and they would disappear; for this reason, I never completed anything: what was the point of telling the end of a story when its beginning had got lost?' (p. 114). Thus there is no development in his writing skills.

His fantasy self, however, cannot be sustained. When the First World War breaks out, events in the real world begin to blur the distinction between fiction and reality (p. 134). Heroism becomes available to anyone: '...courage and self-sacrifice were becoming humdrum virtues; worse still, they were being reduced to the level of the most elementary duties' (p. 133). He realises he is 'relating nonsense that no one would want to believe; in short, I discovered the imagination' (p. 134). Re-reading his writings for the first time brings him face-to-face with the reality of himself: 'Scarlet in the face. Was this really me, *me* taking pleasure in these childish fantasies? I very nearly renounced literature. In the end, I took my exercise-book to the beach and buried it in the sand...I stopped writing' (p. 134). Only later, when he goes to school and begins to develop a sense of the shared reality beyond his isolated childhood world does he begin slowly to discover a more authentic sense of self. When he starts to write again, it is no longer a means to a glorious identity, but writing for its own sake, although it is a long time before the themes of his celebrated later work begin to emerge. Rather than wanting to 'realize myself straight away and embrace at one glance the totality which haunted me when I was not thinking about it' (p. 152), he is able now to make space for 'the slow blossoming of my abilities' (p. 147).

The reader in the text

What we have called the imagined reader-in-the-writing-process, then, can function in a variety of ways: it can act as a motivating force for our writing, accompanying and sustaining us in the difficult space for the imagination; it can be a critic standing in judgement on what we write, at worst inhibiting our progress or causing writing blocks, at best motivating us to engage in an 'internal polemic' within the text; it can be an uncritical admiring audience shoring up our identity as 'a writer' but inhibiting the development of our writing. This imagined entity is not usually made explicit in the text itself, except in instances like the poem 'Pagefright' where the writer takes the relationship with it as her subject matter, but it 'may rather be silently presupposed by [the text]' (Rabinowitz, 1989, p. 85), a subtle, hovering, *implicit presence* discernible only by the writer him- or herself or by someone who is privy, perhaps through the writer's diaries or letters, to the personal context of the writing.

Sometimes, though, elements of these imagined readers become visible as *readers-in-the-text*: as 'implied readers' or 'narratees'. As Wayne Booth points out, just as in the process of writing we automatically and largely unconsciously create a self-in-the-text, a 'second self' or 'implied author' (see Chapter 3), so we similarly create a reader-in-the-text, which he calls a 'postulated reader' (Booth, 1991, p. 138; cf. Gibson's 'mock reader', 1980). Wolfgang Iser subsequently called this the 'implied reader', a term which has gained wide currency. The 'implied reader' constitutes a specific role for the reader, a set of instructions for how we want our writing to be read:

> [It is] a textual structure anticipating the presence of a recipient without necessarily defining him; this concept prestructures the role to be

assumed by each recipient, and this holds true even when texts deliberately appear to ignore their possible recipient or actively exclude him.
Thus the concept of the implied reader designates a network of
response-inviting structures, which impel the reader to grasp the text.
No matter who or what he may be, the real reader is always offered a
particular role to play (Iser, 1978, p. 34; see also Iser, 1980).

A good example, discussed by Ong (1977, pp. 62–5, drawing on
Gibson, 1966), is the way Ernest Hemingway in *A Farewell to Arms*
(1929) casts the reader in the role of a close companion of the narrator. He does this from the very start of the novel by using the definite
rather than the indefinite article:

> In the late summer of that year we lived in a house in a village that
> looked across the river and the plain to the mountains. In the bed of the
> river there were pebbles and boulders, dry and white in the sun, and the
> water was clear and swiftly moving and blue in the channels
> (Hemingway, 1964, p. 7).

Rather than telling us which year we are supposed to be thinking
about, the narrator refers to '*that* year', as if we the readers already
know about it. Similarly, we have '*the* river', '*the* plain', '*the* mountains', not '*a* river' or '*a* plain', not simply '*mountains*'. These are very
specific locations with which we are apparently already familiar.
There is no need for further explanations; the narrator assumes that
we share with him a common past. And we, as readers, are encouraged to take up the position of an intimate, a role which has the
potential for making us feel special, valued by the narrator.

Of course, as real readers with different gender identities and backgrounds in different classes and cultures, we may refuse or be unable
to be positioned in this way (see for example Fetterley, 1978; Culler,
1983; Sommer, 1994). In fact Iser's notion of the implied reader
assumes that there is one correct way to read a given text – the way
the real author intended – and if we cannot read it in this way, then
either the text has failed (it's a 'bad' book) or we have failed as readers
(we are 'bad' readers). Wayne Booth's formulation is rather more
useful. His ideal 'postulated or implied reader' is the reader who
understands the intentions not of the real author but of the 'implied
author' and 'shares all (or most, or the most important) [of his] facts
and values' (Booth 1991, p. 422). He is also able to be flexibly dialogic
in the reading process, on the one hand fully aware of the fictional

nature of the text, and on the other able to pretend 'that it is all true' (pp. 429–430). William Nelles agrees with Booth's formulation, but adds that the implied reader can 'accurately interpret the full signification of the choices made by the implied author' (Nelles, 1993, p. 38). This means that 'very few real (historical) readers can identify exactly with any implied reader' (p. 31), although some literary critics and close readers attempt to do so, in order to ferret out the meaning incorporated into the text by the implied author. (Critics sometimes interpret the implied author's intentions differently on different readings; see for example Bernard Paris's reading, 1965, and re-reading, 2003, of George Eliot.) Others, as Booth says, will approximate to the 'implied reader' depending on the extent to which they share the implied author's 'facts and values'.

The narratee is a rather more straightforward textual agent than the implied reader (see Prince, 1980, for an overview). At its most obvious, it is a character in the text who has been cast in the role of listener. Joseph Conrad often uses the narratee to create an audience within the text, such as in *Heart of Darkness* (1902) and *Lord Jim* (1900), where his fictional narrator Charlie Marlow addresses a group of people who are present during the telling of the stories but who speak very little. Less obvious narratees are often present in a text, their role sometimes overlapping with that of implied readers, although Nelles' suggestion that the 'narratee' hears, whilst the 'implied reader' interprets, helps to distinguish more precisely between them (Nelles, 1993, pp. 22).

The poem 'Pagefright', discussed above, contains both a narratee and an implied reader. The mother-critic is the narratee, with a central role to play. She is a character whose words are present indirectly and who is also addressed indirectly by the narrator. Much less obvious is the implied reader or listener, someone who will recognise the implied author's conflict between wanting to write about her sadness and feeling unable to do so, will sympathise with it and not condemn her as the narratee inevitably will. The writer when writing the poem was clearly conscious of including the mother as narratee, but in all likelihood she would not have been as conscious of incorporating a role for an ideal implied reader. This is more likely to be a product of the partly unconscious implied author. The relationship between the two imaginary listening agents in the text (the narratee and the implied reader), as well as that between them and the two imaginary authorial agents we discussed above (the implied author and the narrator) give the poem its rich ambiguity, and provide a fascinating insight into the tensions between different parts of the psyche in the writing process.

There is disagreement amongst literary critics as to the location of these four 'textual agents' in a narrative communication. As shown below, Seymour Chatman suggests that the implied author and implied reader hover on the edge of the narrative, and have a close and often ambiguous relation with the real author and the real reader who are entirely outside of the narrative. By comparison, the narrator and the narratee are centrally located within the narrative. Chatman believes that all narratives contain an implied author and an implied reader, but not necessarily a narrator and a narratee (Chatman, 1978, pp. 148–51).

Real Author → | Implied Author → (Narrator) → (Narratee) → Implied Reader | → Real Reader

Shlomith Rimmon-Kenan, by contrast, holds that there are always a narrator and a narratee, even if only minimally, but she places the implied author outside of the narrative communication. If, as discussed in Chapter 3, the implied author is the 'governing consciousness' of the text, holding it together, 'it cannot literally be a participant in the narrative communication' (Rimmon-Kenan 1996, pp. 88). Rimmon-Kenan also does away altogether with the implied reader, preferring instead the narratee to cover all the different kinds of readers-in-the-text. Certainly we can discuss the two 'listeners' in 'Pagefright' as two different kinds of narratee, but the distinction between the narratee as a listening character in the text and the implied reader as the interpreter of the implied author's (conscious or unconscious) meaning is nevertheless a useful one.

As will be obvious from the above discussion, we have the opportunity as writers to create different kinds of effects through the roles we incorporate into the text for these various 'textual agents'. Much of the effect created by the implied reader will be done unconsciously or semi-consciously, and being too conscious of it may compromise our writing (see our discussion of 'intention' in Chapter 3). However, the narratee offers lots of possibilities, especially in a postmodern context, where it is not unusual for writers to 'play' with the relationship with the reader (see McHale, 1987, Chapter 14). Here, for example, is John Barth addressing the narratee of his short story 'Life Story':

> You, dogged, uninsultable, print-oriented bastard, it's you I'm addressing, who else, from inside this monstrous fiction. You've read me this far, then? Even this far? For what discreditable motive? How is it you don't go to a movie, watch TV, stare at a wall, play tennis with a friend, make amorous advances to the person who comes to your mind when I speak of amorous advances? Can nothing surfeit, saturate you, turn you off? Where's your shame? (Barth, 1969, p. 127).

This angry outburst comes towards the end of the author-narrator's tortuous and unsuccessful attempts to clarify how to capture on the page the proposition he wishes to write about: that 'the world is a novel' and he himself 'a fictional personage' (p. 117). The levels of complication this proposition opens up – the author-narrator is a fictional construct trying to write about his predicament as a fictional construct in a fictional world through a third person fictional character, who is telling the story of his predicament through a fictional character or 'hero' whose situation replicates his own! – drive the author-narrator to despair. But his outburst at the reader (in the guise of the narratee) clears the textual air, as it were, allowing the hero an insight that has reverberations down the textual levels to the author-narrator himself: that he is his own reader and that as reader he is imposing on himself a task that is torturing him. Attempts to escape this predicament include unsuccessfully bludgeoning his reader-self into killing off his author-self, an interesting twist indeed on Roland Barthes' notion of the 'death of the author' (see Chapter 3).

Being our own reader

Barth's story highlights, albeit ironically and at the level of textual agents, a central feature of the writing process which is not always obvious: our relationship with ourselves as readers of our own writing. Indeed, much of what we have said in this chapter has revolved around that relationship. Paul Michel's 'Foucault', the mother-critic of 'Pagefright', and Sartre's admiring audience are all internalised images of 'others' which have become part of the writers' psyches and strongly influence their sense of identity as writers.

These 'self-readers' inhabit the space for the imagination, so that when the writers write they are, as it were, 'performing' in the presence of themselves as readers (see Timothy Clark's view that creativity involves 'improvised performance, mediated by self-reading', 1997, p. 21). Clearly, some of these 'self-readers' are more helpful than others. Michel's 'Foucault' sustains him as a writer as long as the real Foucault is alive and acts as external referent. Sartre's admiring audience is crucial to his young self to keep in place a much-needed sense of identity, but is positively detrimental to his ability to develop his writing. The mother-critic of 'Pagefright' potentially hinders the writing process but also motivates the writer to explore that hindrance in a creative way.

Obviously we don't have control over the psychic inner mechanisms that bring self-readers into being, and some writers undoubtedly manage to write successful and powerful work in spite of having very unhelpful self-readers. But by becoming more aware of our self-readers, it *is* possible to influence them and sometimes to ameliorate unhelpful effects (see Hunt, 2004a). Ideally, it will make our life easier as writers if we can avoid being the harsh inner critic who damns our words even before they reach the page, or the uncritical admiring audience that applauds our every word, no matter how bad it is. An ideal self-reader would be not unlike Michel's Muse: on the one hand keeping us company in the writing process and encouraging us to allow our deeply felt, often difficult material to emerge, and on the other helping us to critique our work-in-progress constructively, so that we can shape our material into its strongest form. As an ideal reader of our own writing-in-progress, we will be no ordinary reader. We will not, like the implied reader, be looking to interpret the meaning of the implied author in the text; at this stage we will not be sufficiently outside the text to do that. In some respects we will be a little like a narratee in that we will 'listen' to ourselves writing and often be surprised by what emerges into the space of composition. As William Golding says of his own experience as a writer: 'The author becomes a spectator, appalled or delighted, but a spectator' (Golding, 1965, p. 98; in Boden, 2004, p. 28). But unlike the narratee, we will also influence the shaping of what emerges, helping our implied author to make important choices. Indeed once a piece of writing is in progress we become a highly privileged reader. We know the material in a way no other reader can ever know it: we bring our knowledge of earlier drafts and turns of phrase that have now been abandoned; we are aware of connections and motivations behind the writing that will never appear explicitly on the page. In short, we are privy to the 'aesthetic intelligence' of the creative process (Bollas, 1997, p. 167), the rich world of *felt* knowledge in which we become immersed when we are deeply engaged in creative work. At this stage, reading ourselves does not constitute stepping outside of this aesthetic realm; switching into reader-mode is more akin to taking the lead role in the 'trio' of the writing process (Bakhtin, 1986, p. 122), whilst the other two participants – the writer-self and the text – temporarily occupy the background. When the ensemble is working well, we are unlikely to notice the way we engage in this intuitive switching of roles.

Being our own reader-in-the-writing process, then, is an essential part of the dialogic or reflexive relationship with ourselves that the writing process involves. Like authorship at its best, it is a fluid rather than a fixed position, involving us in not only playing an active part in the space for the imagination, but also helping to hold the potentially chaotic creative process in place by retracting and becoming part of the 'frame'. Once a draft is on the page, however, a different kind of readership becomes possible – *re*-reading. We move out of the aesthetic realm in which the work was created, become more like any other reader, at a distance from the writing process. We can leave the writing to stand, as it were, so that when we return to it again we see it with different eyes. When we become *re-readers* of ourselves, we have the opportunity to find out what kind of writing we have written and, like Sartre, what kind of writers we are – perhaps even what kind of selves.

Recommended reading

Andrew Bennett's excellent anthology *Readers and Reading* (1995) is a good place to get an overview of critical approaches to readership. Mikhail Bakhtin's discussions of readership are spread widely throughout his work, but a useful place to start is his discussion of the 'superaddressee' in 'The Problem of the Text' in *Speech Genres and Other Late Essays* (1986). Walter Ong's 'The Writer's Audience is always a Fiction' in *Interfaces of the Word* (1977) continues to be a highly thought-provoking essay for practising writers. Shlomith Rimmon-Kenan's *Narrative Fiction – Contemporary Poetics* (1996) has a useful discussion of different kinds of readers in the text. On reflexivity in the reading process, see Mary Jacobus *Psychoanalysis and the Scene of Reading* (1999); also Georges Poulet's 'Criticism and the Experience of Interiority' (1972). On the developmental and therapeutic dimensions of reading ourselves, see Celia's *Therapeutic Dimensions of Autobiography in Creative Writing* (2000, Chapter 4) and 'Reading Ourselves: Imagining the Reader in the Writing Process' (2004).

Writing exercises

- Spend a few minutes thinking and making a few notes about your sense of audience or readership when you are writing: (a) a diary; (b) autobiography; (c) creative writing: for example, a poem, or a short story or novel.
- Imagine someone whom you would like to read your work – it may be someone you know, a friend or colleague, or an imagined ideal reader. Write down a description of this person. Now write a brief letter to this person about your current writing project. Write a brief reply from this person to you in response to your letter.
- Read a novel or short story and say what kind of reader you feel compelled to be by it. Develop the implied reader role into a fictional character and engage in a written dialogue with him/her.

Guided fantasy on the Reader-in-the-Writing-Process

Notes for facilitators:

1. This exercise is best done in a writing group, with a group facilitator reading out the instructions and participants writing into the gaps between. As it delves quite deeply, it is best undertaken with a group that is well established and on going. If used in a therapeutic context, great care should be taken to ensure that those participating are able to manage the nature of the exercise.
2. It is useful to have short intervals between the three parts, so that participants can have a break and discuss with a partner what they have done so far. At the end of the exercise participants can be asked to select something to read out or simply to discuss an aspect of the exercise that interested them.
3. This exercise works best if participants undertake Parts 1 and 2 in a group workshop and then work on Part 3 subsequently at home.

Part One

I want you to imagine that somehow or other you are able to leave your job and your home and family and to go away to live for a year on your own, to devote yourself to your writing. You are going to rent a room somewhere for a year. You can go anywhere in the world you like. Where are you going to go?

Say something about the location you have chosen. Why have you chosen it? What is it you like best about this particular place?

You have arrived at your destination and are now entering into the room you have rented. What are your first impressions of the room?

You are going over to the window now to have a look at the view. What sort of window is it? How does it open?

You open it, put your head out. What can you see? What can you feel? What can you smell? What can you hear?

Close the window now and come back into the room. You are going to unpack your case. You have brought something with you that is very important to you, something you can't do without. Something that, when it is unpacked, will make you feel that the room is yours. What is it?

You have to find a special place for it in the room. Where are you going to put it?

You are going to organise the room now. Is there a desk or a table that you can use for your writing? Is it in the best position for you? If not, move it to another spot. Have you brought a typewriter or a portable computer? If so, set it up now on your work surface? Or perhaps you are simply going to write by hand? Organise the room in the way that suits you best, makes you feel at home.

(Close eyes) Imagine now that you have settled into your room and that you are preparing to write for the first time. You have assembled your writing materials, chosen a comfortable chair. I want you to sit down. Take a deep breath. Relax. You are not yet writing. This is the opportunity you have always wanted, an uninterrupted space of time in which

to write. And you are free to write the thing you have always wanted to write. I want you to let your thoughts float freely for a moment. And when you are ready I want you to write down a single word or image that floats into your thoughts as you sit there.

Now I want you to associate freely to the word you have written, following wherever it leads without reflecting on it too much.

As you sit there in your room writing, you have a feeling that you are not alone, that there is someone there in the room with you. Not liter- ally there, but somehow present in the moment of writing. You have often had this sense before that someone is present when you write, that in some strange way you are writing for this person or to this person. You may have thought about them before, but now for the first time you are focusing on them more closely. Who is this person? Is it a man or a woman? Is it an adult or a child? Perhaps it is more than one person? Perhaps it is just a vague sense of presence.

What does it feel like to have this person there in the room with you? Are they sympathetic to your writing or antagonistic? Do they help or hinder?

What do you want of this person in relation to your writing? What does this person want of you?

Part Two
I want you to step outside of your role as the writer and think of the writer as a character.

Six months have now passed. The writer who was occupying the room has unexpectedly disappeared before the year was completed. However, the room has been left exactly as it was when the writer occupied it. The writing materials are still there, as well as the writing that was done. There are the writer's clothes and other belongings, but the writer has gone.

Into the room comes the person whom the writer imagined was in the room when the writing was being done. We will call this person 'the reader'. The reader walks around the room, looking at the things the writer has left behind, picks up the writing lying on the desk and starts to read.

Write a piece in the first person from the point of view of the reader as he/she reads the writing left behind by the writer. What does he/she make of the writing? What does he/she think about the writing and the person who wrote it? Try to get into the head of this person and make a first person narrator out of him or her.

(If you were unable to imagine a person coming into the room where you were writing, bring someone else into the room to read the writing, someone associated perhaps with the locale, the person from whom you rented the room, for example.)

Part Three
Whilst the reader is in the room, the writer unexpectedly returns. Write down what the reader and the writer say to each other.

6   Characters and Selves

A character...can always ask a man who he is. Because a character truly has a life of his own, marked by his own characteristics, because of which he is always 'someone'. On the other hand, a man... can be 'nobody'.

Luigi Pirandello, *Six Characters in Search of an Author*, 1921/1995, p. 55.

Much of what we have said so far has emphasised the importance of finding a balance in the writing process between freedom and control, of developing a metaphorical or reflexive relationship with our own material so that it takes on a life of its own within the holding environment we provide for it. This is particularly important when we come to think about the relationship we have as authors with the characters and narrators we create in our fictions. In this chapter we explore several different kinds of such relationships.

Characters as autonomous creations

In Luigi Pirandello's celebrated play *Six Characters in Search of an Author*, the characters of the title – all members of an extended family – arrive unannounced at a theatre where a Director is in the process of rehearsing actors for a play. They are in great distress, having been brought into being by the rich creative fantasy of their author, who has then been either unable or unwilling to give them life within a play. They know that the script is within them and they desperately need to act it out, but they can't do this without the shaping consciousness of an author. Consequently they are forced to search for an author – any author – who will enable them to realise themselves fully, and they see the Director as a possible author-substitute.

Needless to say, the Director is both amused and bemused by the situation. Whilst at first he is inclined to dismiss the intruders as cranks, he is gradually persuaded to try to give form to their drama, and in the interval between Acts I and II goes off with them to get a rough outline down on paper. When it comes to developing the drama on the stage, however, the characters and the Director find themselves in conflict. The Director assumes that, once he has devised a form for the drama, his actors will take on the roles of the characters, but the characters are unhappy about this. The Father, for example, is uneasy about the tone the Leading Man uses to convey his character: 'I am beginning now to… hear my own words ringing false, ringing with a different sound' (p. 34). He is concerned that the characters' way of being, their voice and gestures, should be given full and authentic expression. But the Director is adamant that this is not possible: 'Your expression becomes material here to which the actors give body and form, voice and gesture… here you cannot exist as your real self!' (pp. 35–6).

This exchange embodies one of the main themes of Pirandello's play: the autonomous nature of characters in literary creations and the difficulty this autonomy poses for authors and characters alike. Authors, Pirandello is suggesting, bring fictional characters into being, but once they are created, they have a life of their own which is likely to go beyond what the authors have in mind for them. This means that authors have to develop a particular kind of relationship to their characters. As the Father says:

> When characters are alive, truly alive before their author, he has only to follow them in their words and actions which they precisely suggest to him, and he has no other choice except to want them to be the way they want themselves to be. And he's in for trouble if he doesn't! When a character is born, he immediately assumes so much independence, even from his own author, that he can be imagined by everybody in a number of other situations in which the author never thought of putting him, and sometimes he even acquires a meaning the author never dreamed of giving him! (p. 56).

The dialogic nature of author-character relations

Pirandello is dramatising in this play his view of the ideal relationship between authors and their characters, a relationship characterised by sincerity and spontaneity, which he regarded as the two essential virtues of the artist in the act of creation (Caesar, 1998, p. 7). Sincerity, for Pirandello, meant not only that the writer should be honest to his own experience, not constrained by 'schools, movements, precepts and formulae' which might 'curtail the autonomy of the creative moment' (p. 9), but also that he should 'give his characters the space to think and talk for themselves'. A sincere approach to artistic creation ensures the necessary spontaneity of both creative artist and artwork, and makes it possible for him to carry out his responsibility both to the inner world of the work and 'the outer world as it is in itself' (p. 11):

> ...outside of me the world exists for itself and with me, and in my representation I must determine *to realize it* as much as I can, creating for myself something like a consciousness of it in which it lives, in me as it does in itself, seeing it as it sees itself, feeling it as it feels itself. Then there will be no need for symbol or appearance: everything will be real and living. And I will not make characters think, feel, act in one way, that is to say in my way... but I shall endeavour to give each his own voice, each thing its own appearance and colour, its life in short... (Pirandello, 1897; in Caesar, 1998, p. 11).

Characters, on this view, are not just words on the page but the embodiment through speech of 'real' beings – autonomous 'speaking presences' in the text (Caesar, 1998, p. 2) – and the author, rather than forcing them to fulfil the roles he has determined for them, has to get to know them on their own terms. This does not involve a 'death of the author' in Barthes' sense, where the author removes himself in order to allow the text free play, nor is it simply a 'de-egoization' in Cixous' sense, which at best reduces the author to a weak and rather ineffective minor character (see Chapter 3). Here the author plays a crucial role, imaginatively embodying the characters and realising them through himself to the best of his ability.

It will be obvious from what we have said in preceding chapters how close Pirandello's views are to those of Mikhail Bakhtin. For Bakhtin, characters are 'speaking consciousnesses' (Bakhtin, 1984, pp. 47–77), and the writer's role is not only to create a space in which these consciousnesses can engage in a dialogue with each other, but to join in the dialogue with them, on equal terms, thus creating a true 'polyphony' of voices. By dialogue, Bakhtin does not simply mean a conversation between people with different views; it is a relationship of equals where both parties enter into or, as he puts it, 'live into' each other. This 'live entering' into another is not the same as empathy, which involves merging, nor does it involve a complete loss of the self; rather it is a form of 'creative understanding' (Bakhtin, 1986, p. 7; Morson and Emerson, 1990, pp. 54–5). In Bakhtin's view, this is what Dostoevsky achieves in his novels:

> ...the new artistic position of the author with regard to the hero [i.e. the narrator or character in fiction] in Dostoevsky's polyphonic novel is a *fully realized and thoroughly consistent dialogic position*, one that affirms the independence, internal freedom, unfinalizability, and indeterminacy of the hero. For the author, the hero is not 'he' and not 'I' but a fully valid 'thou', that is, another and other autonomous 'I' ('thou art')... this dialogue [between author and hero]... takes place... in the *real present* of the creative process. This is no stenographer's report of a finished dialogue, from which the author has already withdrawn and *over* which he is now located as if in some higher decision-making position... (Bakhtin, 1984, p. 63).

Bakhtin does not deny that characters' freedom is 'relative' (p. 51); after all they only exist by virtue of having been brought into being by the author. '[Their] freedom... exists within the limits of the artistic design, and in that sense is... a created thing...' But creativity, for Bakhtin, is not tantamount to invention. The creative act 'invents nothing'; it 'only reveals what is already present in the object itself' (pp. 64–5), a discourse with a life of its own. Nor does Bakhtin deny the author a role in relation to the characters; indeed the author's role is crucial. The author must not withdraw his own consciousness or lose himself in his characters' discourse, 'not fuse with it, not swallow it up' (p. 64). Rather he has to reposition himself with regard to his characters: 'The author of a polyphonic novel is not required to renounce himself or his own consciousness, but he must to an extraordinary extent broaden, deepen and rearrange this consciousness... in order to accommodate the autonomous consciousnesses of others' (p. 68).

In omniscient narration, where the author is God and knows everything about his characters, he has what Bakhtin calls a large degree of 'surplus of meaning'. The characters know only their own little worlds and are not privy to the 'dialogizing background' which is contained within the author's all-encompassing 'field of vision'. In the polyphonic novel, by contrast, the author retains 'only that indispensable minimum of pragmatic, purely information-bearing "surplus" necessary to carry forward the story' (pp. 70–3).

The author, then, for both Pirandello and Bakhtin, has to develop a dialogic relationship with his characters, which involves giving up his privileged position as omniscient creator and entering into the fray of language as one amongst many speaking consciousnesses, even though he himself has set those consciousnesses in motion. At the same time he has to act as a container for these consciousnesses, providing a structure for their words and actions. Is this really possible in a work of literature?

Conflict between characters' autonomy and authors' rhetoric

Literary critic Bernard Paris doesn't believe it is, or at least that it happens only rarely. For him, the relationship between authors and characters, or at least the relationship between authors and *mimetic characters*, is more often than not cacophonous rather than polyphonic. By mimetic characters Paris means those that can be thought of as in some ways corresponding to – or mimicking – real human beings. Following Scholes and Kellogg (1966), he distinguishes them from 'aesthetic' characters, which can be understood 'primarily in terms of their technical functions and their formal and dramatic effects', and from 'illustrative' characters, which are 'concepts in anthropoid shape or fragments of the human psyche parading as whole human beings' (Scholes and Kellogg, 1966, pp. 87–8; in Paris, 1997, p. 6). A mimetic character 'usually has aesthetic and illustrative functions, but numerous details have been called forth by the author's desire to make the character lifelike, complex, and inwardly intelligible' (Paris, 1997, p. 7). Paris agrees with Pirandello and Bakhtin that such characters are 'autonomous beings with an inner logic of their own... They say, do, think, and feel things that belong to the portrayal of their psyche but that may have no other function in the work' (Paris, 1991a, p. 28). But rather than seeing the authors' relationship with their characters as dialogic, Paris highlights the difficulties authors have of working with them. He takes E.M. Forster's view that mimetic – or 'round' – characters are 'creations inside a creation... full of the spirit of mutiny... [they] try to live their own lives and are consequently often engaged in treason against the main scheme of the book' (Forster, 1979, p. 72; in Paris, 1991a, p. 28).

As Paris demonstrates in his analyses of novels and plays from ancient Greece to the postmodern (see for example Paris, 1997), authors rarely understand their characters fully, at least consciously, although intuitively they may understand them perfectly well. Authors' 'character-creating impulses work against their efforts to shape and interpret experience, and they must choose between allowing their characters to come alive and kick the book to pieces [as Forster says] or killing their characters by subordinating them to the main scheme of the work' (Paris, 1997, p. 10).

Some celebrated authors, Paris says, certainly bring into being powerful mimetic characters with inner lives and motivations of their own, in the way Pirandello and Bakhtin suggest, but more often than not these characters are in conflict with the authors' own rhetoric. By rhetoric, Paris, drawing on Wayne Booth (1961), means the textual strategies and devices authors use to influence the way readers respond to a work morally, intellectually and emotionally. Sometimes this rhetoric is in conflict with the mimetic portrayal of character and sometimes it is in conflict with itself; sometimes it is in conflict with both (Paris, 1991a, p. 29; see also 1991b). This means that novels and plays are more often than not inconsistent, but this does not necessarily detract from their power, or rather, with their striking mimetic characterisations, they continue to be powerful in spite of their inconsistencies.

Paris's discussion of the character of Dorothea Brooke in George Eliot's *Middlemarch* (1872) provides a good example of what he means by the conflict between the mimetic portrayal of character and the author's rhetoric (Paris, 2003, pp. 23–57). From the Preface onwards, Eliot portrays Dorothea as a woman with a 'passionate nature' who longs to do something special with her life. Eliot's rhetoric, Paris suggests, strongly encourages the reader to see these characteristics as a natural and healthy endowment, which places Dorothea on a par with as elevated a person as Saint Theresa. But whilst St. Theresa found an outlet for her 'spiritual grandeur' in reforming a religious order, Dorothea is hampered by the 'meanness of opportunity' in her time and culture: 'Here and there is born a Saint Theresa, foundress of nothing, whose loving heart-beats and sobs after an unattained goodness tremble off and are dispersed among hindrances, instead of centering in some long-recognizable deed' (Eliot, 1971, pp. 25–6). That

Dorothea doesn't manage to centre herself in a 'long-recognizable deed' is not because of problems in herself. Eliot is keen to dissuade readers from tending toward the view that her heroine is odd or mad; Dorothea, she wants readers to be aware, is a superior being, with a spirituality and goodness that go far beyond that of the ordinary mortals by whom she is surrounded. If she makes mistakes, as she does when she marries the older and patently unattractive Reverend Edward Casaubon, we are given to understand that this is inevitable, given Dorothea's 'spiritual grandeur' and the 'meanness of opportunity' (Paris, 2003, p. 30). By anticipating in the Preface our possible negative impressions of Dorothea and constantly reminding us in the remainder of the novel of her specialness, through favourable comparisons to biblical figures, Eliot seeks to 'exculpate her in advance by putting what might be seen as her mistakes and flaws of character in a favourable light' (p. 27).

Looking at Dorothea as a mimetic character rather than through the lens of Eliot's rhetoric, Paris sees 'her desire for intensity and greatness and need for an epic life [not as] manifestations of spiritual grandeur but of a compulsive search for glory' (p. 31). She fixes on Casaubon because 'her search for glory leads her to idealize him' (p. 32). Paris accepts Eliot's argument that it is the attitudes towards women in her culture that hinder her character's ability to fulfil her potentialities, but criticises her for not seeing that Dorothea's desire is not for self-realisation but for self-glorification through doing good for others, a defensive self-effacing strategy that arises out of her 'self-alienated development' (pp. 32–3). A healthy striving for self-realisation would not be so compulsive and would not involve the sense of superiority to and contempt for ordinary mortals which Dorothea constantly expressed. Blinded by her idealised image of herself as 'an ascetic who scorns worldly pleasures' (p. 34), Dorothea cannot contemplate marrying an ordinary man. But marrying Casaubon helps her to fulfil her idealised image: sacrificing herself to the great cause of helping him complete his 'great work', *The Key to All Mythologies*, will be a living testament to her 'goodness'. When Dorothea realises that this path will not enable her to achieve her goal, she has to 're-define her idealized image and seek glory in a different way' (p. 39), through philanthropy and her later marriage, after Casaubon's death, to Will Ladislaw.

As an imagined human being, then, Paris suggests, Dorothea does not illustrate what she is supposed to: 'The [author's] rhetoric affirms

that it is good to be like Dorothea... the mimesis shows that it is not'
(p. 210). By seeing Dorothea through her own 'religion of humanity',
an atheistic philosophy that glorifies living for others (see Willey,
1950), Eliot creates a conflict between her own conscious intentions
and the spontaneous life of the character she has intuitively created.

Characters as imagined human beings

The idea that characters have spontaneous lives of their own is starkly
at odds with the postmodern view that, like selves and authors,
characters are no more than a textual function or 'word masses'
(Docherty, 1983, p. 34). So what exactly does this mean and how do
characters acquire their spontaneous lives? To explore this question,
we need to look not so much at the finished text, but at the 'real
present of the creative process', as Bakhtin calls it, to see what actually goes on in the imagination of the author whilst a work is in
progress.

The recorded experience of many writers supports the view that in
the process of creation characters are often much more than words
on the page. They can 'arrive' in the writer's imagination fully developed or quickly develop a presence beyond that required of them to
fulfil their roles in the text. Here's Deborah Moggach describing the
'arrival' of the main character of a novel she was planning:

> He sprang into life once I had pinpointed where he lived: one of those
> sooty blocks of mansion flats on the Edgware Road. For days I sat in my
> car, opposite the building, and pictured him shuffling out – big,
> bearded, wearing espadrilles with the backs squashed down and pulling
> along one of those matted little dogs that looks as if it has been run
> over. By this time his name had come to me – Russell Buffery. I knew he
> would shuffle along to the local pub, because he was a boozer. I knew
> he would shuffle along to the chemist's, because he was a hypochon-
> driac... I followed him to the bottle bank [where he] glared at people...
> (Moggach, 1993, p. 134).

The process she describes is spontaneous, beyond her conscious
control: he 'sprang' into life', his name 'came' to her, she 'knew' his
idiosyncrasies. Moggach is clearly a writer with a strong autonomous
visual imagination. All she has to do is to fix on a location and her

character 'shuffles' onto the scene. Indeed, that her dominant sense of him is of his shuffling gait is highly significant. In spite of Bakhtin's and Pirandello's view of characters as '*speaking* consciousnesses', when we are in the process of creating characters for fiction it is often not their words that come to us first but their physicality. Even before Moggach's character speaks, he *feels* to her like a living, breathing human being, simply from the way he moves.

The novelist John Banville experiences something similar, although he is 'inclined to laugh' when he hears other writers talking about their characters having a life of their own and taking over the action. For him, characters are 'made of words, not flesh; they do not have free will, they do not exercise volition. They are easily born, and as easily killed off. They have their flickering lives, and die on cue, for us, giving up their little paragraph of pathos' (Banville, 1993, pp. 107–8). Paradoxically, he then goes on to say that 'the only way to portray life in art is to be as lifelike as possible. All that the writer has to work with is human being, his own and that of the mysterious others, what little he can know of it, or them'. No matter how abstract art is, being – or even Being – keeps breaking in (p. 109).

Banville does not explain what exactly he means by 'being', with or without an initial capital, but he is probably referring to Wallace Stevens' understanding of this term, which Hillis Miller sums up as 'the universal power, visible nowhere in itself, and yet visible everywhere in all things. …it is what all things participate in if they are to exist at all. All Stevens' later poetry has as its goal the releasing of the evanescent glimpse of being which is as close as man can come to a possession of the ground of things' (Hillis Miller, 1965, p. 157). The example with which Banville illustrates his use of the term 'being' – the final section of Wallace Stevens' poem 'Credences of Summer' (Stevens, 1965, p. 84) – indicates that it has a lot to do with *bodily feelings*:

> The personae of summer play the characters
> Of an inhuman author, who meditates
> With the gold bugs, in blue meadows, late at night.
> He does not hear his characters talk. He sees
> Them mottled, in the moodiest costumes
>
> Of blue and yellow, sky and sun, belted
> And knotted, sashed and seamed, half pales of red,
> Half pales of green, appropriate habit for

> The huge decorum, the manner of the time,
> Part of the mottled mood of summer's whole,
>
> In which the characters speak because they want
> To speak, the fat, the roseate characters,
> Free, for a moment, from malice and sudden cry,
> Complete in a completed scene, speaking
> Their parts as in a youthful happiness.

The poem evokes the way an author brings his characters into being. Contrary to Banville's view that the author is wholly in charge of the creation and despatch of his characters, the author in the poem is passive; he simply 'meditates' his characters into being and watches them 'play'. Stevens describes his author as 'inhuman', which has echoes of Eliot's and Barthes' impersonality of the writing process, but in fact he is not simply a vessel for the play of the text. The characters, it seems, arise out of the author's *felt sense* of what summer means, and he is more concerned with embodying this *sense* – his own felt truth or truths, as the word 'credences' implies – than in creating characters in their own right. At first the author 'does not hear his characters talk' but 'sees them' hazily in half-tones, shapes and shades – 'half pales' of red and green, 'mottled', 'moody', 'fat', 'roseate'. His experience of them has more to do with the vague, felt quality of the imagination than with clear-cut images or particular voices. Only when they have been *felt* into existence do they begin to speak, and not because the author wills them to, but 'because they want/To speak...'. They have become 'Complete in a completed scene' and in their completeness they are momentarily 'free' from negative emotions and 'speak their parts' in the image of 'youthful happiness', which is presumably what the author is attempting to conjure up out of his own bodily memory.

What we see in Stevens' poem is the beginnings of the emergence of characters out of the author's felt, emotional memory. The characters are not mimetic or rounded, rather they serve an aesthetic function within the poem. They are material in the metaphorical process of transposing feelings into words, for which purpose it is not important to characterise them more closely. Essentially, this is the same process we see at work in Moggach's character creation, except that for the purpose of her novel she will go on to develop her character more fully.

The experience of Moggach and Stevens (and by implication also Banville) demonstrates the important role of bodily feelings in the unconscious metaphorical process underlying the imaginative creation of character. Metaphor, as discussed in Chapter 1, is not simply a literary device but a form of thought. It is a neurophysiological process at work both in our conscious and our unconscious lives, a mapping or transfer of meaning between different sensory domains, primarily between sensorimotor experience – our sensing of the body's movement – and our experience of how we feel. A good example is our tendency to link happiness with 'up' or the upright posture of the body. When we feel good we say 'I'm feeling *up* today' (Lakoff and Johnson, 1999, pp. 45–59).

Whilst Freud did not understand the role of metaphor in the unconscious, he identified two modes of mental functioning operating in dreams: 'condensation', where two or more separate elements or ideas are compressed; and 'displacement', where the intensity and significance of an unconscious wish is transferred into an indifferent object (Freud, 1976). It was Jacques Lacan, influenced by the literary theorist Roman Jakobson, who later pointed out the connections between Freud's concepts and literary categories: condensation was the same as metaphor, which conflates two different things or ideas (for example, love and red roses), and displacement was the same as metonymy, where the part stands for the whole (for example, the 'bench' for the law) (Lacan, 1977). In dreams, the unconscious metaphorical process, freed from the constraining 'autobiographical self' and the distractions of the everyday world, operates autonomously, using memories both from the immediate and from the long-term past (Modell, 2003, pp. 62, 66). Dream characters are created both metaphorically and metonymically; sometimes they are a mixture of elements of ourselves or people we know, characters from fictions we have read, seen or heard, or, as Carl Jung suggests, archetypes deeply rooted in our cultures; sometimes they stand for something larger of which they are a part. Because our conscious intention is suspended in dreams, our autonomous unconscious imagination enables dream characters to operate of their own volition just as if they were real people.

Fictional characters as they are being created can similarly be understood as products of our autonomous unconscious imagination; and, as with dreams, the material is drawn from a variety of sources in our memory and knowledge and brought together metaphorically. But what dreams do involuntarily, or by means of unconscious intentionality (Modell, 2003, pp. 92–110), creative writers do partly voluntarily and partly involuntarily. As we said above, we may initiate our characters intentionally, but if they are to be fully developed as imagined human beings, we have to suspend conscious control over them and let them develop a life of their own, a life that can only come from our own knowledge and felt bodily memory, and the power of our imagination, both conscious and unconscious. As the novelist Muriel Spark says about her characters: 'I think I must crop up through every character in a way... I don't see where, otherwise, one's knowledge comes from. *One has to feel things*' (Tusa, 2003, p. 230, emphasis added). According to aesthetician Elaine Scarry (1999), when writers create fictional settings and characters they intuitively use techniques that imitate perceptual mechanisms in the brain's visual cortex, and this enables readers, and presumably the authors themselves as well, to experience these fictional creations more intensely through the felt quality of the 'mind's eye'. Amongst these techniques, the use of colour and movement are key. As we have seen in the above examples, Stevens, by focusing on colour and shape, and Moggach, by focusing on movement and gesture, stimulate their imagination to create, metaphorically and metonymically, characters who, only after they have been felt into being, start to speak.

In the process of creation, then, characters in their most developed form are largely a result of our felt bodily experience. They are 'imagined human beings' (Paris, 1997) or 'revenants of the dream work of life' (Bollas, 1993, p. 61). The extent to which characters *act* like real human beings will depend on the power of our imagination, the extent of our insight, and also the extent to which we can feel ourselves into them empathically, empathy being another form of unconscious bodily metaphor (Modell, 2003, p. 187).

Characters as experimental selves

Whether fictional characters can be said to be like real people or are simply 'word masses' is not something that preoccupies the Czech novelist, Milan Kundera. Characters are useful to him in that they allow him to explore states of being, to help him answer the question: 'What is the self? How can the self be grasped?' (Kundera, 1990, pp. 23). Rather than allowing characters to emerge spontaneously, he starts with a 'working hypothesis, a definition', and then places characters into situations where this hypothesis or definition can be explored (p. 32). In his novel *The Unbearable Lightness of Being*, for example, he invents the character of Tereza in order to explore the hypothesis that vertigo – or 'the insuperable longing to fall' (Kundera, 1985, p. 61) – is a possibility of existence. Tereza, we are told, desires to transcend her origins, to go beyond the emptiness of her mother's life, and is always striving for higher things, which means that she has to be strong and assertive. But in moments of weakness and uncertainty she is powerfully drawn to her mother and is therefore always in danger of falling back into the emptiness (pp. 60–1). The novel charts the consequences of this 'existential problem' (Kundera, 1990, p. 35) for her life, as well as for that of her husband, Tomas.

Kundera does not employ techniques of mimetic characterisation to bring Tereza alive, nor does he attempt to create her as a speaking presence: 'It would be senseless for the author to try to convince the reader that his characters once actually lived. They were not born of a mother's womb: they were born of a stimulating phrase or two or from a basic situation' (Kundera, 1985, p. 39). If he tells us something about her past or the way she looks, this is not so that we can imagine better her physicality or understand her psychologically, but because these things are amongst the main themes of her existential problem (Kundera, 1990, pp. 34–5). Tereza is an 'experimental self', created solely for the purpose of facilitating the author's 'meditative interrogation' (p. 31). In this sense she is an 'illustrative' rather than a mimetic character, 'a part masquerading as a whole' (Scholes and Kellogg, 1966, p. 88), although by virtue of the amount of information we are given about her – details of her relationship with her mother, her desire to learn and to find fulfilling work, her suffering at Tomas's infidelities, and the contents of her dreams – she does have the potential to come alive physically and emotionally *to some extent* in the reader's imagination. But this is only what Kundera would expect: '...the reader's imagination automatically completes the writer's' (Kundera, 1990, p. 34).

Tereza's husband, Tomas, is much more difficult to complete imaginatively, as we are given less access to his inner life and comparatively little information about him. We know he is a surgeon, that he was married and divorced before he met Tereza and has a son, and that he is torn between the desire for freedom from commitment to a woman – the lightness of being which for him is characterised by casual sex – and the unbearable nature of the aloneness that is the consequence of this lack of belonging. His role in the novel is to illustrate the old German adage 'Einmal is keinmal' (literally 'once is not once'), which, for Kundera, implies that we cannot make decisions on the basis of experience if we only have one life (Kundera, 1985, p. 8). Tomas is a 'flat character' in Forster's terms, '...constructed around a single idea or quality', expressible in a single sentence and unable to develop (Forster, 1979, p. 73). However, Rimmon-Kenan's suggestion that characters are best classified 'as points along a continuum... [with] three... axes: complexity, development, penetration into the inner life' is more useful for understanding Tomas textually (Rimmon-Kenan, 1996, p. 41; drawing on Ewen, 1971 and 1980). It allows us to see him as at the low end of the 'complexity' scale, being constructed around one dominant trait; somewhere in the middle of the 'development' scale, as he does eventually begin to liberate himself from his 'existential problem'; and low to middle on the 'penetration into the inner life' scale, as we are allowed a limited access into his internal conflicts.

However we classify Kundera's characters on the page, his relationship with them as author-narrator is controlling and authoritative, far from Pirandello's and Bakhtin's ideal dialogic engagement. Sometimes he is a cruel scientist impassively watching his research subjects undergoing a painful experiment, his 'surplus of meaning' (Bakhtin, 1984, pp. 70–3) giving him complete power to move his characters around. For example, rather than allowing Tereza to *show* readers how *she* feels, through her own words and actions, he spends a good deal of time *telling* us about her feelings in ways that seem rhetorically controlling (on the uses of 'telling' and 'showing' in fiction, see Booth, 1991). He also makes sure that readers are clear about *his view* of her thoughts and actions. Speaking of her first year with Tomas, he says that: 'Screaming [during intercourse], *as I have pointed out*, was meant to blind and deafen the senses' (Kundera, 1985, p. 161; emphasis added); readers are not encouraged to come to their own conclusions. Yet occasionally, he seems to acknowledge that his characters *do* have a life of their own and that his role is to try to understand them. 'I have been thinking about Tomas for many years', he says, 'But only in the light of these reflections did I see him clearly' (p. 6). Similarly with Tereza: 'I find it difficult to explain what she had in mind when she compared a nude beach to the Russian invasion [of

Czechoslovakia]' (p. 69). In spite of his view of his characters as tools in his investigation and his desire to keep them under strict control, sometimes he has to allow them a degree of freedom, otherwise he wouldn't be able to find out how they act and feel in the situation in which he has placed them. Even though the characters are not fully mimetic, they do indeed begin to develop a little bit of their own spontaneous life.

As the novel nears it end it becomes clear that for the author-narrator the experiment is not, in fact, a disinterested exercise, but a sort of auto-fictional exploration. Like Muriel Spark, he confesses that all his characters are in a sense himself, in that he has experienced the very situations and conflicts his characters find themselves in, but what they allow him to do is to circumvent his own borders and to experiment with a self beyond the confines of his own 'I': 'The novel is not the author's confession; it is an investigation of human life in the trap the world has become' (p. 221), or perhaps even the trap that the author's own psyche has become.

Characters and selves

The idea of characters as 'experimental selves' that allow us to go beyond the confines of our own 'I' brings us back to Pirandello's play and the question contained in the epigraph to this chapter: whether characters can be thought of as in some sense *more* real or *more* true than human beings. Clearly characters are not real in the sense that they are not living, breathing creatures in the way human beings are, although, as we have seen, they can acquire an autonomous life in the imagination of the writer whilst a work is in progress, and similarly in the imagination of the reader whilst reading. But what does Pirandello's Father-character mean when he says that a character is always someone, whilst a man can be nobody?

Early on in his stage directions Pirandello tells us that each of the characters is 'fixed immutably in the expression of [his or her] own fundamental sentiment' or emotion: *remorse* in the case of the Father, *grief* in that of the Mother, and *revenge* in that of the Stepdaughter, and he recommends that they should wear masks to emphasise this fixity in 'created reality' (Pirandello, 1995, p. 10). It is as a consequence of this 'created reality', the Father explains later in the play, that the characters know absolutely who they are, the intensity of their feelings driving them to find a context in which they can act out the 'eternal moment' of their particular drama (p. 51). By contrast, he says, the reality of human beings changes from day to day; the feelings they had in the past are no longer the feelings they have in the present; therefore their sense of who they are, their identity or 'personal truth' is much more difficult to grasp (pp. 54–6). Could it be, then, that by creating characters out of ourselves, embodying in them our own feelings and preoccupations, we may have the opportunity, as Kundera seems to imply, of experiencing ourselves more intensely and the possibility of finding a deeper sense of identity and personal truth?

For Israeli novelist Amos Oz, his personal truth lies not just in the characters he creates out of himself and his preoccupations, but also in his engagement with them, as he discovers when, in true Bakhtinian fashion, he writes himself into his novel *The Same Sea* (2001a) as a character. The novel operates in a kind of dream world, where the author appears as himself and engages in conversation with the characters, and where the characters also engage in conversation with each other across boundaries of time and space. The characters struggle with feelings and emotions that are very much the author's own (Oz, 2001b). Rico, the son of small time accountant, Albert Danon, is struggling to let go of his mother, who has recently died of cancer. He has left Dita, his girlfriend, and the family home in a small Israeli seaside town for Tibet, where he tries to lose himself in the wide-open spaces and in sexual abandon. In a similar way, Oz tells us, he himself has been struggling all his life to let go of his own mother who committed suicide when he was twelve (Oz, 2001b). At one point in the novel Dita upbraids the author for continuing to mourn his mother after forty-five years. It is ridiculous, she says, insulting to his wife and daughters. He should give her up, let her wander the underworld on her own (Oz, 2001a, p. 134). Engaging in this 'mono-dialogue', this conversation with himself via a community of characters, some purely imaginary and some based on real people, helps the author to open himself up to his own pain and difficulties (Oz, 2001b). He realises how important is the link with other people but also how important it is to let them go in one's mind, to accept the ultimate aloneness and the overwhelming nature of desire and grief. He recognises too the necessity of relinquishing the drive to do and to be, to accept life as it is and the ending of it all in death, the ultimate return to the oneness of the same sea (Oz, 2001a, pp. 41–2).

The novel is a tool in his own 'peace process' (Oz, 2001b); in the reflexive dialogue with his community of selves he identifies his own deeper truth, a felt emotional truth, and becomes more real to himself.

Recommended reading

Bernard Paris's *Imagined Human Beings* (1997) explores the tension between authors' rhetoric and the mimetic characters they create, as does some of his other work, e.g. *Character as Subversive Force in Shakespeare: the History and Roman Plays* (1991a). Elaine Scarry's *Dreaming by the Book* (1999) is a fascinating discussion of the way writers stimulate the reader to imagine characters and scenes in fiction. Christopher Bollas's *Being a Character: Psychoanalysis and Self Experience* (1993), which explores how we 'dream' ourselves into existence, is richly relevant to the way the writer creates characters in fiction. Shlomith Rimmon-Kenan's *Narrative Fiction – Contemporary Poetics* (1996) provides a useful introduction to narratological thinking about character. Alan Palmer's *Fictional Minds* (2004) explores what he sees as the central role in novels of fictional consciousnesses.

Writing exercises

- Buy a piece of clothing in a jumble sale or second-hand shop and create the character who wears it.
- Take a physical characteristic, such as a limp or a nervous tic, and create a character who possesses this characteristic, showing how the characteristic manifests itself in movement and engagement with other characters.
- Write a poem that captures the sense of a particular atmosphere or quality (such as Wallace Stevens' 'youthful happiness') primarily through the evocation of character rather than place.
- Identify a particular social, political or religious discourse and create a character who embodies this discourse. Enter into the fictional world of this character as a first-person narrator and engage the character in conversation; try to give both textual creations as much freedom as possible.

- Use a character from one of your dreams to create a poem or short prose piece.
- Read a short story, paying particular attention to the way the writer evokes character. What devices does he/she use? What attitude does the implied author have to the characters he/she has created?
- Following Kundera's example, identify a 'state of being' such as vertigo or the fear of falling, and allow a character to emerge out of it (wait and watch as the character emerges).
- Create characters out of people you know by immersing yourself in what you experience as their dominant 'feeling tone'. Do something similar for yourself. As a character, enter into engagement with the other characters you have created.

7   Memory and History

> I have resolved on an enterprise which has no precedent, and which, once complete, will have no imitator. My purpose is to display to my kind a portrait in every way true to nature, and the man I portray will be myself.
>
> Jean-Jacques Rousseau, *The Confessions*, 1988, p. 19.

To some extent we always write out of our own experience. If this is the case, what's different about writing specifically autobiographical material? Is there anything special about the way we remember, about the relationship between personal and shared worlds of experience? And what of the reflexivity of *re*-membering: does it have anything to show us about the writing process in general?

At the opening of the *Confessions*, Rousseau declares his project is a scientific one: he will be 'true to nature'. Despite the religious overtones of his title and the romantic revelations the book will contain, this is to be writing based on experiential knowledge: 'Simply myself. I know my own heart,' he continues. When Rousseau goes on to invoke the 'sincerity' of religious confession in this experiment, we need to remember that eighteenth-century science centred on the *thought processes* of 'natural philosophers' such as George Berkeley and David Hume,[1] rather than on objectively repeatable *techniques.* It was subjective in the fullest sense of that term: a sense referring not only to agency but to a process of meaning-making which centres round the individual. As Roland Barthes points out, the present-day status of the author's name as *part of* the text, a kind of brand, has its origins in this earlier, wider context: in which scientists' names were important because they identified thinkers who might be trusted to *make sense* of the physical world (Barthes, 1964).

Nevertheless, Rousseau's challenge is an interesting one. He makes the paradoxical proposal that a writer can achieve disinterested inquiry – what we think of as something like omniscient narration –

by looking at himself. It's a paradox which is at the heart of the book you're reading now: and of the writing process itself. For we're suggesting that, through exploring and owning the reflexivity inherent in our writing process – the way it's necessarily engaged with who we are – we can 'manage' what's individual in both process and product and move it outwards to the unknown reader. In this chapter we'll look at the way memory and history ask us to *tell the story of* this reflexivity; and how this poses special challenges for us as writers.

The paradox of situatedness

History is an account of something which *went before* the moment of writing. Writing about history therefore always declares a temporal relationship with its material, even if it doesn't put it into words. Very often, however, history-writing does locate author or at least narrator in the 'present day' (not the reader's present, of course, but a textual present); and locate this 'present day' in relation to (another) narrative time. For example, Germaine Greer's *Daddy We Hardly Knew You* is set in three time 'zones': the 'present day' in which the narrator tries to find traces of her father in various archives, the 'short past' of her childhood memories, and the 'long past' of her prehistory when Mr Greer was not yet anybody's father (Greer, 1990). This is a complex set of parallel manoeuvres – carried out in the oral and written texts which record Greer senior's life – of the kind dramatised by A.S. Byatt in her Booker-prize-winning novel *Possession* (Byatt, 1991). In Byatt's novel, the love affair of a nineteenth-century poet, discovered by present-day researchers, partly mirrors but also *generates* the researchers' own affair.

But of course, not all reflexive locations are so romantic. Scholarly forms – including literary biography and some history-writing – increasingly bring the processes of research, the 'present day', into the text in a way analogous to contemporary reflexive practice in anthropology (see Introduction). For example, Simon Schama's *Landscape and Memory* looks at what the primeval European forest (Transylvania, the Polish *puszca*) has represented, across boundaries of time and nation state, to the continent's inhabitants, including himself (Schama, 1996).

This overt location of the moment of writing in relation to (other) narrative objects is particularly pronounced in autobiography; where an additional temporal and textual relationship, that of *memory*, is being established between the moment of writing and what we write about. Autobiography says both 'I am here' and 'I was there'. Its temporally bifurcated narrator stabilises him or herself by 'having a foot in' *both* these moments of narrative time. This is William Wordsworth's 'emotion recollected in tranquillity.' Re-collection, the calling back *together* of a former whole, is also the process Wordsworth talks about as shaping and completing lyric verse (Wordsworth, 1973, p. 608). Because it's a *doubling* of sources of authority, temporal bifurcation paradoxically reinforces the conventional contract of 'good faith' between reader and writer, in a way similar to apparatuses such as epistolary forms, which *locate* narrative authority (see Chapter 9).

That it's a paradox is significant. The metaphysical poets of another expansively scientific age, the seventeenth century, used paradox both to approach what cannot itself be put into words and to suggest the doubled, or reflexive, nature of experience. In 'Song', John Donne declares the impossibility of finding a faithful woman. His injunction to the reader to (imagine) a series of impossible tasks illustrates the 'impossible nature' – that is, paradox – of women:

> Goe and catche a falling starre,
>   Get with child a mandrake roote,
> Tell me, where all past yeares are,
>   Or who cleft the Divel's foot,
> Teach me to heare Mermaides singing,
>   Or to keep off envie's stinging [...]

(Donne, 1969, p. 24)

This extended paradox situates the reader as *both* apprehending and necessarily failing to apprehend the poem's object. Rather than a God's-eye or Ideal Reader, it stages the limits of individual understanding, the reader's *subjectivity*.

Although we might associate it with Modernism and with T.S.Eliot's idea of poetry conducting 'raids on the inarticulate', the paradoxical use of paraphrase to *indicate without naming* what is unspeakable – for example the holy or mysterious – would have been familiar to seventeenth century poets. The God of the Old Testament cannot be named but only referred to. Paradox is also closely identified with the sonnet form, which George Herbert and Henry Vaughan, as well as Donne, use for poetries of sacred rather than secular love at this time.[2] Sonnets such as Donne's 'Batter my heart...' from the 'Holy Sonnets' refer, through this formal association with romantic love, to *individual* rather than ritual spiritual experience:

> Yet dearely' I love you,' and would be loved faine,
> But am betroth'd unto your enemie:
> Divorce mee,' untie, or breake that knot againe,
> Take mee to you, imprison me, for I,
> Except you'enthrall mee, never shall be free,
> Nor ever chast, except you ravish mee.[3]
>
>   (Donne, 1969, p. 172)

As British Church and State settled into constitutional cohabitation in the sixteenth century, religion became both a necessarily *common* social denominator and, at the same time therefore, less of a force binding *particular* groups together. While the space for religious experience became more public and secularised, the private secular model of love poetry became available for religious reflection.[4] In an analogous movement, when we write history or memoir we locate our 'private' writing self in relation to the 'public' space of past time.

So Rousseau's challenge at the opening of his *Confessions* uses paradox: a trope[5] associated with the reflexivity of the narrative I, with its *related situatedness*. It's useful to hold onto this *knowing* use of a reflexive trope when we question Rousseau's confessional project. Because the idea of a unitary self has been problematised in Western thought since the nineteenth century,[6] we understand that the lived self and the self on the page are not the same; and this seems to be a reason to mistrust the project of the *Confessions*. But Rousseau, by introducing the *paradox* of disinterested self-examination, and by positing himself – another paradox – as both exceptional and exemplary, is already acknowledging and staging just this possible non-identity of selves.

Rousseau is significant for our own writing from memory and history because he represents the juxtaposition of two traditions: religious confession, and the secular tradition of Romanticism in which the new metaphysical foundation is the self. As the role and meaning of religion is changed by explosive scientific developments in late eighteenth century Europe, Romantic philosophy – developing in that very space for private experience which, as we have seen, the religious

reforms of the sixteenth century had opened up – poses a new metaphysics. In what is essentially the same conservative gesture as Descartes makes in the *cogito* (Descartes, 1989) (see also Chapter 9),
Romanticism relies on the world of immediate 'sensory apprehen-
sion' – in other words, the *world of individual experience* – as the basis
of its meaning-making. Nietzsche's model of the transcendent self,
the *übermensch* with his endless resourcefulness, is, in the end, no
more than a development of the journey of self-discovery Schiller's
Young Werther makes.

Confession and the boundaries of the text

This status of the Romantic self as a *metaphysical* foundation is
important when ideas about the self are taken as the basis for action,
as they are in political philosophy. Rousseau's self-portrait (Rousseau,
1986) assumes particular importance because he bases his philosophies of human rights and education on his ideas about the 'nature'
of the self (including the gendered self; see our Chapter 10). But the
other textual tradition by which Rousseau's *Confessions* are inflected,
and which they break apart – the confession of spiritual experience –
also sites texts *in relation to* a realm of consequent action. A confession declares itself to be part of a process which also takes place in the
world, beyond the text, of such actions as ethical decision-making
or the carrying out of penances. Literary memoir or 'kiss-and-tell'
exposé, though secular, declare a special kind of relationship with the
world beyond the text too. All writing reflects the world it comes from
in one way or another. But forms which use memory always bring one
aspect of confessional with them: which is that they *posit* their telling
as a *continuation* of action *beyond* the page.

To understand this mechanism (and where it might lead us),
we need to look a little more closely at some examples. In the six-
teenth-century Spanish *The Life of Saint Teresa*, confession is itself a
spiritual exercise. But her confession is also a record of specific spiritual exercises completed (St Teresa, 1958). The text shifts between
confession in the first person, third person reflections on the nature
of God, and second person prayers addressed to Him. These shifts
characterise not only personal inner process but also collective religious observance (both preaching and private reflection may characteristically lead to or include prayer). Moving between the worlds of

inner and of collective outer experience in this way, the *Life* describes that bridge which, as we discuss elsewhere (in Chapter 9), all writing makes between inner and outer experience.

The overtly didactic *Life* is another kind of model too. Like the *Poems* of St Teresa's colleague[7] St John of the Cross, it also functions as a work of spiritual instruction (St John of the Cross, 1960). Here for example is St Teresa's description of the 'prayer of the quiet':

> This entails a gathering of the faculties within oneself [...] but they are not lost or asleep. The will alone is occupied in such a way that it is unconsciously taken captive [...]. The other two faculties – the memory and the imagination – help the will to make itself more and more capable of enjoying this great blessing [...]. (St Teresa, 1958, p. 98)

This description of meditation surprises us because we tend to associate such practice with non-Christian traditions like Zen Buddhism. But as the 'bridging' role of *The Life* indicates, this description of contemplation also partly describes the process of writing the confessions themselves. The idea of writing as continuous with meditative action beyond the page is central to one of the most influential of contemporary creative writing handbooks, Natalie Goldberg's *Writing Down the Bones*. In fact, Goldberg tells a story about having practised Zen for six years until her *Roshi* pointed out that writing could be her meditation (Goldberg, 1986, p. 3). Goldberg's book is a charismatic and supportive writer's companion. It also offers a model of the writing process as a practice which goes on beyond as well as on the page:[8]

> This is the practice school of writing. Like running, the more you do it, the better you get at it. [...] You don't wait around for inspiration and a deep desire to run. It'll never happen, especially if you are out of shape and have been avoiding it. But if you run regularly, you train your mind to cut through or ignore your resistance. You just do it. And in the middle of the run, you love it. (Goldberg, 1986, p. 11)

T.S. Eliot made one of St John of the Cross's instructions for practice from 'The Ascent of Mount Carmel' – that 'In order to arrive at what you are not/You must go through the way in which you are not' – famous by identifying it with a key Modernist idea: an individual, or a society, must first be broken down in order to be rebuilt (Eliot, 1985,

p. 201). It's the idea, inherited from the Romantic ideal of undivided
subjectivity, of the revolutionary subject; and of that subjectivity
multiplied to the nth degree in national or societal renewal through
revolution. Leo Tolstoy's attempts to build a utopian lifestyle on
Christian beliefs about the importance of individual ethics are one
literary-social example of this nineteenth century phenomenon
(Tolstoy, 1984). Transcendence, which we might otherwise associate
simply with spiritual practice, is in this view a subjectivity which over-
comes its own current form and remakes itself (see Chapter 10). In the
later twentieth century, post-structuralist unease with the consequences of essentialist and totalising aspects of this idea led among
other things to the idea of the *sujet-en-procès* (subject in process), a
continuing (individual) experience which is acted upon by and acts
upon the world around it: which, though it has responsibility for its
actions (agency), does not change solely as the result of conscious
choice (see Chapter 10).

Yet this is not the way the authorial 'I' of St John of the Cross's
Poems is constructed. A first person narrator addresses passionate
love poetry to God. This first person *singular* is the lover; it is also
each *individual* reader participating in the (spiritual) process of
reading this text. The use of first person demonstrates a blurring
of the boundaries of self in two directions: between the 'I' of the
writer as public individual – as an 'everyman' speaking to and for a
constituency – and the readerly 'I' for whom the text claims to speak
(for more on this intimacy between writer and reader see Chapter 10);
and between the first person of the text and that second person to
whom it is addressed, the God with whom the speaker merges. Here,
for example, the poet uses that tool in the repertory of love-poetry,
paradox, to express this move away from self:

> Vivo sin vivir en mí,
> Y de tal manera espero,
> Que muero porque no muero.
>
> En mí yo no vivo ya,
> Y sin Dios vivir no puedo [...][9]
>
> (St John of the Cross, 1960, p. 50)

Like *The Life of St Teresa*, this text is a 'confession' of loss of self.
Also like *The Life*, it emphasises process rather than the individual

undertaking it.[10] The fourth century St Augustine's *Confessions*, however, represent an altogether different project: the *record* of a whole life as it is affected by spiritual process (St Augustine, 2002). Here the portrait of the authorial 'I' becomes *pluri*-dimensional. We see not only intentions but outcomes: the way different experiences (the secular and the spiritual, inner and outer) have to be fitted together by the *individual* located at their juncture. This representation of a plurality of personal aspects constitutes the first steps towards what we may call characterisation. It constructs an idea which is sufficiently 'in the round' to imply how that character may appear in contexts other than ones the author actually uses (see Chapter 6). As the phrase 'come to life' points out, there is a sense of the writer's having produced an idea capable of independent existence.

Characterisation as three-dimensional autonomy is also key in drama. Bertold Brecht says, 'Standing in a free and direct relationship to it, the actor allows his character to speak and move' (Brecht, 1964, p. 143). Key across art forms, too, is the idea of the three-dimensional human self located *across* outer and inner worlds of experience. Writing on Bauhaus theatre, Oskar Schlemmer says that, 'The history of the theatre is the history of the transfiguration of the human form. It is the history of *man* as the actor of physical and spiritual events. [...] The arena for this transfiguration is found in the con-structive fusion of *space and building*' (Schlemmer, 1961, p. 17). Barthes talks about music becoming more than mere performance ('*pheno-song*') when it 'comes from [the] inner body' ('*geno-song*'). 'The "grain" is the body in the voice as it sings, the hand as it writes, the limb as it performs' (Barthes, 1977, pp. 188, 189).

In other words, a text comes to life when *embodied* experience (of the author) meets the textual (narrator). In confessional forms this continuity is performed to the fullest possible extent. But St Augustine's narrative in *Confessions* is also more than merely programmatic in the way that instructive texts, such as those of SS Teresa and John of the Cross, must be. This produces an additional density, an excess of textual material, as if the world of experience it (re)creates had 'a life of its own'(see the idea of 'play' in Chapter 10). This margin of excess, latency and plurality is what 'characterises' our texts as literary rather than simply documentary.

Testimony and authority

Another genre which makes the link between the inner and outer worlds of writing experience explicit is testimony. Like confession, testimony may claim to do both more and less than a conventional literary text. In claiming to be 'unembellished' truth, the genres of confession and testimony are free to sidestep *apparently* literary devices. However, while confession professes to report the true actions of an individual, testimony also reports on the experience, including witness, of actions involving or perpetrated by others. The authorial 'I' no longer represents the limit of responsibility and meaning, as if it were a Romantic subject, but is responsible for identifying other people's roles and ascribing significance to them.

The importance of the extra-textual in determining the *genre* of a text becomes clear when we look at the reception of Binjamin Wilkomirski's Holocaust 'memoir'. Wilkomirski was fostered prior to adoption by a Swiss couple, the Dössekkers, in Zurich in 1945. The Dössekkers died in 1986. In 1995 Wilkomirski's *Fragments* – whose English subtitle is *Memories of a Childhood, 1939–1948* – was published in Germany (Wilkomirski, 1998). Critical acclaim and editions in several European languages, as well as Hebrew, followed. The book won the autobiography/memoir category of the American National Jewish Book Award. It is a short work which tells the story of a boy, Binjamin Wilkomirski, born in Riga in 1938/9, who escapes the massacre of Jews in that city, but loses his parents, by being taken on board a boat to Gdansk; is captured and imprisoned in Majdanek and then Auschwitz-Birkenau camps; and taken to a Jewish orphanage in Krakow on liberation and thence to Switzerland, where his memories are repressed and disacknowledged.

However, in 1998 Daniel Ganzfried, a young writer who had himself published a Holocaust novel, published documentary evidence which seemed to suggest that Wilkomirski had been born Bruno Grosjean in Biel, Switzerland, in 1941 and placed in care as the child of an unmarried mother. The controversy became highly developed. As Elena Lappin points out, Wilkomirski, who had become involved in Holocaust survivor conferences and events, seemed convincing because of his anguished personal manner and because of his book's clear, sparse diction (Lappin 1999). Carl Tighe, on the other hand, writes that he mistrusted the book even before its status was exposed because of its 'concentration camp kitsch': 'after ten pages I threw it at the wall' (Tighe, 2005, p. 92). Another way to say this was that *voice*, rather than the story it told, was what convinced Wilkomirski's readers.

In other words, as this example demonstrates, for a characterisation such as 'sincerity' to be read from a text it must itself be a *textual* (literary) device. And yet, unlike memoir or confession, testimony relies on extra-textual but *not* literary authority; and the figure of its author is constructed accordingly. It does not need a reader to ensure its status. It may not even be published: some archived testimony is read only by individuals with prescribed roles, such as researchers or the judiciary. Testimony can also be collected by oral historians, who become the 'authors' of other people's words both through such interventions as editing – they may transcribe verbatim, but it is they who decide what constitutes an interview – and by lending the authority of their name. The contributors to Studs Terkel's highly influential collections do not become known as *authors* (Terkel, 2004): as Jack Goody points out, literacy is what masters and fixes the oral elements in a society (Goody, 1987).

So testimony and 'false testimony' raise particular questions about the relationships of text to memory, and of memory to lived experience. These questions include the status and nature of 'truth' in our writing; and how close the relationship between our lived experience and the text we produce can be.

Emmanuel Levinas says that all art, including writing, is a kind of black 'Magic':

> We find an appeasement when, beyond the invitations to comprehend and act, we throw ourselves into the rhythm of a reality which solicits only its admission into a book or a painting. Myth takes the place of mystery. The world to be built is replaced by the essential completion of its shadow. (Levinas, 1987, p. 12)

If this is the case, if in writing we always turn away from *engagement with* the world to *model* that world, then writing is not an action *in* the world. But genres such as confession and testimony, which continue the trajectory of action in the world *through* what we write, dramatise the essential failure of Levinas's vision of the hermetic text. Writing a novel or keeping a journal are particular kinds of actions in the world, just as building cars or making soup are. The completeness of the soup or the car doesn't make either of them a *refusal* of the world; although they may be what Ioan Davies calls a 'counter-ritual, which is the basis for any textuality' (Davies, 1990, p. 109). This is something it's easy to experience when we set ourselves an observation exercise. The *writing* which results may work all the better for being full of detailed observation of the *world around* us.

Once again, then, we need to relocate our writing selves and the world of our experience in relation to what we're writing. Other genres which refer to the external world of experience for meaning and status, and which we may therefore call *non-autonomous,* include reference, academic and text books. Their authorial 'I' may not be strongly evident – in self-help books it may be characterised as an exemplar – for these texts work with the world of *shared* experience, unlike autobiography, testimony and memoir, whose authority is located in the *individual* experience of the author. Even so, the locus of authority in memoir may be unstable. Laurie Lee's cycle of memoirs, whether of an impoverished Cotswold childhood in *Cider with Rosie* or of the exceptional conditions of Spain as it moved towards civil war, in *As I Walked Out One Midsummer Morning* and subsequent volumes, dealt with experiences which had not previously been literary staples (Lee, 1959, 1969). However, the books remained in print and on the school curriculum because of their 'poetic' style. In 'Dear Mr Lee' another Gloucestershire writer, the poet U.A. Fanthorpe, has a young reader make this link between writerly voice and the life of characterisation:

> [...] Dear Laurie, I want to say sorry,
> I didn't want to write a character-sketch
> of your mother under headings, it seemed
> wrong somehow when you'd made her so lovely,
> [...] I'm not much good at terse and cogent,
> I'd just like to be like you, [...]
> see everything bright and strange, the way you do [...]
> (U.A. Fanthorpe, 1987, pp. 22–3)

So in memoir, *literary* talent may blur the boundary between the individual and the experience they record. Does Anne Frank's *Diary of a Young Girl* move us so much because we know it was written by a young person who didn't survive the events she writes about; or because of the clear yet intimate prose in which it's written (Frank, 1996)?

In his consideration of the distances narrative can open from bare fact, Richard Kearney argues that where important historical events, like the Holocaust, must be remembered, it is the authority of the experience which matters.[11] 'Veridical recall claims primacy' over fictionalisation or literary shaping. 'Testimonial narrative' needs to stay close to particular recall in order to avoid dangers including the totalising narrative which subsumes actuality, or narrative reifications such as relativism or reductivism (Kearney, 2002, pp. 67–9).

But is experience by itself enough to allow us to posit ourselves as a source of real authority when we write testimony or memoir? Susan Kavaler-Adler suggests that creative work, especially by women writers, may represent repetition rather than reparation of difficult formative experiences (Kavaler-Adler, 1993). Among her examples are Sylvia Plath, Emily Dickinson, the Brontë sisters and Anaïs Nin; whose diary, which developed into both her literary source-book and a primary text in its own right, does show, Kavaler-Adler argues, the work of reparation being carried out through reflection and, in the fiction which originates in the diary, through explicit working-out. Metaphor allows Nin to work *through* themes including her relationship with her father. Nevertheless, one of Kavaler-Adler's conclusions is that most of the writers she studies:

> become the victims of their most valuable assets, their creative talents. Without the capacity to mourn though the creative process, artistically gifted people can remain endlessly trapped, unable to experience how creativity can move them towards a richer interpersonal life (Modell, 1975; 1976). (Kavaler-Adler, 1993, p. 103)

This is remarkably close to Levinas's idea, as we have seen, that the writer is turning away from engagement with life to enact an imaginary revenge on it – 'Revenge is gotten on wickedness by producing its caricature' (Levinas, 1987, p. 12) – and, like Levinas's position, seems to stem from an uncertainty about how the boundaries of texts work. Where do the things we write become the things we live, and *vice versa*? If I create an angry character, or use an embittered first-person narrator, am I necessarily doing so because that anger or bitterness *is my own experience*? Mightn't I be responding to *textual* needs such as motivation or narrative tension?

Kavaler-Adler also begs the question of whether we write memoir or even testimony *primarily* for personal developmental rather than textual reasons.[12] An alternative way of locating these texts in their author's personal development is through the idea of scapegoat transference: the written or recorded text is a *physical* record of an unhappy memory or reaction, though which that memory is *placed outside* the witness who experiences it. This separate object can be 'scapegoated', or treated in the ways its author would like to be able to treat the original memory: for example, it can be thrown or given away (Schaverein, 1999). Confession or testimony may have a posterior relationship to the public world beyond the text too: for example their use by Peace and Reconciliation Commissions in Argentina and South Africa as the first stage in social and individual forgiveness and a movement beyond war crimes. These texts, and the actions which surround them, may in turn re-enter fiction, as in Achmat Dangor's Booker shortlisted novel, *Bitter Fruit* (Dangor, 2004).

History and fiction

If the *relationship with* extra-textual experience is key to the status of autobiography, testimony and memoir, what happens when that relationship is explicitly distorted? We often use memory or history when we're writing fiction. New Historicism was a form of critical approach which repositioned the text within the writer's own world of experience in order to trace contextual influences and authorial presence. In doing so it claimed to find extra dimensions *of* the text. Analogously, when we write historical fiction we may use literary tropes to try to find extra dimensions of that history. In *Black Water* Joyce Carol Oates tells the story of Kelly Kelleher, a girl drowned when a drunken Senator goes off the road after a 4th of July party (Oates, 1994). This short work, almost a novella, has a series of correspondingly fragmentary chapters told from the girl's point of view. Each returns us to the moment of drowning as to an unacceptable fact which must be disbelieved over and over again, as the narrator disbelieves it. This repetition expands a small scandal of twentieth-century American political history into something which must be repeatedly faced.[13]

A different strategy is adopted by Michael Cunningham in *The Hours* (Cunningham, 1999). Using the title of an earlier draft, Cunningham's novel retells the Virginia Woolf novel now famous as *Mrs Dalloway* (Woolf, 1992), setting it in late twentieth-century

America. He transmutes the schizophrenia of Septimus Smith in the original into maternal depression and AIDS-related dementia; and interleaves scenes from Woolf's own suicidal depression between those of the fiction. Cunningham is making an explicit *analogy* between Woolf's own life and state of mind and those of her characters. But, although in doing so he positions the author *within* the composite text, he is not arguing for a necessarily *auto-biographical* connection between Woolf's experiences and those she portrays.

A more complex relationship between memory and text is that in which the writer fictionalises memory. Marcel Proust, in *À la recherche du temps perdu*, studies his own process of recollection and the recording of memory not only in the famous trigger of the madeleine, the little cake whose smell brings back the world of his childhood, but by making conscious a *process* of 'bringing-to-mind' (Proust, 1996). This explicit reflexivity, which is always *supplementary to* the incidents remembered, adds an element of unfinishability to the project to record the incidents of a life up to the always receding horizon of the present day. When we write about ourselves writing, in other words, we problematise the borders of the text in two ways. It's not only that we have made the link between what we do off the page and on it explicit; there's also the question of *where* to draw the borders. When do we *stop* writing?

Anthony Powell's twelve-volume *A Dance to the Music of Time* is another fictionalised version of a life (Powell, 1995). Though his brisk, realist prose is less overtly Modernist than Proust's, it preserves the trope of reflexivity in the way characters recur from volume to volume, often reintroduced by social or other circumstantial coincidence. Widmerpool, the school scapegoat, recurs in conversation in the characters' adult life even in volumes where he isn't an actor. The sequence records historical events and the changing fashions and *mores* of the mid-century decades in which it's set. Unlike Proust, Powell also wrote a memoir, *To Keep the Ball Rolling* (Powell, 2001). To read it is to enter the characteristic tonal world of Powell's fiction; yet its mere existence defines the *Dance* as *comparatively* fictional.

Both Powell and Proust might be said to record not so much testimony as life-worlds, the generalised and shared experiences of their generation and class. As we'll see elsewhere (see Chapter 10), some writers assert an especial responsibility for recording the experiences of the group to which they belong, often for social or political reasons. For example, Toni Morrison recreates unwritten slave histories through fictional testimony in her novel *Beloved* (Morrison, 1997). As the novel, in which the Beloved of the title is gradually forgotten – *de*-loved – makes clear, this is a work of *social* reparation. The significance of process in the narration of testimony – and its personal character – are emphasised by the way this novel's eponymous heroine re-visits incidents, each time revealing more about them. Testimony, even when it bears witness to the experiences of a whole group, retains a special relationship to the *individual* who narrates it.

But is this relationship 'truth'? Jacques Derrida reminds us that 'the *contingent* [is] what touches on touch, on the tangible, on what touches' (Derrida, 1987, p. 200). The *contingent* is what happens to be the case. It is what happens. This occurrence, both in and beyond the text, is the way in which experience, and the testimony or confession which arise *in relation to* it, are linked. It is an intrinsic relationship but not one which necessarily engenders truth: if I misapprehend something I think I've witnessed, that misapprehension will be in what I write too.

Another way to say this is that testimony, autobiography and memoir are also *genres* shaped, as is all *genre*, by elements of authorial identity and reference *within the body of the text*. These *genres* are no more unaware of what they're doing than is a detective novel or lyric verse. Even testimony may be explicitly shaped by its author in order to achieve the authority of *textual* completion. Diana Friel McGowin's *Living in the Labyrinth: A Personal Journey Through the Maze of Alzheimer's*, a patient's memoir of living with Alzheimer's, is testimony *shaped* on '"my" friend, the word-processor' as well as, given the challenges of that disease, such necessary aids to memory and structure as prompts from colleagues and family members (Friel McGowin, 1993).

To sum up, then, testimony and memoir allow us to use our memory and experience in particular ways. They are *genres* which position themselves partly in the textual and partly in the experienced world; and posit identity between the authorial and narrative 'I'. In shifting our attention beyond the text – not only during the process of writing but in that of reading – testimony, autobiography and memoir link themselves to the world of experience. They fit into that world through relations of reaction and consequence, whether scientific, spiritual, moral or political. Alone among literary genres, these non-autonomous texts demand not (only) to be read on their own merits. Their particular link with the world of experience marks a teleology of which literary texts are characteristically innocent. Even the 'purpose' of Rousseau's 'display' in the *Confessions* is tendentious; which is why his claims of scientific impartiality ultimately fail to convince. It is not because of the eighteenth century's close identification of science and subjectivity but because of the memoirist's 'eternal return' to his own identity and experience – a failure of transcendence or reparation – that the Rousseau of the *Confessions* remains essentially a participant within literary tradition. For us as knowing participants, however, testimony, autobiography and memoir remain *genres* which allow us to explore the links between our lives and what we write about them; and to bridge the inner and outer worlds of our experience.

Recommended reading

Michael Cunningham's *The Hours* (1999) marries a well-known novel by Virginia Woolf with the well-known story of the novelist's death, in a fiction which forces the reader to think about the importance of retelling. Ioan Davies's *Writers in Prison* (1990) is a theoretical overview of the role of writing in prison. *The Levinas Reader* (1989) provides an introduction to one of the few twentieth-century European philosophers to retain a moral dimension to epistemology. Rousseau's *The Confessions* (1988) is one of the foundational texts in the genre. Simon Schama's *Landscape and Memory* (1996) locates the history of a region in and through the cultures of the people living there. *Writing and Responsibility* by C. Tighe (2005) surveys the importance of responsibility in writing through a range of examples.

Writing exercises

- Write down one of your earliest memories, the kind that's one of Wordsworth's 'spots of time': a snapshot rather than a story. It can be about a paragraph or so long. Now have a look at how you've written it: have you used present or past tense? First person? Retell the memory from each of the following viewpoints: a nearby adult; an animal (there is always an animal, even if it's a dust-mite, present); the voice of your child-self; as myth or folktale. Notice how what you have to say develops as viewpoints are added.

- Take a passage of well-known autobiographical writing – anything from Anaïs Nin to St Augustine – and rewrite it in the third person, from your own viewpoint. What can you make sense of and where do you find it difficult or impossible to bring the writer's *own* experience to life?
- Write a poem or short piece of fiction in the persona of a historical character.
- Have you ever been disbelieved: for example when as a child you swore it wasn't you who stole the chocolates – and it wasn't? In discussion or on paper, try and identify what felt so awful about being disbelieved; and how this made you feel about the links between speech and agency.
- Conversely, pick an account which you don't believe – it might be a celebrity talking about their private life, or a politician making promises, for example – and 'talk back to' it, either out loud or on the page. How does this change the way you 'hear' their story?

8   Geography and Culture

> One must penetrate into the country [...]. Sharpen one's eye on the land.
>
> Hélène Cixous, *Stigmata: Escaping Texts*, 1998 pp. 3, 19.

What happens when ideas and themes are transmitted between cultures? When I read a book written out of another culture and under conditions I haven't experienced, how much of what's going on in it can I really understand? Can I ever fully know what the relationship is of that book to its cultural context? I may have been told that a particular novel presents a radical viewpoint, or that a poet's style is characteristic of his generation or school. But to some extent I have to take this on trust. 'Often if you just read poems by someone from another country you don't know where you are – you've got to situate them in their context,' as the Editors of *Modern Poetry in Translation* acknowledge (Sampson, 2004b).

Conversely, how much of what I write must be perfectly comprehensible to every reader, regardless of context? Can good writing rely on shared cultural assumptions – whether that's an understanding of the myths of Ovid or of British TV programming in the 1970s – or must it always assume no prior knowledge? To put it another way, can there be such a thing as context-free writing; or is writing which is filled up with local cultural meanings actually more filled up with human meaning, since all humans live at least partly within local cultures? In this chapter we'll look at how relationships between cultures inform the ways we write or read them; at what translation means for our writing; and at the difficulties inherent in *cross*-cultural reading and writing.

Culture as power

The transmission of ideas and themes takes place within a cultural power relationship. When Lord Elgin took the famous frieze from the

Parthenon to Britain, an act of cultural appropriation was probably taking place. When the North European folk figure of Santa Claus got dressed in the colours of Coca-Cola, a powerful extension of North American culture was arguably achieved. In other words, whichever *direction* cultural material is transmitted in, it's the more powerful culture which is *enlarged* by it.

The literary marketplace can work in much the same way. Writers, such as the Nigerian Ben Okri or Czech novelist Milan Kundera, who *are* widely published in the Anglophone West, become incorporated into the canon of contemporary writing in English. Meanwhile, translations of English and American *genre* fiction (including thrillers, fantasy, and 'shopping and fucking' novels), dominated East European publishing in its first decade of freedom and of market economics. The proportion of translated titles published in the region is 40–50%, compared to roughly 3% of US publishing. Translations published in the US have such small readership that they are not considered viable unless they attract a subsidy (O'Brien, 2003). As a result they're often published by smaller independent presses and so may be less-well distributed and passed over for review, thus ensuring their readership does indeed remain small. Emigré essayists Slavenka Drakulić and Dubravka Ugresic, who both identify as former-Yugoslav, are telling exceptions (Drakulić, 1996; Ugresic, 2003). Since Yugoslavia no longer exists, these cultural identities are conceptual rather than actual; in other words, both writers locate themselves *within* Western textual practises and *in relation to* their former Balkan experiences. Within the text, this strategic *ostranie* allows the resistance to clichés from both cultures.

But this apparently straightforward power relation becomes more complex when we try to imagine what might 'rectify' such a situation. Why should a notional reader in Poland be denied access to what his peer in the States reads? Isn't this a way of keeping the more powerful culture closed to outsiders? If I'm reading from a less powerful culture mightn't it benefit me to see how a range of things including my *self* are figured in the Anglophone world? And to whom should I myself be accountable when I write?

Two recent novels published to critical acclaim in the US – Jonathan Franzen's *The Corrections* and Jonathan Safran Foer's *Everything Is Illuminated* – use Lithuania and the Ukraine, respectively, as a background for explorations of American family life. These are indeed highly literary novels, whose American protagonists are portrayed with subtlety and ambiguity. The East European backdrops for substantial portions of this portrayal, however, revisit some of the clichés of the Hollywood of the Cold War era. Franzen's Lithuania is so corrupt the whole country has been bought by an illegal outfit with which one of his protagonists becomes associated (Franzen, 2002). Safran Foer's Ukraine is peopled by credulous provincials whose English is a running joke – and forms a key part of the book's narrative style (Safran Foer, 2003). The Ukrainian past is presented as a series of magical realist tableaux which suggest that, rather than European history functioning as a discrete sequence of causes and effects, the continent is merely the collective 'dreamtime' or 'unconscious' of North America (as the Mediterranean region has functioned as the 'unconscious' of British literary culture (Sampson, 2003)). The Ukraine is not a protagonist in international politics but a passive *ground* on which visitors or spectators can figure its identity.

One of Safran Foer's strategies is to use beauty in prose. Beauty functions here as a form of rhetoric: it serves as an intensifier, engaging the reader's attention and 'drawing them in' to a particular view of things, in the same way as repetition or ascending emphasis can. It is also self-referential. Metaphorical phrases stage their own distance from familiar idiom. So Safran Foer's prose here is knowing: it claims full responsibility for what it does, in a manner similar to the strategic play in some women's writing (see Chapter 10). Safran Foer's second novel brings European history into America, with a story of immigrant Holocaust survivors (Safran Foer, 2005). Here his protagonists are allowed to tell their own story. They are the story's *agents*. Once 'otherness' begins to participate in a writer's *own* culture, in other words, it can figure as *experience*.

Location and preconception

Safran Foer's work shows us something about the way meaning gets *located* in writing. It may not be easy to write from a set of experiences we don't have. On the other hand, it's surely not difficult to write as if everyone *has their own* experiences. So what's happening here? Jacques Lacan points out that cultures are partly built on a terror of their own foundations, for there is always a point at which culture stops and its absence – the absence of the set of symbols and values with which that culture gives meaning to experience, and represents itself – begins. The *differences* of other cultures show us that our own is contingent and that there's nothing necessary about our way of going on. That meaning is arbitrarily founded on what Lacan calls the 'catachretic' substitution of a cultural thing – a metaphor – for the nothing which is prior to it (Lacan, 1973).

As a result, every cultural point of view resists the idea that other viewpoints hold meaning *in the same way as* it does. We can see this as a form of transference[1] which, as in psychoanalysis, both holds the key to and blocks potential understanding of that terror. As writers, then, we need to recognise that the ways we imagine other cultural or literary traditions are *constructed by* how we experience our own discursive position (Chaitin, 1996).

A related problem occurs if we write *for* an 'outsider' readership and what we figure as their preconceptions of us. The Greek Cypriot Niki Marangou's poems, which present folkloric images from Greek life, can be read as a symptom of the cultural contest for Cyprus (Marangou, 2003, p. 198). In the same way, the British-based Guyanan Grace Nichols has a body of poems which sometimes seem to simplify the lived complexity of life in the Caribbean (Nichols, 1984). Any society is a complex form of life whose strengths and weaknesses are modulated and interrelated. In the postcolonial context, reductive pastoral may serve to placate a dominant culture.

What happens when we deploy cliché like this? Because clichés are predictable they don't tell us – as readers or writers – anything new. Instead, the reader's attention slides over them to something told in more interesting terms: in both Franzen and Safran Foer, the unfolding emotional life of their North American protagonists. Clichés appeal to an already-established common ground of preconceptions. This isn't the same as speaking to what Alisdair MacIntyre calls a 'communication community', the group created by shared interests and viewpoints (MacIntyre, 1984). As readers and writers we may be members of several such communities – from the community of our political orientation to that of our professional discipline – but we don't expect to *already* know everything we read or hear within those groups. When we use clichés, however, we disrupt and pre-empt the mechanism of *telling*.

Richard Kearney summarises Paul Ricoeur's 'circle of triple mimesis' as ' 1) the *prefiguring* of our life-world as it seeks to be told; 2) the *configuring* of the text in the act of telling; and 3) the *refiguring* of our existence as we return from narrative text to action' (Kearney,

2002, p. 133). Kearney is making the point that narration is an *extended process* rather than a product. Enlarging on Plato's idea of mimesis,[2] Ricoeur says that story-telling explores the *connectivity* of experiences or ideas. As Charles Taylor points out, the *spelling out* of story allows us to place one thing after another in order to connect them (Taylor, 1992). We are probably most familiar with this mechanism in the process of *catharis,* in which a story *brings us to* a moment of emotional realisation.

Cliché, then, is a form of premature release of meaning – interpretation or conclusion – into the text. Because such tropes use what is already thought rather than discovering what there may be to think, they *pre-empt* the text we think we're producing. In other words, when we use preconceptions in our writing we also disrupt our own and our readers' curiosity. The literary critic Pierre Pachet argues that lack of curiosity is a depressive inability to move beyond the self (Pachet, 1993).[3] French producer of documentary interviews Isabelle Yhuel puts this another way when she suggests that curiosity is a form of human life (Yhuel, 1993)[4]. Curiosity, then, is one of the ways in which our writing moves beyond solipsism to engage with the 'otherness' beyond the self; whether that is the unassimilated in our own experience or a world of the experiences we've never had.

A counter-example demonstrates this process. Arundhati Roy's *The God of Small Things* brings its precise location to vivid life not because where the author *herself* is located acts as a kind of demonstrable authenticity, nor because her text employs what we may call the 'self-orientalising' strategies of Marangou or Nichols, but because its language, far from being clichéd, is alive with the neologisms and dialects of childhood (Roy, 1998). The child's eye view is necessarily local; and Roy creates a kind of private language which demonstrates its foundations in the local as it indicates the limits of specific kinds of understanding.

Creating a character who is so embedded in a particular context as to be unable to comprehend what's beyond it may be a risky strategy. Roy creates 'growing room' by allowing her narrator to return as an adult to her childhood memories. This doubling of narrative voice allows us to see the individual as both situated and fully individuated: she is not limited to a 'character role' but can exert narrative authority (see Chapter 9).

However some narratives locate certain characters *in order* to set their personal and cultural limits. Lawrence Durrell's extraordinary though problematic *The Alexandria Quartet* (Durrell, 1986) exploits the shifting ground of limited viewpoint. Durrell, who was himself a (colonial) diplomat in Egypt, nevertheless uses four narrators who are Westerners or 'honorary Westerners' and shows us their final defeat by their own accultured inability to fully understand the members of indigenous communities. As Jean Rhys's *Wide Sargasso Sea* demonstrates, this is what Charlotte Brontë does with the first Mrs Rochester in *Jane Eyre* (Brontë, C., 2003; Rhys, 1980). Because she is from the Caribbean, and partly non-white, in Brontë's version Antoniette Cosway's marriage to Rochester seems to be almost beyond the law of 'civilised society'. Because she is 'mad', she does not quite count as an autonomous – or comprehensible – individual against whom Rochester can be fully said to contemplate adultery. Moreover, in the earlier novel these facts seem related. The passionate instability of the imprisoned woman seems of a piece with her (non) *appearance*. Rhys's 'prequel' to *Jane Eyre* shifts the narrative territory from appearance to experience. By locating both Antoniette's despair and her cultural difference from her English husband within her *experience* of becoming a young woman and his bride, Rhys makes narrative sense of her character in a way Brontë does not.

Of course, all narratives have boundaries which are not merely chronological (the story starts and ends at points we chose) but lateral. Not everything our characters encounter is fully developed: if it were, novels would be paralysed by limitless lateral connection. Nevertheless we need to be confident that, if we do use ciphers in our writing, we are not excluding important material such as characterisation. What is excluded returns not only as the repressed[5] but, within the text, in the emphasis omission gives:

> Figuration turned against itself ever turns back toward itself, so that in the end what emerges is not the negation of figures but their affirmation as inescapable, in a positive necessity. (Wolosky, 1987, p. 184)

'Authentic experience'

In a related paradigm however, writers – especially in non-Occidental traditions – have turned to representations of Rousseau's noble savage, the peasant or the *idiot savant* for a viewpoint 'guaranteed' by authenticity. The nineteenth-century rise of the nation state in

Europe tried to provide itself with a foundation (what Lacan might call a 'primary catachresis' and Plato a 'founding myth') in the idea of 'the land' – both physical environment and way of life – as embodying both ethnic and cultural identity. Many Slav languages use the same word, *narod,* in some ways similar to the German *Volk,* for both the people who work the land (peasants) and the people who 'belong to' a particular Land (population).[6] In Martin Heidegger's version of this tradition, *die Heimat* is both originary, care-taking 'Motherland' and the scope and limit for its individual inhabitants' expressions of identity. Heidegger proposes that 'man dwells authentically' in his match with his native landscape (Heidegger, 1990). Since migration and cultural mix have been intrinsic to human settlement throughout history, this 'jargon of authenticity', as Theodor Adorno called it, is itself inauthentic (Adorno, 1973). Nevertheless, the *mystification* of the necessary relation between identity and experience – between the happenstance of being born and living in a particular environment and the accrual of local knowledge – is an expression of insecurity, a desire to tighten a contingent into a causal relation between elements of identity.

The mystification of rural life by writers as diverse as the Estonian poet Jaan Kaplinski (Kaplinski, 2004) or the Australian novelist Patrick White (White, 1965) suggests a pronounced distance – perhaps discontinuity or even alienation of meanings – between the literate urban middle class, in which writers are necessarily situated, and a largely peasant rural population. For example, while the Egyptian feminist Nawel el-Saadawi's *God Dies by the Nile* is a specific critique of traditional rural society (el-Saadawi, 1985), Ben Okri's *Famished Road* fills the even greater cultural distance opened up by its author's situation (Okri is a Nigerian writer based in Britain) by ascribing supernatural insights to characters leading traditional village lives (Okri, 1992). The fluency of the passages about hunting in *Anna Karenina* remind us that Leo Tolstoy even went so far as to try living out the pastoral ideal:

> Noticing the special way Laska was searching, pressed flat to the ground, as if raking it with her hind legs in big strides, and with her mouth slightly open, Levin understood that she was after great snipe [...]. In a space between two hummocks, close to one of them, he made out a great snipe. It was listening, its head turned. Then, fluffing its wings slightly and folding them again, it wagged its behind clumsily and disappeared round the corner. (Tolstoy, 2001, p. 617)

What makes this more than simply lyrical is the power of observed detail: Tolstoy, like the Ted Hughes of *Moortown* or *River* (Hughes, 1979, 1983), animates the creatures he writes about because he records both what is key ('as if raking it with her hind legs') and what is apparently inconsequential ('between two hummocks, close to one of them'). However, as Raymond Williams points out, the pastoral *genre* is an urban fantasy of an 'authentic' way of life which was always 'Just back, we can see, over the last hill'. Edward Said's critique of *Orientalism*, too, sees this *displacement* of essentialism onto the Other as what Williams calls a 'persistent problem of form' (Said, 2003). Williams talks about 'what seemed like an escalator' taking this fantasy, part of the recorded culture of every century, back without pause: 'Where indeed shall we go before the escalator stops?// One answer, of course, is Eden' (Williams, 1993, pp. 9, 11–12). Williams' own answer takes us to the ninth century BC and the birth of the pastoral genre in Hesiod's *Works and Days.*

Then how can we write acknowledging the culture we come from without disappearing into fantasies of authenticity? A radical alternative to the noble peasant is the antiheroic everyman. At first glance, he seems to escape cultural specificity. Examples from the Czech Republic, Hungary, Scotland and the US, respectively, include: the hapless *Good Soldier Svejk* (Hasek, 1990); Jancsi Hes, the unemployed alcoholic former factory-worker in Sándor Tar's *Our Street* (Tar, 1995); James Kelman's chaotic Glaswegians, whose streams of consciousness are slowed by alcohol and a kind of uncomprehending literalism (Kelman, 1994); and the solipsistic Henry of John Berryman's *Dream Songs* (Berryman, 1969).

These figures pose their own limits *in the same moment* as they work as cultural intensifiers. In Ardal O'Hanlon's *The Talk of the Town*, it is the narrator's laddish small-town persona, partly expressed through dialect and slang, which secures the reader's eventual complicity in his crime (O'Hanlon, 1999). There's also a second narrator in the novel: some chapters are 'written', by the girlfriend Patrick ultimately kills, in the 'inauthentic' reported speech of a diary. It's a juxtaposition which reveals the intimate authority of the first-person narrator: because he *totalises* the narrative (see Chapter 9), this narrator can override questions about his own *location*. We know *where* the murdered girl is addressing the reader: in her diary. But Patrick's narration itself already 'frames' the incidents of the novel: this narration will not in turn be given a framing context.

Translation and authority

Narrative techniques like these strategise the relationship between writer and reader. Readerly autonomy can be difficult for us as writers to accept. Isn't it like letting strangers roam around your house, fingering and displacing objects? Of course one difference is that a text is a form of thought but a home a form of life: homes have their primary meaning for the people who make them. There's also a category difference between the visitor who acts appropriately (sits in a chair, looks at a book) and the one who doesn't (stands on a chair, rips a book to pieces). Readers don't have any choice but to act appropriately with our texts. All they can do is read or not read them: they can only interact with them in a *textual* way. In this sense the text is uni-dimensional, it *is* a guide for its own use. Nevertheless, within these constraints readers do read texts in their *own* ways. What we write can be misremembered or misquoted; or the reader may use it to represent some part of her own experience to herself. She 'carries across' the text into her own version.

Some discussion of literary translation has focussed on the process as a form of reading. It can be seen as the re-making of a text in the translator's own image. Vladimir Nabokov argues against fluency in translation, suggesting that this may be a process of cultural appropriation in which a complex of native resonances which characterise the text in its original language are lost by the unreliable translator. His proposed solution, echoed by Ortega y Gasset (Ortega y Gasset, 1992), is that the translated text should not 'languish[...] in "poetical" versions, begrimed and beslimed by rhyme' but should read as characteristic of its original language – for example retaining informal metrical characteristics of the original – and be supplemented with 'copious footnotes, footnotes reaching up like skyscrapers to the top of this or that page' (Nabokov, 1955, p. 512).

Nabokov belongs to a small group of distinguished writers who are themselves doubly-located. Generally, it is migration which has caused them to produce literary work in what Mehmet Yashin calls a 'step-mother tongue' (Yashin, 2000). Poets like Joseph Brodsky, Charles Simic and George Szirtes have been able to produce appropriate *bi-vocal* literary translations of writing from, respectively, Russian, Serbo-Croat and Hungarian. The British poet Gwyneth Lewis is distinguished in both English and Welsh (Lewis, 1995). However, this isn't a particularly useful model if we ourselves work out of only one cultural location. Once again, the gap which Gillian Rose calls *The Broken Middle* opens between cultural meanings (Rose, 1992). How do we resist the 'horror' of our cultural illiteracy when it comes to the Other? If we can't read or write *as* the Other, how do we read, and write, the Other without misrepresentation?

Despite his own double-location as an émigré, Nabokov's views, based on the paradigm of translating a classic – Pushkin – fail to take into account the bi-located processes of *co-translation*, particularly widely used in poetry. Here, the author of the original and their peer – a fellow *writer* – in the target language work together to re-create a text. The co-translator may not understand the original but can work from a literal version in the target language (sometimes created by a third partner, who understands the original language but lacks the skills to produce a finished text). Examples of collaborations like these include Ted Hughes's with Yehuda Amichai and Sarah Maguire's with Mahmoud Darwish (Amichai, 2000; Darwish, 2004).

Writing about her involvement in translating texts by colleagues from the Indian sub-continent who work in languages other than English, Gayatri Chakravorty Spivak suggests it is a practice of intellectual 'hospitality' to enable texts by non-Anglophone feminist theorists to enter the arena of Western theoretical debate. She argues for the need for *fluent* translations if these texts are not to be shouted down by virtuoso native speakers and of those Western feminists, for example from France, who are already adequately translated (Spivak, 2000, p. 399).

For when we get involved in translation practice we assume a 'gatekeeping' role. We exert a form of textual authority: as do any of our writing practices which involve representations of cultures or places other their own discursive centre. Whether I write in Delhi or Darlington my text is at the centre of its own discursive affiliations. (Is it fiction? Or fictionalised autobiography? Is it full of researched material? Or first-hand anecdote?) But when I'm engaged in literary translation, or in presenting something from another cultural norm (writing about Darlington in Delhi, or Delhi in Darlington), my mediating authority *goes up to the edge of* the text. This authority, like narrative authority, takes over the available discursive space. Unlike mediating narrative structures, however, my mediating role as translator or cultural translator may be signposted by the apparatuses of footnotes, forewords or quotation marks. Moreover, the discursive space may be troubled by its own non-homogeneity. 'There is in the life of a collector [of texts] a dialectical tension between the poles of disorder and order,' as Walter Benjamin says in his essay on book collecting, 'Unpacking my Library' (Benjamin, 1992, p. 62).

Discursive power relations

As writers we enter into particular relationships with other discourses *whenever* we embark on writing our own. Texts *locate themselves* in specific discursive contexts; and this location is often a performance of discursive power relations. As we've seen both Kearney and Williams argue, it is a question of *genre*. Scholarly texts, for example, use quotation to *appropriate* material to the dominant discourse – as example or source-material – rather than enter into the destabilising dialectic of *equal* voices in dialogue. As Gemma Corradi Fiumara points out, discursive competition evolves from discursive defensiveness (Corradi Fiumara, 1990). It's not merely that, as we saw in Lacan's argument, cultural differences point out the arbitrariness of our own forms of thought. In order to think through our topic in a particular way, we must be reasonably confident that it constitutes a way of *knowing* rather than self-delusion. So, ways of thinking compete to be *the way to know* about particular topics; and texts characteristically expel alternative discourses beyond their own margins. In Arthur Grimble's *A Pattern of Islands* – a colonial governor's view of the Windward Islands which was still on the British school curriculum in the 1970s when the Islands already had independence – the viewpoint of *islanders* is not explored (Grimble, 1952). Nor do we hear *from* the neighbours in Peter Mayle's affectionate but clearly Anglocentric *Toujours Provence* (Mayle, 2001).

The relationship between discourses can also be one of desire. When bell hooks writes on 'Yearning', she is talking about discursive exclusions and nostalgias but also about the im/possible desire to marry-up two apparently incompatible languages and viewpoints: a black vernacular with an often-white-led academic discourse (hooks, 1990). However, Emmanuel Levinas suggests that what marks out 'poetry', or literary writing, is the way in which, resisting simple 'signification' of ideas or objects – particularly by using obliquity or beauty – its language, though it makes sense, 'relinquishes' its claims on those ideas and objects. He calls this oscillation between language's appropriative practices and this kind of self-staging 'scintillation'. It is a sign like a 'star' which, because it's situated *beyond* what a particular text claims to be telling, is an introduction of the Other into that text (Levinas, 1989, p. 156). For Levinas, working after Kant, the arrival of the Other is the ethical moment: the moment when 'meaning' is created. So we might say that the writer of a self-consciously literary text problematises both language and whatever it is she writes about: problems, like questions, imply the possibility of an outward turn, of incompletion, of the arrival from elsewhere of a solution.

In other words, when we succeed in writing a literary text, unlike in minutes or technical reports, we create Virginia Woolf's 'living halo of uncertainty'. It is the text's project to underdetermine, even as it supports, itself. This uncertainty is hospitable to that stranger, the reader; and in particular to the reader's own meaning-making within the text. For example, book club members discuss *aspects* of motivation and characterisation which are not *spelled out* in the text of a novel. This reading-into-the-text of the hinterland of under-expressed characterisation, not dissimilar to that practised in daily life, is *dialogic*. The reader interacts with – creates dialogue with – the text (Bakhtin, 1981).

If readers and writers are in dialogue, might the cultural and geographic location of readers influence not only the *reception* of a novel or collection of poetry but its actual *form*? In *Writers in Prison*, Ioan Davies gives examples of writers producing narratives specific not only to their own contexts but those of their readers, both their peers in prison and other individuals (visiting tutors, the 'liberal' readership supporting political prisoners), who can *place the author as* writing from prison. Certain narrative structures and tones seem to predominate, as do collective codes (Davies, 1990). A similar phenomenon can be observed in mental health care units (Sampson, 1999) and creative writing groups. It's the *mutuality* of these developing discourses which reveals them as reader- or peer-led rather than simply a form of writerly self-location. The author is not *appropriating* local tropes but *assimilating himself to* a particular local set of discursive practices, which are carried out by readers as well as writers.

The colonial phrase 'going native' indicates some of the sense of indignation felt by (formerly) powerful discourses when individuals move away from them like this. The discursive struggle is an uneven one: at any moment, certain viewpoints have the support of educational and political structures while others, because they lack these platforms, may be constructed as unauthoritative. The colonial tradition, of violent appropriation of cultural and geographic spaces by groups on the basis of self-limiting viewpoints, is a brutal example of this. In essays collected in *In Search of Our Mothers' Gardens*, Alice Walker argues for the importance of black women writers' reclaiming these spaces by allowing themselves to be used as role models (Walker, 1984, pp. 3–14, 130–8).

Some of the most challenging postcolonial critiques unpick these violent limitations from apparently seductive textual examples. It may be easy to recognise that Joseph Conrad's 'dark continent' reflects back nothing so much as the question of *where the light is situated:* though the image of cosy lamp-lit authorial study it generates is perhaps slightly unfair, since Conrad did in fact travel in Africa (Conrad, 2004). However, it can be harder to see in Marco Polo's enthusiastic exaggerations an early manifestation of that orientalism which locates both the speaker's own situation, and the 'otherness' of its subject matter, by dwelling on *dissimilarities* between cultures or groups of individuals (Polo, 1997). In fact, Polo's sponsorship by European royalty allows us, if we look closely enough, to see the links between his writing and the British eighteenth and nineteenth appro-priations of 'exoticism', for example in the ostentatious splendour of the Royal Pavilion at Brighton, as an opulence *so far removed* from customary experience only fabulous wealth could achieve it.

A scrupulousness similar to that exercised in close reading demands that we continue to attempt cross-cultural communication. Despite the risks of failure – through sloppy or excessively context-dependent translation; through cultural gate-keeping or the abuse of power relations by writers; through discursive limits both owned and unacknowledged – there are more profound risks in omitting the attempt. It's hard to imagine the kinds of claims for authority which could be made by a literary canon that included writers from only one cultural background; or in which no text speculated about cultural and geographical alternatives.

We might look for examples of successful cultural negotiations among those which confound the conventional direction of flows of cultural information. Derek Walcott, the St Lucian poet who has some-times been condemned within the Caribbean for writing from his 'imported' Catholic education as well as local experience, and using Received English rather than patois (King, 2000), appropriates the Greek myth of Ulysses *to* the experience of island life in *Omeros* (Walcott, 1990). His archetypal narrative, albeit in contemporary and local costume, indicates that *what happens here* has the same scale of meaning as in Ancient Greece – or in a Jungian consulting room in any European capital. In another verse novel, *Fredy Neptune*, Les Murray appropriates European twentieth-century history for the Pacific region in his story of the eponymous Australian everyman who serves through both world wars (Murray, 1998). Authors, from backgrounds as diverse as Fred D'Aguiar's, Caryl Phillips's and Toni Morrison's, of fictions based on the experiences of slavery, use the European, nineteenth-century conventions of the realist novel: the culture of its perpetrators. (Morrison, 1997; Phillips, 1995; D'Aguiar, 1997).

Cultural mediation is transgressive, in other words. It resists the conservative imperative to limit its attention and instead engages in unconventional acts of dialogue with other cultures. When we borrow or mediate against the grain of our particular cultural limitations, we engage in dialogue with what is repressed in our own ways of thinking and writing. We also destabilise our relationship with our readers: this becomes less hierarchical, more a form of dialogue. At these moments we are, in fact, listening *over the margin* of our own text.

Recommended reading

bell hooks' *Yearning: Race, Gender, and Cultural Politics* (1990) collects her recent essays – passionate, polemical and theoretical – about discursive positioning. Richard Kearney's *On Stories* (2002), is a theory of narrative. The authoritative reference book for psychoanalytic terminology is J. Laplanche and J-B. Pontalis, *The Language of Psychoanalysis* (1988). Edward Said's *Orientalism: Western Concepts of the Orient* (2003) could be called the founding text of postcolonial theory. L. Venuti (ed.) *The Translation Studies Reader* (2003) provides an introduction to ways of thinking about translation. Raymond Williams' *The Country and the City* (1993) is a classic text that traces the hold of the pastoral genre – and related concepts – on the Western imagination.

Writing exercises

- Using a dictionary, try and translate a six- to eight-line passage of a poem, in a language you may or may not know, into your mother tongue. (You can find poems in their original language in most good bookshops, libraries and on the internet. Try to chose one by a poet you are interested in, as this is an opportunity to get close to their work.) How does the poem change in translation? What were the problems you had to solve? Were there puns or ambiguities in the original? Were there passages where it was hard to make your version graceful?

- Take a short poem, of between 12 and 20 lines. List what you think are the most important ideas and symbols in it. Now make your own poem combining these elements. Compare it to the original.

- Take a short passage – 2 or 3 pages – from a piece of fiction or literary non-fiction written from a culture other than your own. Try and retell whatever happens in it – trivial or significant – as if it were happening in your own culture. Compare your version with the original and, if you're working in a group, with the other new versions.

- Write a short poem or passage evoking your own original culture for other members of that culture. For example, you might take a street scene, family meal or other conventional activity as the starting point. Then write something in a similar genre which evokes it for 'outsiders'. How does your story change? Do you find yourself 'making the familiar strange'? Is it less or more interesting to write for 'outsiders'?

9   Embodied Selves

Yet thy eternal summer shall not fade
Nor lose possession of that fair thou ow'st;
Nor shall Death brag thou wand'rest in his shade
When in immortal lines to time thou grow'st.
                                        – Shakespeare, Sonnet 18, 1971 p. 1311.

We can think about books as a form of virtual reality. All writers have bodies. And yet books are often read as if they do not; as if there were nothing beyond the margin. Reviewers and academic critics may talk about a text being what the writer themselves 'says' or 'believes', as if the writer were only a characteristic way of thinking, a self on the page. Even when it is in evidence – at public readings or signings – the writer's body may become merely a function of the text. As Roland Barthes says, with irony, of the personal myth-making which surrounds much authorial hype:

> To endow the writer publicly with a good fleshly body, to reveal that he likes dry white wine and underdone steak, is to make even more miraculous for me, and of a more divine essence, the products of his[…] inspiration. (Barthes, 1981, p. 31)

And literary criticism presents itself as discussing fiction and poetry in an impersonal, disinterested way, as if they were ideas floating in disembodied space rather than a series of achievements by particular individuals, perhaps known to the reviewers. All of this poses a problem for us as writers: should we, too, be writing as if we did not have bodies?

Being embodied both permits us to write – and may determine the ways in which we can. Posy Simmonds's *Literary Life* cartoons for *The Guardian* newspaper embodied the contemporary writer in clearly recognisable types. There's the woman novelist writing in middle-class comfort in the countryside; there is an older male novelist jealous of his reputation; an endearingly messy poet's mascara runs when she eats the pre-reading Tandoori Mix. Simmonds's 'Paradise' consists of a single image of the woman novelist at her laptop. She's sitting in the garden of what is clearly a holiday villa in Southern France, a bottle of wine and flip-flops at her feet. Other people are relaxing by a pool. In the passage she's typing, the survivors of defeated army, ambushed during a snowstorm, are being mown down (Simmonds, 2004).

It's this potential for radical discontinuity between what we write and the circumstances in which the embodied self writes it – a discontinuity called 'fiction' (from the Latin *fictio*, make), or 'making it up' – which creates confusion about the writer's embodied self. But this discontinuity needn't be amusing or ironic. As Irina Ratushinskaya's 'No, I'm Not Afraid' demonstrates, poems by political prisoners may resist the damage being done to their authors' bodies (Ratushinskaya, 1986, p. 137).

Yet, in this title poem and others in this first translated collection published on her release, Ratushinskaya adopts a different strategy from those of the well-known earlier group of Soviet dissident poets, the Acmeists surrounding Osip Mandelstam:[1] although she situates her writing in relation to them (Ratushinskaya, 1986, p. 139). She addresses her prison experiences directly rather than transmuting them into a symbolic register or incorporating them into meta-narrative. Her strategies include realism – she lists the mud, thaw, wind, which surround her – and use of the vocative. 'No [...]!', the poem's opening word, isn't part of an internal dialogue within the poem's body. It's denial: turned outwards from the text like a hand raised in the stop sign, it addresses not merely the reader but whoever, situated as it were *behind* the reader, she needs to resist. The poem, ostensibly addressed to her lover, in fact addresses whoever defines and observes her life: it speaks to her captors too. These techniques create an impression of a transparency or lack of separation between the suffering body and the composing mind; yet the transparency's an illusion. The voice on the page, which is in any case *translated*, has been *deferred* through both time and space to what is its first reliable publication: oral transmission and *samizdat* or 'forbidden' reproduction characteristically reproduce the 'fingerprints' of the individuals involved through minor errors.

So some discontinuities between what we write and the body we write with are useful or even necessary. But – as that 'with' implies – there are obvious continuities too. This chapter asks how we can think about writers as embodied selves; and looks at ways in which embodiment may shape the text we produce.

The mutuality of embodiment

The limits of the embodied self have traditionally been questioned in ways which link them to problems of identity. One problem the body poses is the manner in which it seems to be both continuous with and separate from that part of our self which thinks and, in particular, wills. Fumiaki Nakamura, theorist of the Japanese dance-philosophy Butoh,[2] writes about the bodily experience of gravity as our experience of the physical limits to the mental world:

> Because we lose the control over our incessant self-consciousness we feel the fear of bottomless existence. We know that something about 'my' body has nothing to do with 'my will', 'my ego'. In other words, in Butoh the body in crisis has to grasp the knowledge of power from downwards; the moment when one feels 'the body is not mine, it belongs to the other'. (Nakamura, 1999, p. 62)

Nakamura articulates the way in which the body is both essential – it is the vehicle for 'bottomless existence' – and other. We experience the world through it and yet sometimes (for example when it's tired) it resists our attempts to respond to that world. It is this complex status of the physical self – as something which is not fully *coterminous with* the self that thinks and yet which seems *inalienable from* it – which makes its bearing on thinking and writing such a puzzle. Is it just a medium through which thought must pass in order to be expressed as a text? Or does it play a part in shaping that text? Does the body itself come into play on the page; and if so, whose body is it?

In literary genres, the self which is in question may or may not be embodied: as an individual character, whose experiences demonstrate the limits or scope of human nature; or as a narrative persona, whose identity can only be demonstrated through the limits or reliability of what he or she tells us. However, the *writer's* self is always embodied. We look at the effect of writers' locations in Chapter 8; later in this chapter we'll look at ways in which *particular* bodies restrict individual experience. These particular cases throw light on ways in which embodiment is *in itself* always a specific location.

But we can trace authorial embodiment even in anonymous composition, where we cannot identify the *particular* writer. Oral texts and those, such as pre-Norman Welsh praise poetry or Anglo Saxon epic verse, originating in oral tradition, betray, in their reliance on patterns of alliteration and use of interchangeable periphrastic expressions,[3] the physical limits both of an individual poet's memory and of the listener's powers of attention and comprehension within a single hearing. Formulaic epithets ('kennings') are used in *Beowulf* both to 'buy time' for the speaker who recites the poem from memory; and to reinforce the listener's understanding of what's going on. Like crampons left in a rock face, they record their own instrumentality and delineate the embodied selves who used them. Memory and attention may be shaped by cultural habit, but they also chart the physiological limits of the individual human brain.

These traces of the embodied writer and reader have survived into the age of the book. For example, the traditional Welsh *cynghanedd* ('kung-hán-eth'), or 'sounding together', is another poetics with its origin in the oral: it's still used for spontaneous oral composition competitions, called *Talwrn y Beirdd* ('táloon u báerth'), today. On the page, it developed into the classical *cywydd* ('cú-wuth'), or rhyming couplet, under the fourteenth century *prifardd* ('pri-várth') (court poet; literally the First Poet) Dafydd ap Gwilym, who had access to the European Romance tradition.[4] The *cywydd* is marked by alternative patterns of stressed assonance between the half-lines of a fourteen-syllable couplet. Such formal patterning works like a kind of 'spam-guard' both to 'contain' the memory and reduce the options within a text not only as it is being composed but as it's being transmitted.

Paradigmatically, in other words, the process of composition progressively *reduces* creative options. The more formal requirements the word needed to complete a line must satisfy, the less choice the poet or reciter has. It may feel as though it's the 'ear', rather than conscious reflection, which completes the metrical pattern in a line. This pattern of *cynghanedd* from Dafydd ap Gwilym's 'Morfudd Ageing', for example, is called *Groes* or 'cross':

Breuddwyd yw; ebrwydded oes![5]

(ap Gwilym, 1982, p. 51)

It's not necessary to be able to pronounce Welsh to *see* the pattern of repeated consonants here; but the English poet Gerard Manley Hopkins, who learnt Welsh during his time in St Beuno's Jesuit seminary in North Wales, developed a complex assonantal technique of his own in response to *cynghanedd*, whose dense diction he also imitated.[6]

Although Hopkins' techniques were too radical to ensure easy publication in his lifetime, attention to alliteration remains a widely-used poetic. And in general, poetry's structural stress on the aural elements of language allows it to demonstrate the creative impact of embodiment. This is as true of free verse, where line-breaks can make the difference in emphasis and meaning, as of the overtly formal villanelle or sestina. Poetry shifts the meaning and experience of texts *further into* the physical world: it's because we're sensory creatures that we can experience and enjoy sound. Writing which *embraces* the aural elements of language moves outward from the merely instrumental to celebratory engagement with both writers' and readers' embodiment.

Jacques Lecoq, founder of European post-war physical theatre, writes that, 'I always look for an actor who "shines", who develops a space around himself in which the spectators are also present.' (Lecoq, 2000, p. 18). It is this *mutuality* of embodiment which is implied by its traces in the texts we produce. It's a mutuality which seems both paradoxical and necessary, and which exerts pressure on us at the moment of composition because of the way 'writing' is both something which happens as we make our texts and also 'happens' – it 'comes to life' – when it's read. Derek Attridge calls this double life of the text both an act and an event:

> In so far as it is an act, reading responds to the *written*, performing interpretative procedures upon it [...]; in so far as it is an event, reading is performed by the *writing*. (Attridge, 2004, p. 105)

This double instantiation of writing mirrors the noun/verb tension in 'reading' which, as Peter Stockwell points out in *Cognitive Poetics, an Introduction*, is both something we do (to a text) and something – a version of a text – we have as a result of doing it. Stockwell bases a case, for texts having sufficient interpretive stability to sustain this process, on embodiment too:

> Most simply, we think in the forms we do and say things in the way that we do because we are all roughly human-sized containers of air and

liquid with our main receptors at the top of our bodies. (Stockwell, 2002, p. 4)

In other words, despite the individuality which we celebrate in reading and writing practices, what *contains* this plurality of meanings and versions, like the waist on the hourglass of a text, is the mutual embodiment of reader and writer: what they can cope with and enjoy *as a result of the way* they are embodied. *Textuality* draws these embodiments together. When we write we're summoning up the reader's body, without which our text won't continue as active 'writing'. Stockwell argues that literature works by refreshing forms – the shape of a story for example – which have already been laid down in the neural networks of the brain. Bodies are thus an immanent physical ground on which text grows. And in this sense all texts could be called vocative. They call up the reader: *Reader, I married him.*[7]

Walter Benjamin quotes Brecht as saying, 'in one of his didactic poems on dramatic art', 'The effect of every sentence was waited for and laid bare. And the waiting lasted until the crowd had carefully weighed our sentence' (Benjamin, 1973, p. 150). Benjamin talks about this *conjoined* waiting as a form of 'interruption' to the text; but says that this 'interruption is one of the fundamental devices of all structuring' *(ibid.)*. It sews together rather than fragments the drama. In other words, it is a form of textual inter-relationship *and* of interaction between audience and performers.

So there's a more than contingent historical connection between the traces of embodiment in literary forms and our physiological make up. Rhythm seems peculiarly placed to record this embodied relationship. In his essayistic 'novel' *The Song Lines,* Bruce Chatwin speculates that narrative is a form of motion. The human moves through the world, giving it meaning for himself; and the experienced world only comes into being, like the line of a narrative we write, when it's given meaning in this way (Chatwin, 1994). It's a bit like the impossibility of properly experiencing a scent until we recognise that – oh yes! – it's Eau de Cologne grandmother wore: we need to name the experience to have it 'come in focus'.

Chatwin is writing about Aboriginal Australians: whose Song Lines are routes retraced on foot, and in narrative verse which links the sacred sites associated with the founding myth about their group's totemic animal. We make the link between walking and the walking-pace – the *feet* – of poetic metre whenever we pay attention to the rhythm a poem enacts (Carper and Attridge, 2003; Fabb, 1997). In an era of 'public and community' funding for the arts, walking remains a contemporary point of access to poetry. High Wycombe has a metrical poem, carved in letters of appropriate size so that it 'reads' at normal walking pace, in its Riverside Park (Peever and Sampson, 1997). Maria van Daalen's poem painted on the wall by St Gertrudiskerk in Bergen op Zoom comes into focus as we walk towards it (van Daalen, 2000).

Despite this, oral texts embody the physical limits of the individuals who produce and use them in ways recorded texts do not. A novel doesn't need to be composed, or be performable, all in one sitting: *because it is written down*. Writing mediates the limits of the human body by allowing us to delegate some of the processes involved in composition – such as holding in mind what's happened to all the characters so far – to the page: a form of, as Daniel Dennett says, 'off-loading' parts of the mind from the brain to other parts of the physical environment (Dennett, 1996). In a further example of this kind of extension, what cyber-guru Steve Harnad calls 'skywriting' is the simultaneous production of a text by both its original author and intervening readers – potentially as many as have connection to the web world-wide – when it is posted for peer review in cyberspace (Harnad, 2004). The linear arrangement of footnotes on a scholarly page can be replaced by a virtual third dimension of hyperlinks.

These are strategies embedded in the technological nature of paper and pen, computer chip and telecommunications, rather than the human individual. But what *is* such a human? Who am I when I sit down to write?

The ideal of disembodied thought

It was Descartes who proposed that the self was located *within* thinking: the self *is* consciousness (Descartes, 1984) (see Chapter 1). He did so using the tools of rationalism, the seventeenth and eighteenth century movement which worked to replace faith in a revealed religion[8] with a view of the world which derived from, and so centred on, human powers of thought. Descartes uses pre-existing techniques of logic – paring an argument down to a statement we can be certain of because it demonstrates its own truth – and dialectic (building his argument through a series of questions) to create his revolutionary idea that I know I exist, even when I doubt that I can know or prove it, because I experience my *thinking*, including those very doubts, *going on*. In other words, for Descartes self-experience is primarily mental.

Contemporary critics, equipped with experimental knowledge, are able to argue, among other things, that the thinking Descartes experiences is demonstrably a physiological function of the brain, and that therefore the mental and physical cannot be separated. However, some current critique of dualism is unfairly *ad hominem*. As Andrea Nye points out in her work on its gender assumptions, logic has, at least since the pre-Socratic Parmenides in the sixth century BC, been a form of thought which claims to be context-innocent and innocent of affect (Nye, 1990). In claiming to work in the same way no matter where it is done, or by whom – and to afford no scope for emotion or personal bias – logic has always proposed a model of disembodied thought.

Critics of logic, however, point out that this is disingenuous. Apart from anything else, since logic is carried out using the brain, the logical arguments of children, healthy adults and people with dementia do differ from each other. More pertinently, wherever logic moves from pure mathematical structures to linguistic axioms with their extra-linguistic referents,[9] the relationship between term and referent, between language and what it names, is one of meaning. And these meanings are locally applied – they mean different things to different individuals involved in doing logic – and produce local distortions both within the axioms themselves and within the roles they can play. For example the sentence, *There are three men in the household therefore there are three electors in the household*, which makes a particular kind of sense in an Athenian context of male-only citizenship, reads nowadays as not merely denaturalised but logically unstable.[10] We see the same failure of universalising assumptions when we try to protect an element in our writing by saying, 'But that really happened!' It's an appeal which doesn't understand how irrelevant our individual *experience* is to the relationship our *readers* have with our text.

When he reaches logical conclusions, then, Descartes is merely using *pre-existing* logical techniques. On the other hand, he chose to employ those techniques; and did so in relation to a question – about the nature of the human self – which to us as contemporary readers may intuitively seem far removed from the ideal of disembodied argument. In a contrary tradition to the ideal of disembodied thought, realist fiction had traditionally extended what John Ruskin called the pathetic fallacy – using descriptions of physical objects to 'reveal' mental states – from landscape to the physical appearance of characters (Ruskin, 1985). For example, the 'tall, dark, handsome' hero of popular cliché has his roots in romantic fictions from Jane Austen's *Pride and Prejudice* to its homage, Helen Fielding's *Bridget Jones's Diary* (Fielding, 2001). In a virtuoso telescoping of connotation, Fielding's hero was not only tall and dark, but named for Austen's Darcy (who, at his first entrance into literary history, 'soon drew the attention of the room by his fine, tall person, handsome features, noble mien; and the report... of his having ten thousand a year.' (Austen, 1992, pp. 7–8). Mark Darcy therefore embodies a whole freight of cultural meanings, not least (as the novel makes clear: Bridget Jones watches the video when she is feeling low) those of the 1995 BBC TV *Pride and Prejudice*, in which Mr Darcy is played by Colin Firth (Langton, 1995). In a further piece of telescoping, Firth plays the contemporary Darcy in the 2001 film of *Bridget Jones* (Maguire, 2001).

Another well-known example of this physical coding of characters is Emily Brontë's, in *Wuthering Heights*, where safe, good, lowland, Edgar and Isabella Linton are blond; and dangerous, sexualised, *craggy* Heathcliff matures from a 'little black-haired, swarthy thing, as dark as if it came from the Devil' into a gentleman landowner who is still 'a dark-skinned gypsy in aspect' (Brontë, 1965, pp. 40, 47). This formula was familiar enough for Stella Gibbons to be able satirise it in *Cold Comfort Farm* where, among 'pathetic' landscapes, the orphaned incomer Flora Poste encounters dark, brooding Adam Lambsbreath and 'earthy' sons of the soil Reuben and Seth (Gibbons, 2003).

Selves as agents

It's only when we turn to ideas of agency that there seems any chance to mend this mind-body rift in our writing selves. The idea that we as human individuals have the status of what for much of the twentieth century was known as the Subject – that which generates meaning – has always been linked to ideas about the *capacities* of that human individual. These particularly human capacities – significant because they are human and because they make the human significant – traditionally centre round two kinds of mental capacity: reflexive thinking, and its entailed moral capacity; and free will, with its entailed moral responsibility. It's because we can *reflect on and identify* what we do as well as just doing it that we *can* exercise moral judgement; it's because we can *choose* what we do, rather than being over-determined by instinct or destiny, that we *ought* to exercise that judgement. Language, which enables these capacities by providing the tools – a symbolic register – in which to process them, is often also identified as key to human identity. And the capacities for reflection and selection are so significant for the writing process they suggest we could think of writing as a form of *responsibility* to our material.

As Simone de Beauvoir was among the first to point out, social groups have often adopted this idea of capacities, rather than inalienable worth, to exclude other groups from the club of Subjectivity (de Beauvoir, 1988). Aristotle, for example, argued that different kinds of people have 'the excellence of the rational' in different degrees which are reflected by their position in society:

> [...] although the parts of the soul are present in all of them, they are present in different degrees. For the slave has no deliberative faculty at all; the woman has, but it is without authority, and the child has, but it is immature. (Aristotle, 1988, p. 19)

Maya Angelou's title for the first volume of her autobiography, dealing with an abusive childhood – *I Know Why the Caged Bird Sings* – does more than link voice to the limits of embodiment: it shows us, through the speeded-up transaction of a metaphor, that people are not always treated as fully human (Angelou, 1993).

Models of democratic participation, which also model *perceptions* of the right to self-determination, map exclusions of these kinds. If our capacities for reflexive self-understanding and free will are innately human, surely they are as universal and universalisable as human rights?[11] This is clearly logically true; but one weakness of the capacities model is that, being concerned largely with the internal, mental world of the framing of experience, rather than the external, physical world of action and appearance, such capacities are easily denied. What we think is always private. Meanwhile, just by looking at you, I can jump to all sorts of conclusions about what you're thinking. Of course writing, in *both* Attridge's senses of the word, bridges the mental and physical worlds by making thought concrete. It leaves a trace of *what was thought* within the physical world.

For example, in Doris Lessing's first novel, *The Grass is Singing*, a white settler's young wife becomes obsessed by the Otherness of the black handyman until he fulfils cultural stereotype by having sex with her, shifting her mental harassment of him into physical harassment (Lessing, 2002). Just as it is not clear whether or not the narrator blames the individuals involved for what may or may not be a consensual act, it is not clear whether the man's sexualised presence is a construction by character or author. The narrator, created by an author who was herself a young white woman in the African bush, may or may not believe that both characters have moral autonomy, the capacity to make choices.

Like Lessing's protagonists, women and members of poorer communities, traditionally the last groups in any society with access to literacy, may lack the rhetorical skills, developed by education, which allow them to *demonstrate* that they can 'think for themselves'. Rationality, like its cousin logic, is built of a series of thinking *techniques* (such as resisting fantasy, managing anger), and may overwhelmingly reflect social opportunity.

Can writing escape authorial embodiment?

Even creative writing, despite its traditional identification with the emotional and embodied life of characters, has fantasies of disembodied thought: the ideas of 'pure fiction', composed in complete detachment from the writer's experience or agenda; and of the context-independent literary 'genius'. Virginia Woolf's well-known invention, in *A Room of One's Own*, of the character of Shakespeare's sister, and her analysis of the impossibility of that young woman being taken seriously as – or even becoming – a professional playwright, is a simple demonstration of how dependent on *physical context* our emergence as a writer is (Woolf, 1985). In pointing out that a young woman from Shakespeare's background would have lacked the grammar school education which gave him not only the stories on which many of his plays are based but the highly developed literacy to write them – and that she would have been treated as a sexual object if she had turned up in London's theatre-land – Woolf is debunking the idea that 'genius' is simply in the *nature* of what Wordsworth calls a man 'endued with more lively sensibility, more enthusiasm and tenderness, who has a greater knowledge of human nature, and a more comprehensive soul, than are supposed to be common among mankind.' (Wordsworth, 1973, pp. 601–2).

Yet the idea that we may be able to write 'pure fiction' still requires more than the perceived necessity for authorial disclaimers of 'any resemblance to persons living or dead' to debunk it. Literary biography isn't just premised on the idea that there's something interesting about the life of an individual because of the books they've written; it also tries to show a *link* between the life and the texts. At its extreme, it may treat all texts as a *roman à clef*, a coded autobiography or fictionalisation which needs to be deciphered. For example, Diane Middlebrook's biography of Ted Hughes, *Her Husband*, argues that Hughes learnt from Sylvia Plath's work, as he edited it for release throughout his life, how to engage in psychotherapeutic and thence poetic terms with his own experiences of their marriage and beyond (Middlebrook, 2004). However, this is a double deciphering whose very ambition suggests there may be limits to how far a text 'contains' the embodied author. In *The Haunting of Sylvia Plath*, Jacqueline Rose goes further and suggests the leakage of the figure of Plath into the life of her poems – the way they're read and received – is *uncanny*, in the particular Freudian sense of *not being normal* (Rose, 1991).

Freud's term for what his patients experienced as inexplicable or 'uncanny', *unheimlich*, literally means 'unhomely'. When we encounter something which isn't part of the world of our experience, we feel it's inexplicable simply because we don't already have the explanation. For example we can be astonished by extreme achievement – whether in gymnastics or poetry – and feel it's more than human. This sense of the uncanny is one of the mechanisms which produces the idea of genius.

As writers, we may say of a particular image or phrase, 'I don't know where it came from'. This sensation of not having 'worked it out' – of not being 'in control', as Nakamura says, even within the mental realm – is another of Freud's *unheimlich* experiences. The word 'genius', from the Latin *genus*, meaning *a being*, identifies this experience using the metaphor of possession by a spirit. In order not to worry about whether we can do it again, it's tempting to believe that it's not ourselves, but some other force, which produces these parts of our writing. The idea of 'genius' works as a charm against self-consciousness; a form of magical thinking which we use to protect our writing process from scrutiny by others or ourselves.

But, as we've seen in Chapter 7, no literary text, even autobiography, is coterminous with the author's lived experience. Toby Litt's *Finding Myself,* a novel which takes the form of the editor's proof (complete with marginal notes and excisions) of a book by fictional chick lit novelist Victoria About, plays with this idea. Litt's fictional writer tells what happens when she takes a group of friends to Southwold for a month's preparation for a 'reality novel' (Litt, 2003). Since things go wrong in the 'Big Sister' house, About never gets to fashion a novel out of her journal entries, an 'unfictionalised' narrative which her editor steals, cuts and publishes as a novel.

Although it breaks with visual convention, Litt's novel belongs to the tradition of epistolary and journal novels. The epistolary novel was a popular genre in the C18th, when the form of the modern novel was still emergent[12]. It's significant for our writing from our own situated and embodied selves because of the discomfort it stages with the totalising narrative of the realist novel. Even in the nineteenth century, novels including *Wuthering Heights* and Wilkie Collins's *The Woman in White* used fictional inter-textuality – their authors introduce auxiliary narrators and the idea of 'found' rather than 'owned' narratives – to introduce and justify the sweep of narrative action which follows (Brontë, E. 1965; Collins, 2004). Paradoxically, these multiple textualities and limited standpoints are what ensure each book's narrative stability. In both novels the 'objective' viewpoint of the realist project is endangered by the pull towards an individual character's personal viewpoint needed to express supernatural experience. Without compensatory strategies to locate these individual viewpoints *within* the novel as a whole, the books could easily become psychodramatic or – to use the nineteenth century term which 'embodies' such viewpoints – *hysterical* narratives. It's only by incorporating the embodied figure of the narrator him- or her-self that these fictions can return to the safe ground of *apparent* objectivity.

So might we stabilise our own texts by representing our embodied selves in them? Developments in British travel and non-fiction writing since the 1980s, led by William Dalrymple and Bruce Chatwin, use reflexive forms in which the *inner* world of authorial reflection and experience is reported alongside the *outer* world of action and interaction (Dalrymple, 1990). The figure of 'the writer' – that 'double agent' who both moves within the text and moves the text along – has become a bridge between inner and outer experience. However, it's not always clear whose side such a figure is on. Does he problematise the realist narrative about uncompromisingly physical adventure? Or has that narrative become a mirror in which to represent the heroic endeavour of Important Writing?

Travel writing which 'encounters' the authorial self has become linked to a British renaissance in literary auto/biography, which, like fiction, uses literary techniques to explore portions of often in-them-selves-unexceptional lives. Linda Grant's and Blake Morrison's moving books about their parents fall into this category. Both Grant's *Remind Me Who I Am, Again?* and Morrison's *And When Did You Last See Your Father?* take a parent's terminal decline as the starting point for exploring who that person has been (Grant, 1999; Morrison, 1993). Grant's portrait of her mother and Morrison's of his father both reveal the writers' difficulty in thinking about a parent in terms independent of that relationship: P.J. Eakin calls this practice 'relational auto-biography' (Eakin, 1985). Both are reflexive self-portraits as well as parental life-stories.[13] Death, as an ultimate limit of embodiment, seems to work as a powerful engine for representing the physically lived life by the way in which, in our binary system of 'metaphysics of presence' (Derrida, 1982), absence throws presence into relief.

In his thinking on drama, Raymond Williams points out that 'to write an action [...] is not simply to write a report of an action, or even its detailed description; it is also to write the movements as they are to be made' (Williams, 1972, p. 186). In other words, we can resist the inner/outer distinctions of Cartesian dualism by suggesting that all writing about an action *causes that action to be staged*, even if in the mind's eye. Writing literary auto/biography then becomes a writing against death. It causes the dead to 'walk again'.

The narrators of these kinds of reflexive nonfictions are textualised *characters* whose *embodied* limits the texts explore. However, such delineated limits may destabilise the reader's belief in authorial omniscience. They suggest that we will be *necessarily* embodied, located and limited to specific intellectual and emotional capacities. While this may be appropriate for domestic drama, it runs the risk of falling short, into whimsy, when faced with larger material. How, then, do we retain authority when we write non-fiction, in particular?

Primo Levi's accounts of the Holocaust, including *The Periodic Table* and *If This is a Man*, are profound, magisterial and universally acknowledged (Levi, 1959, 1985). This may be because Levi provides little in the way of moral commentary, so that he seems to present his readers with an unmediated account of physical experience (a strategy we saw at work in Ratushinskaya). Despite being a text which has been *formed*, using such literary devices as chapters, *If This is a Man* presents itself as unreflexive. Although these are autobiographical accounts, Levi's affectless tone – his prose doesn't change rhythm, nor his vocabulary register, whether he is writing about selections for the gas chamber or his return home at the end of the war – functions in the same way as an omniscient narrator. It creates a contract which, in return for the reader's unconditional trust, promises to show what happens 'beyond' individual emotion and experience.[14] Luckily, most of us are unlikely to have any experience approaching this to write about. But Levi's model serves to remind us of the limits to endlessly reflexive writing. Sometimes the friction of bodily surfaces is unnecessary to animate what we write.

Embodiment, disability, illness

There remains one special category of embodiment. Cartesian dualism reflected the development of medical science in the seventeenth century: earlier ideas about illness did not make such a separation between the mind and the body.[15] Today, the disability or illness of a writer still raises questions both of Subjectivity – or meaning-making – and agency. Some of these are questions of authorship; others are questions of authority. Under the first category come questions about technological intervention and where this begins to amount to co-authorship: many of these queries concern writing by people with physical impairment. The second category largely concerns the experiences of people perceived to be suffering from mental health problems or learning difficulties, and revolve around reception of work as a symptom rather than a literary text.

When Christie Brown, whose story was dramatised in the film *My Left Foot*, published his book of that name, he already had a precursor in Christopher Nolan, whose story was told in *Under the Eye of the Clock* (Brown, 1990; Nolan, 1987). Both these Irish writers have cerebral palsy; both achieved literary prominence with accounts of how they overcame this impediment to their writing. Neither has since produced a body of fiction; it is the feel for language which makes the telling of their life-stories distinctive. Although they live in a highly verbal culture, neither author can speak: in a well-known moment from *My Left Foot*, Brown demonstrates to his parents that he understands them by managing to grasp a pencil/crayon with the eponymous left foot and trace his initials. The Nolan method is to write by pressing the keys of a keyboard with an implement held in Christopher's mouth while his mother steadies his head.

In a society in which literature has a relatively high status,[16] to write a book which achieves literary critical success is regarded as desirable. Nolan has faced allegations that it is his mother who writes his work. However, the painstaking spelling-out of text has produced literary success elsewhere, too. *The Butterfly and the Diving Bell* is a memoir of Locked-in Syndrome by Jean-Dominique Bauby (Bauby, 1998). In a process somewhat akin to predictive text, his amanuensis transcribed the memoir by running through the alphabet until he blinked yes at a letter, repeating the process until it became possible to guess a word. The book, originally written in French, became a bestseller because of the spare, elegant style which it is easy to read as the result of distillation by laborious dictation. Paradoxically, it is also easy to read the metaphorical flamboyance of Nolan's texts as a dam being burst on a young man's sensibility. We're tempted to read both, in other words, with not so much the author as their disability in mind. This is close to seeing the text as symptom of that disability, rather than measuring it by literary criteria.

This tendency may be still more pronounced in the reception of texts by people known to have mental health problems or to have experienced distress. A rapidly-developing literature suggests that creative writing is an intrinsically therapeutic activity (Hartill, undated; Mazza, 1999) (though a related literature argues that creative writing may be used within the therapeutic context but is not in itself a therapeutic activity (Downie 2004; Flint, 2004; Sampson, 1999)). The argument is either that writing practice, unlike other forms of thought, accesses the part of the mind where traces of psychological damage, or at any rate of a personal prehistory, may reside; or that giving literary shape to such material works in much the same way as therapeutic practice. 'Yet a person expressing himself is not necessarily being creative. [...] The difference between the act of expression and the act of creation is this: in the act of expression one plays for oneself alone rather than for any spectators,' as Jacques Lecoq says (Lecoq, 2000, p. 18). This stress on the *action* of creative writing reminds us that the premise that material simply 'presents itself', like a symptom, is a surprising restatement of the superstition of the 'uncanniness' of literary ability.

However, there are texts which occupy a transitional territory between symptom and literary production. These texts make us uneasy because the contract of authorial trust has been eroded by the margin of embodiment which frames them. For example, are the last texts of Nietzsche, whose terminal syphilis caused a psychotic dementia – of which the grandiosity which is his hallmark is a characteristic symptom – philosophy or delusion (Nietzsche, 1979)? Shortly before she was diagnosed, Iris Murdoch – the brilliant scholar and novelist now ironically better known as the object of her husband John Bayley's memoir, *Iris*, about her death from Alzheimer's Disease – announced that she had found her last book, *Jackson's Dilemma*, difficult to complete and would not be writing more (Bayley, 1999; Murdoch, 1995). Can we be sure that this novel, written by someone with Alzheimer's, was in no way limited or defined by her illness? And what would happen to our own writing self if we fell ill?

These questions return us to the embodied self with which we write. As we said at the outset of this chapter, embodiment both limits and enables our writing process. Some strategies – including the use of genres such as logic which claim to be independent of their users, the superstitious belief that writing emerges without authorial intervention, literary achievement in the face of ill health or disability – destabilise assumptions about the embodied writer. Others, such as the developing genres of reflexive literary non-fiction and celebratory traces of human physicality, embed that embodiment within the text. Some writers create ambiguity about the separation between embodied writer and authorial self on the page; others explore questions of human embodiment through the use of the pathetic fallacy in characterisation, or in their poetics. There are many strategies open to us as writers wishing to explore what Laura Riding calls 'the good-will of the body'; but the contract of embodiment between writer and reader remains the ground on which each of these strategies is mapped (Riding, 1980, p. 285).

Recommended reading

Roland Barthes' 'The Writer on Holiday' (1981) demonstrates the difficulty of *characterising* ourselves as writers. I. Jack's 'Introduction', in *Granta: The First Twenty-one Years* (2001) is a short introduction to the rise and role of the reflexive school of 'dirty realism' in the UK.

The Twentieth Century Performance Reader (edited by M. Huxley and N. Witts) is a compendium of extraordinary essays by performers, writers and theoreticians about performance, including pieces on its relationship to text. Virginia Woolf's *A Room of One's Own* (1929) is the classic work addressing the dilemmas of the embodied woman writer.

Writing exercises

- What voice do you ascribe to your body? Try writing short anecdotes told by different parts of your body – a toe, your liver, your nose. You may find you ascribe limits to their viewpoints but you'll probably also find you characterise them.
- How do you experience the idea of a split between your mind and your body? Try and concentrate on being 'really present' and do a five-minute freewriting. Now do another five-minute freewriting and concentrate *primarily* on your bodily sensations. If you're working in a group, discuss how you feel about a possible mind-body split *after* doing this exercise.
- Pick a poem to memorise (sonnets are an ideal length and form). Notice where, using things like internal rhyme or alliteration, the *form* of the poem, even if free verse, *prompts* you to remember it.
- Either alone or in a group, read two or three pages of a story or novel you don't know. Now see how comprehensively you can retell what you've just heard or read.
- Write about a physical activity you engage in. This needn't be a sport: it could be walking to work. You may chose to *explain* how the body performs the activity, or to *evoke* the experience.

10 An Essential Self?

I am; yet what I am none know or cares.

Clare, J. 'I am' 1972, p. 601.

Much of the time, when we reflect on ourselves as we are engaged in the writing process, we do so as individuals. We think in terms of developing an *individual* voice; of the *particular* life experience which we want to inform our writing; or of the character or image we have thought up ourselves. However sometimes – perhaps when we read about an experience we recognise, or when we have the sense of writing on behalf of a constituency – we experience ourselves as part of a group. In particular, we may have this experience because of aspects of our identity which seem inalienable. These characteristically include race, sexuality, gender and disability or illness (see Embodied Selves). But such identities, seen as being of our *essence*, are frequently as much thought about by people not being actively categorised in these ways as by those who are; and they may limit – or exaggerate – perceptions about our roles as writers or about our texts.

As we saw in the chapter on Culture and Geography, thinking about race is culturally relative: that's to say, it varies from culture to culture and also according to the perceived racial identity of the thinker. Very often the writer positions himself as a member of a particular culture in order to establish his authority to carry out a specific critique. This is as true of Laurens van der Post's mid-twentieth-century orientalism, which in books such as *Testament to the Bushmen* contrasts the apparent wisdom of the bushmen with the materialism of the author's native culture (van der Post, 1985), as it is of bell hooks's refusal of those forms of academic discourse which exclude or discredit the discursive forms of contemporary black culture (hooks, 1990).

Gendered identity, on the other hand, is seen as essential in very similar ways both by some feminist women and by those who argue against the idea of women as equal human agents. In this chapter we look both at some of this kind of essentialist thinking, using the paradigm of gender, and at thinking which resists essentialist constructions of identity. We'll also look briefly at related questions of sexual identity.

Identity as difference

How might these questions be related? Let's start with an example. In contemporary Britain, soccer is still largely a male preserve. Although the film *Bend It Like Beckham* (Chadha, 2002), about a British Asian girl with a talent for football, records the development of girls' teams at youth level, Bill Forsyth's *Gregory's Girl* covered similar ground in the 1980s: yet a generation later every major competition remains male-only. In the male-dominated community of supporters, common insults include 'The ref's a woman'.

In an essay subtitled 'A Phenomenology of Feminine Body Comportment, Motility and Spatiality', Iris Marion Young uses the old insult 'Throwing Like A Girl' as a starting point for her argument *both* that the fact that women typically move in certain ways shows they have a particular set of typical experiences of being in the world *and* that those experiences are characteristically those which *develop* 'feminine hesitancy' (Young, 1989, p. 60). 'Feminine', in this argument, means a characteristic set of *experiences* rather than an innate and potentially mystified way of *being* (Pope, 2005). Merleau-Ponty's phenomenological approach is a philosophical attempt to define things in terms of the meaning established by their *phenomena,* or physical manifestation in the world: in practice, this means that the primordial structures of existence, the way things are, must be measured from the human subject *as it is embodied,* rather than from a disembodied subjectivity (Merleau-Ponty, 1962). Young reads the specifically female body's occupation of and action within space, and the (inhibited) relationship to intention of both these modes of its being, against Merleau-Ponty's (ungendered) model. She suggests that feminine existence in the body is less extended, more passive and more disrupted by 'the wasted motion resulting from the effort of testing and reorientation' (*loc. cit.*).

Meanwhile, camp has brought the idea of 'throwing like a gay' into the cultural mainstream. In a 2001 episode of *Will and Grace,* Will, the heroine's gay flatmate, chucks away the American football, 'symbol of heterosexual oppression', which Grace's boyfriend has brought to a picnic in the Park, with an exceptionally good throw underlined by canned laughter and expressions of astonishment by the character himself. In a 2004 episode of his chat-show, the camp British TV presenter Graham Norton showcased a gay basketball team to similar hilarity.

Both these responses to the apparently hetero/sexist challenge thrown down by the football terraces, then, take it up on its own terms, embracing rather than ducking issues of difference. And essentialist feminisms are characterised by their appropriation of this territory of perceived gender difference. There is a great deal of 'common sense' evidence to support them in this: after all, men and women have differently-shaped bodies and different reproductive roles; and conception in particular requires one individual from each of these groups, thus committing them to biological difference. Of course, there are many exceptions to these rules: transvestites, transsexuals and transgendered people suggest gender identity may not be fixed *by* birth identity, even if it *is* fixed *at* that point (further questions are thrown up by children born with the reproductive characteristics of both genders). And developing reproductive techniques mean both that more than one woman may be involved in a live birth (where an egg donor or surrogate mother is used); and that, as we move into the era of genetic engineering, conceptual parents' genetic material may be removed from a fertilised egg. *Junior*, the Arnold Schwarzenegger film in which he plays a father bringing an ectopic pregnancy to full term, dramatises actual clinical research which destabilises assumptions about women's necessary role in pregnancy (Reitman, 1994).

These interesting cases, which may or may not suggest a continuum within rather than a divide between gender identities, are less radical all the same than the question of whether, since essentialism founds many of its claims on reproductive 'fact', we think gender has any meaning beyond these facts. For example, do we think that a woman who cannot or chooses not to have a child is not a woman? It's true that a woman who has a problem conceiving may say, 'I feel I'm not a real woman'. But, in a world made up of only two identities, does such a woman really become a man? And, whether or not we have children, what about our gender identity when we take part in activities other than childcare? Are we women when we drive a car? Go to a conference? Eat supper? Write?

Constructing identity

To put it another way, then, is there such a thing as 'writing like a girl?' Virginia Woolf argues that there is. Her analysis, in her essay on 'Women and Fiction', of the limits that the young woman novelist's experience imposes on her writing ability, is surprisingly analogous to Young's feminist phenomenology (Woolf, 1990). Although Woolf's essay was published decades before Merleau-Ponty's *The Phenomenology of Perception*, she was able to link ways of being in the world and what they 'mean'. She makes the connection between prevailing traditions – both of prosody and in women's social roles – and the difficulties the women who were her contemporaries may have had in adopting the role of authoritative novelist. Women's experiences as dependents and carers have made them unfit for the 'sentence made by men: it is too loose, too heavy, too pompous for a woman's use' (*op. cit.* p. 37). More profoundly, Woolf sees women's future as enfranchised wage-earners as the chance for them to move their concerns outwards from the personal to the political and, beyond that, the poetic. As a Modernist, she sees the poetic as what works with impersonal universal questions about the meaning of life (abstract thought), rather than personal questions about particular individuals and their choices (domestic preoccupations).

Like Young, Woolf suggests that, with more time and space available to them, women would become protagonists of a different kind: their writing technique would become 'bolder and richer'. This throws down a challenge to us as writers today, and we'll return later to how contemporary writers negotiate it. One way to side-step it has been, however, to 'write as a man'. Not only George Eliot and Georges Sand but also the Brontë sisters originally had male *noms de plume* to ensure publication and to meet the demands of respectability. Sand retained hers even after she was not only known but notorious as the bohemian novelist who became Chopin's last lover (Sand, Flaubert and Eyre, 2003).

In twentieth-century Britain, writers as different from each other as the poet U.A. Fanthorpe, the crime novelist P.D. James and best-selling children's author J.K. Rowling have resorted to the gender anonymity of initials for authorial identity. Perhaps particularly significant is their use by Ursula Fanthorpe. Although sexual orientation is fully part of her public professional persona, when she writes about relationships, their lesbianism is either unstated or codified. In

'7301', for example, she writes about 'learning to hide/The sudden shining naked looks of love' without spelling out why the protagonists feel those looks have to be concealed (Fanthorpe, 1987, p. 33). In 'Christmas Presents' the protagonist, recovering from an operation, holds hands with her partner and wonders why 'next bed's visitors were staring'. The poem is built around the graceful idea that these neighbours were staring because they couldn't bear to watch their own loved one dying; and also, in a turn towards transcending that death, 'because we were...human' (Fanthorpe, 1995, p. 65); but its clarity contains a private ambiguity about whether the reader should understand that this is a gay couple, who may have been stared at for other, perhaps homophobic, reasons. The separation between authorial identity and the writer's self on the page remains fragile.

Another way to 'write as a man' is to assume a male narrative persona. As we've seen in Embodied Selves, Emily Brontë prefaces the main action of *Wuthering Heights* with a male narrator who is told the story of the lovers by a woman, Nelly Dean, Catherine's old nurse, to whom he offers hospitality (Brontë, E., 1965). It is this male narrator, Lockwood – his name reminiscent of the impasses of a Dantean mid-life crisis[2] – who experiences Catherine's ghostly rapping on his bedroom window. Once he has established this personal link with the story he recounts, Nelly Dean's first-person narration takes over. Why, then, was it necessary to insert him into the novel? The answer is that Lockwood functions as a stabilising figure for the narrative in much the same way as an omniscient narrator. Convention dictates that the *source* of such a story be a woman because, as Woolf's essay points out, at least until suffrage women were associated with the domestic and personal spheres and might be expected to be their more assiduous observers. But, by the same token, a woman character could not function as *omniscient* narrator because she is *gendered*.

The figure of the omniscient narrator carries with it traces of the ideal of a disembodied discourse not limited by any particular personal viewpoint. To be gendered is to be associated with only a part of human experience. A male narrator is of course also gendered; but, as Simone de Beauvoir first pointed out in *The Second Sex*, a male-led society characteristically defines attributes perceived as masculine as the norm from which the feminine deviate (de Beauvoir, 1988). Women are constructed as gendered in moments when men are not. This kind of gender demarcation may be defined as *difference from* rather than simple difference *between*.

So how can we write from and beyond the group to which we may belong? Alice Oswald's book-length *Dart*, which traces the course of the Devon river from source to sea, is a *persona* poem which attempts to defeat this 'difference from'. In it, the river speaks but so do the people who live and work on it. Many of them (forty-two out of the fifty-six listed by name in the Acknowledgements) are men; and when, at the poem's end, the river speaks again – 'This is me, anonymous, water's soliloquy, // all names, all voices' – it nevertheless gives itself the *male* identity of Proteus (Oswald, 2002, p. 48). The reader's experience of ventriloquism – the female poet speaking through male personae – is particularly pronounced because Oswald uses prose poetry and verbatim interview transcription alongside conventional blank/free verse.

As we saw in the chapter on the Reader, Patricia Duncker's *Hallucinating Foucault* is a passionately engaged polemic about writing. Her protagonist is a young researcher whose girlfriend urges the turn from examining texts to tracking down the writer himself, a brilliant Frenchman to whom Duncker gives French philosopher Michel Foucault's real name. He has also loved Michel Foucault and been incarcerated in a psychiatric hospital. When Paul Michel seduces our narrator, the girlfriend turns out to have loved this charismatic protagonist since she was a child. In Duncker's novel, the contract between reader and writer is an intimate form of love which 'can never be proved' as Paul says (Duncker, 1997, p. 154). Invented character Paul Michel has a real name: one belonging to his lover, the real figure with the invented name Michel Foucault. In this entirely *textual* relationship, the fictional Paul Michel has loved the historical Foucault as his ideal reader: 'he was the man I loved most. He was the man for whom I wrote' (*loc. cit.*). This is a novel whose many layers of correspondence require its own reader to pay intimate attention to what it has to say about reading and writing as forms of love. In other words, the reader is forced to enact the novel's message. At the heart of this process is the figure of the young researcher, agent of readerly comprehension and both Michel's new ideal reader and our narrator: and Duncker *does not let us know* the gender of this figure.

At one level this generates interesting questions about sexuality; but Duncker has done something much more radical than this. She has used homosexuality – *one* of the narrator's relationships must be same-sex – not only to explore orientation but in a technical way: as a trope with which to force her reader out of assumptions which flow from having a gendered narrator. This narrative is neither omniscient nor particularly reliable: as well as declaring affect – showing its own emotion – the plot requires that it is ill-informed. Nevertheless, this is the story of a sentimental education in which Duncker's strategies allow us to see the narrator as a reading, writing agent emerging regardless of gender.

Hallucinating Foucault destabilises the reader's sense of what experience unlimited by gender may be, and therefore of what gendered experience is.[3] We can see how important this project is for all these writers – from Brontë and Woolf to Duncker, Fanthorpe and Oswald – when we look at Carol Shield's last book, *Unless* (Shields, 2003). Once again a (woman) novelist prepares the ground for an exploration of agency in and beyond the page by establishing a complex set of *textual* relationships within the story. Reta Winters, the protagonist, translates distinguished French feminist philosopher Danielle Westerman, and is herself a wife, mother, author of a romantic comedy and at work on a second novel. Reta's eldest daughter Norah has dropped out of student life in search of Goodness, a search which takes the form of begging on the streets of Toronto; a reaction, we eventually learn, to being unable to save another young woman from self-immolation. Much of the novel is taken up by her mother's struggle to come to terms with what has happened to Norah; and with her developing certainty that Norah has been damaged by the female sense of responsibility for the cares of the world. The novel becomes a search for an alternative feminine subjectivity. At its climax, the phone-call which starts the process of the family's recovery of Norah breaks in on a conversation between Reta and her new editor in which he urges her that her new manuscript is a Serious Book rather than simply a novel for women; and that she must therefore make the male, rather than female, lead the main character whose emotional development is explored.

Duncker's strategy for destabilising gender expectations is plainly not essentialist; Shields on the other hand seems to be exploring the possibility of a specifically female subjectivity whether or not essential in origin. Essentialism is never far away from these arguments. Another way to say this is that if gender is a construction, a set of ideas and expectations projected onto women, what is it that the group onto whom these ideas are projected have in common? How are human individuals selected to belong to one or other gender? One answer might be: through behaviour. Transvestites show us that sometimes gender may be constructed in this way, regardless of *appearance*. As the American choreographer Bill T. Jones says, 'We don't have to have a Giselle, a prince, a dying swan. Nothing. Just what these two bodies do' (eds Huxley and Witts, 2002, p. 75). If roles aren't essential, they can be *established* in ways similar to any other form of social action which 'requires a performance which is *repeated*' (Butler, 1990, p. 278). Judith Butler, whom we might describe as the leading *constructivist feminist* theorist, argues that gender is not, in fact, a role but an act: it does not *fit into* a narrative of meaning but *enacts and creates* it.

Essential identities?

Essentialist feminists may also write from the performance of gender. Their writing may adopt extravert and rhetorical styles. The title of Luce Irigaray's *This Sex Which Is Not One* sums up her look at what 'woman' is. In it she tries to resist the Aristotelean view of the world as a series of entities *being* themselves (Irigaray, 1977).[4] For Irigaray, this is a metaphysics which arises from the male experience of the self as unitary individual, who does not give birth and who is constructed as a free agent in society; but who *because of the unitary shape of his genitals* needs there to be an Other in order to experience (sexual) fulfilment: this produces an 'autistic, egological, solitary love' (Irigaray, 1991, p. 180). Woman, on the other hand – who does give birth and whose identity is profoundly constrained by social construction (as Irigaray shows us in analyses of Plato's myth of the cave and Freud's idea of the castration complex (Irigaray, 1985)) –, has no need of an Other because of the plurality at play in her genitals. She is able to experience continuing pleasure and to encounter the world as multiple and undivided. Crucially for us as writers, Irigaray also argues that women enact this essential self by expressing the world as multiple and by resisting the unitary line of logical argument. Her essentialist critique is quite other than the one we looked at in Embodied Selves, in which logic is seen to be limited because it proposes the fantasy of disembodied discourse.

In other words, one of the ideas she is turning on its head is Sigmund Freud's notion that a woman (visibly) lacks what a man has (a theory first developed in the case history of 'Little Hans' (Freud, 1977, pp. 169–305). Instead, she points out the metaphysics – ontologically

prior beliefs, held without justification through proof or argument –
which underlie it. These are sophisticated arguments, working with a
substantial canon of Western philosophy, and Irigaray carries them out
in non-linear form. Her language uses a great deal of play:

> ...'she' [...] speaks about the dazzling glare which comes from the
> source of light which has been logically repressed, about 'subject' and
> 'Other' flowing out into an embrace of fire that mingles one term into
> another, about contempt for form as such, about mistrust for under-
> standing as an obstacle along the path of *jouissance* and mistrust for the
> dry desolation of reason. (Irigaray, 1985, p. 191)

Here as elsewhere, she returns to positions and ideas from several
conceptual directions. Above all, she seems to 'show rather than tell',
in the familiar dictum of creative writing workshops. This writing isn't
only consistent with her ideas about gendered discourse: it is performative. The structure of *Speculum of the Other Woman*, for example,
mimics that of the gynaecological mirrors it's named for: with analysis of Plato on one side – and of Freud on the other – of a mid-section,
acting like the mirror's *tain* or silvering, in which Irigaray speaks
about the woman who generates these images.

Writing at almost the same time as Irigaray, the critic Hélène Cixous
proposed the idea of *écriture blanc* – 'white writing' – an idea in which
breast milk becomes the essential female substance (see Chapter 3).
There's nothing milky, however, about Cixous's most famous essay,
The Laugh of the Medusa, in which the writing woman is seen (once
again in a mirror, this time the shield Achilles used in order not to
look directly at the Medusa and be turned to stone) as monstrous,
transgressive, discursively excessive (Cixous, 1981).

Cixous gives us the flamboyant return of the woman writer as the
dangerously multiple, tricky and playful self who, because she turns
'men' to stone, is in fact responsible for the fixity of certain discursive
conventions. This is the powerful return of the repressed, both in the
socio-political (Gilbert and Gubar, 2000) and psychoanalytic senses of
that term. It's the latter sense which is most significant for us as
writers. For Freud, play, especially play in language (punning) was a
form of *parapraxis*, what we call the Freudian Slip, in which repressed
material breaks through the links of conventional and grammatical
meaning (Laplanche and Pontalis, 1988, pp. 300–1). In *Creativity*,
Rob Pope enlarges this idea to suggest that the excess which is

creativity is itself the return of this repressed material (Pope, 2005). This is the opposite of Kavaler-Adler's idea, which we looked at in Memory and History, that creative writing is inadvertent repetition. In Pope's model, it is both advertent and useful.

This suggests that when we write fiction, poetry or literary non-fiction, something additional or excessive is going on. We are doing more than what the rules tell us to do: these rules by themselves simply produce formulaic writing. They may also circumscribe local literary taste. Jeanette Winterson is one of the most transgressive fiction writers in contemporary British literature. Her fiction breaks the realist contract – she has moved from magical realism, in *Sexing the Cherry*, to postmodernism in *The PowerBook* – and she uses a playful narrative voice in which irony, dream and straightforward narrative are difficult to distinguish (Winterson, 1990, 2001). Like her precursor Angela Carter, whose novels of female identity also moved from scenes of working-class life to fantasy derived from folktale and Shakespeare, Winterson's narrative voice often employs asides.[5] It is also arch (Winterson, 2001, p. 49).

This knowing playfulness is an enactment of *jouissance* (lit: playfulness), the play of surplus which may be said to represent the female body or to enact female bodily experience. It can also, however, represent 'play' in the secondary sense of *range* of creativity in a *textual* body regardless of gender. Jacques Lecoq writes of teaching physical theatre that:

> Of course there is no such thing as absolute and universal neutrality, it is merely a temptation. This is why error is interesting [...] The north pole does not quite coincide with true north. There is a small angle of difference, and it is lucky that this angle exists. Error is not just acceptable, it is necessary for the continuation of life [...] Without error, there is no movement. (Lecoq, 2000, pp. 20–1)

Readers can make creative errors too. A Winterson narrative may not proceed in chronological order. *The PowerBook* moves between an e-correspondence, in which two apparent strangers invent a series of sexual and romantic scenarios, and a love triangle set in a series of non-virtual European spaces. In this story, the destiny of the lovers seems to be constantly under threat of being re-written. As if to stabilise this unstable narrative, the scenarios which originated in cyberspace are filled in, before the novel ends, with what happened next.

The PowerBook's leitmotif is that: 'You can change the story. You are the story.' This echoes the idea of the subject-in-process with which thinkers like Denise Riley oppose the stasis of essentialism, 'a positivist position where everything simply was as it was' (Riley, 1992, p. 123). In 'A Short History of Some Preoccupations' Riley borrows Foucault's idea of doing 'archaeology' on discourses to see the *processes* by which they construct identities: 'to distinguish what different forms of description were active at what levels. This was surely a fully historical and indeed a materialist undertaking' (*loc. cit.*). Identities are continually *being made* rather than arrived at or discovered.[6]

Yet aphorisms like Winterson's can seem knowing to the point of return to an omniscient narrator. There's a tension, in other words, between the very ambition of the novelist's 'play', and the artlessness of *jouissance. The PowerBook,* though its complex structure is reflexive, still *tells a story*, albeit one whose end the reader may be required to supply. To some degree, therefore, it does tell rather than show. In *Aspects of the Novel* E.M. Forster called what he saw as the necessary structural evil of story 'a backbone – or may I say a tapeworm, for its beginning and end are arbitrary' (Forster, 1979, p. 34).

That Winterson has attracted hostile as well as extremely positive critical attention may indicate the extent to which such textual conventions are policed. One of the more surprising aspects of essentialism is the extent to which its proponents seem keen to police it. As Sarah Kofman points out, if something is 'natural', in the sense of inalienable rather than contingent, why would it need to be enforced? Kofman uses deconstruction to point out the 'cauldron logic' in Jean-Jacques Rousseau's argument that girls *must* be limited to what suits their female 'nature'.[7] Rousseau is a particularly pertinent example for Kofman to have identified for this kind of analysis, since, as we've seen in Chapter 7, he is a significant figure both in the development of Western political philosophies of human rights and in the eighteenth-century's relocation of meaning in the individual Subject. Rousseau's work was carried out in the context of the development of 'natural philosophy', or epistemology. He took its idea of a *general* inalienable nature, which could be rationally deduced from *particular* observations, as his starting point for arguments about the inalienability of human nature and therefore of human rights. However, this whole method comes under pressure from the anti-essentialist argument that you cannot deduce the true nature of individuals from the way they operate in the world because of formative and existential constraints that world places on them.

Writing identity

This presents a two-fold problem for us as writers. Questions of human rights are too important to be trivialised by appropriation to a specialist argument: yet they necessarily work through generalisation. We can't make arguments for universal human rights without making the related case about a universal human nature. What does this mean for ideas about the *construction* of identity? Does it make it more or less likely that we can chose whether or not to write out of a shared identity?

Second, a premise of characterisation is that, especially in *persona* narration, the character of an individual can be *construed from what is shown* of their actions. We don't usually show (let alone tell) the *inner experience* of other than the main character in fiction. This literary strategy relies on the normative human assumption that we can indeed 'read' character from action: and that what we read is stable enough to serve as some kind of indicator of future (and past) actions. Even a novel which traces the *development* of a character's consciousness relies on our being able to believe, on the basis of what we've been shown so far, that the character's reactions to each new situation, though developmental, are consistent with 'who they are'. For example, the eponymous hero of Vladimir Nabokov's *Pnin*, the exiled *literati* who at the novel's outset is seen almost missing a lecture because he has tried to be cleverer than the official train timetable, remains naively and pedantically self-engaged throughout the book and its progress towards his betrayal by long-term colleagues, revealed only after Pnin and his reader believe safety to have been finally achieved. It's the very same qualities which caused him to bungle the opening journey, we realise, which allow him to 'lose his way' in life as a whole (Nabokov, 1989).

Like Heidegger's dream of authentic *Being*, this retrospective construction of character looks backwards from the phenomenon of action for something necessary or true-to-itself on which a continuing belief in identity can be based (Heidegger, 1990). But wherever we find characterisation 'inauthentic' or schematic we're recognising how an excessively stabilised identity is fantasy. The protagonist whose badness or goodness is unmodulated has stepped out of melodrama, not literature. We expect character *development* as a story acts on its fictional participants; we experience characterisation without this kind of development as two-dimensional.

When we write, we also create a narrative self on the page. All writing creates such personae. Even this chapter has a narrator, which uses the first person plural – 'we' – to locate itself as co-authored and as complicit with you the reader, who may also be a writer. The *standpoint* may be impersonal, but this narrator is shaping a particular intellectual *narrative*. Each chapter draws you through or past certain viewpoints to the narrator's own synthesis, analysis and conclusions. This narrative, the way what we write is *put together*, creates order in two senses of that word. It's not only the order in which we present ideas, one after the other; it's also order in the sense of form, correctness, manageability. An 'order' is also a command; and in this putting together of narrative we *direct* the reader's thinking.

Narrative personae have a different relationship to our writing selves than does our writing voice. They aren't continuous with or in some kind of necessary relationship to our own self off the page. Narrators are *textual* constructs which enable our writing process and determine our texts. But those which are less fully characterised often refuse, or fail, to locate their own stake within the text. When we use an omniscient narrator, for example, one thing we're asking the reader to accept is that our narrative viewpoint isn't from within the drama of the text. It doesn't have the bias of a lover or the motivations of a rival. And yet *all* narrators are *characterised* by certain traits. How do we characterise a viewpoint if we're not to give the apparently-omniscient narrator individual human characteristics?

It's here that the narrative persona becomes useful. A *per-sona*, that which is *for letting sound through*, functions as a mask. It is *characterised* but is not *a character*. When we think about masks, whether from Japanese *Noh* theatre or Venetian carnival, we can see that this characterisation isn't life-like but stylised. It may *suggest* an individual character – the wise old man or the young soldier off to war – but this isn't done through realism. A mask covers only part of the body: we can see that it's not 'a real person' in itself. A mask enables the performance of a role – whether on stage, at a party, or in ritual – rather than *being* that performance itself.

Among such performances, the conservative, fatalistic characterisation of melodrama finds its opposite in the conscience of the avant-garde, which sees each idea as time-specific and -limited by the events which will necessarily succeed its moment of invention. Jean-Jacques Lyotard writes about the postmodern as an accelerated form of this kind of conscientiousness, against the grain of an 'epoch [which] is one of slackening'. It works:

> ...to present the fact that the unpresentable exists [...] The artist and the writer [...] are working without rules in order to formulate the rules of what *will have been done* (Lyotard, 1983, pp. 77, 82).

But postmodernity is also associated with play, not necessarily in the excessive sense of *jouissance* but in the sense of transgressing the unitary authority of a particular way of going on: whether that is consistent typeface or single narrative viewpoint. Among its literary forebears, the French writers who made up the Oulipo group in the 1950s and 60s played with both (Calvino, Queneau and Fournel, 1995). Oulipo resisted the pull of *genre* although, like the Surrealism which preceded it, in doing so it drew attention to the *genres* it devised: these included childish lalations alongside exceptional formal constraints such as a novel written without using the letter e (Perec, 1996).

The result is a strange kind of authorial anti-authority, in which the writer uses the text like a mask. He performs it fully but it may 'express' nothing about his 'essential' self. The Argentinian Jorge Luis Borges (1899–1986) used the fascination of genre to confuse the politico and liberate the reader in ways which continue to influence non-Anglophone postmodernisms. The younger generation of European fiction writers in this tradition include Macedonian short-story writer Aleksandar Prokopiev (Prokopiev, 2002), Natashe Goerke from Poland (Goerke, 2001) and Austro-Romanian Herta Müller, whose *The Land of Green Plums* tells the story of a group of young students living with the unrealities of Ceausescu's reign (Müller, 1998). Indeed an increasingly systematised postmodernism has dominated Romanian fiction and literary theory of the last twenty years. Writers living under the totalitarian regimes of communist Europe codified their socio-political insights; in Romania and Bulgaria, in particular, this strategy also tends to produce a kind of 'affect-less' text, of narrative games rather than explorative story, which seems to capture the depersonalising experience of post-/totalitarian society.

In other words, by omission such texts seem to suggest a link between explorations of our own identity *as* writers and explorations of identity through characterisation.[8] It may be that not only our beliefs about individual identity – I choose the gender of my main character according to whether or not I believe I can write 'beyond' my own gender – but the way we ourselves *perform* identity – I put off doing the hoovering until I've finished my chapter; I have a particular *female* critic in mind as my ideal reader – may create *implied identities* within a text. What animates characters in a fiction in ways which we experience as being true-to-life may be a whole network of things we use, not entirely consciously, to orient ourselves in relation to the people we're 'reading' off the page.

It may be our *ideas about* other people, rather than simply the finely detailed observation of human behaviour, which enables us to project a fully-individuated humanity onto characters which – as writers as well as readers – we encounter only through their actions. For example, the measured, extended sentences of W.G. Sebald's novels, including his unparagraphed masterpiece *Austerlitz*, give us the voice of a strangely under-emotional narrator (Sebald, 2001). This is how Sebald characterises the refugee, who as a child had his 'true identity' hidden from him. The narrator recalls how, after arrival on a Kindertransport, he was raised in a Welsh vicarage by the couple who denied his former name and history. The narrative voice create a textual space for the kind of damage this denial of identity may do to such an individual; it also carries over an echo of Theodor Adorno's famous dictum that there should be 'No poetry after Auschwitz'.

Postmodernity also suggests that play remains key in the continual revitalisation and destabilisation of ideas about identity. The carnivalesque possibilities of deliberate transgression, as much as inadvertent error, are, as Cixous and Irigaray suggest, key (Bakhtin, 1993). That free play of representation which is the sexual transgression of gender roles allows us a way to see such play as more than 'essential' duty. Orientation and gender come together again, then, to suggest how expectations and experiences of the ways our texts speak for an essential self may be distortions – or amplifications – of what's going on when we write. If group identities such as gender and sexuality are always a construction, we write as a member of a group even when we are not aware of doing so. It is a writing position full of possibilities.

Recommended reading

Feminists Theorise the Political (1992), edited by J. Butler and J.W. Scott, is a Reader which introduces some of the key debates about agency and identity through essays by some of the leading thinkers. *A Reader in Feminist Knowledge* (1991), edited by S. Gunew, is an unusual collection of material on the topics covered in this chapter. *The Irigaray Reader* (1991), edited by M. Whitford, introduces this complex philosopher, largely using work from her middle and later periods. Not yet superseded as a collection of some of key texts from a highly-influential moment in French thought is *New French Feminisms: An Anthology* (1981), edited by E. Marks and I. de Courtivron. *Adrienne Rich's Poetry and Prose* (1975), edited by *B. Charlesworth Gelpi and A. Gelpi,* brings together Rich's best-known essays and poetry.

Writing exercises

- Free-write on any topic for five minutes. Now rewrite the passage trying to be as hyperbolic as you can. Notice where the text becomes ridiculous or ironised, as well as where it slips out of control.
- In discussion or in a list, identify the ways in which you 'control' what you write, for example by observing the rules of grammar or the realist contract. Are any of these 'controls' things you demand from *everything* you read, or can they be waived sometimes? Do you need the same things from a post-modern fiction as you do from a bank statement?
- Take a poem in strict form – ballad, sonnet, villanelle etc – and write it *out of form.* Remove all traces of the form by inserting synonyms, adding material, changing from voice to voice, etc. How does your finished text hold together, and how much does form hold the original together?
- Do you consciously write from or for any group viewpoint? How do you feel about writing which does? Discuss; or try to articulate your ideas in a short reflective essay or piece of fiction.

Conclusion

'To admit that [the self] is elusive...is not at all to concede that it is fictive'.

Barry Olshen, 'The Self' in *Encyclopedia of Life History*, 2001, p. 801.

In this book we have endeavoured to show how reflexivity is a central feature of the writing process, and indeed, of the creative process in general. Whether we are thinking about what it means to find a writing voice, or our stance as authors in relation to our work in progress; whether we think about our relationship to imagined readers in the writing process, or to ourselves as readers of our own writing, or to the characters and narrators we create in our fictions; whether we think about our relationship as writers to history and memory, or to geography and culture, or to our bodies; reflexivity – the ability to move fluidly back and forth between an inside and an outside view of ourselves and our material – runs throughout as a theme. We have suggested that exploring this reflexivity, both through understanding it conceptually and entering into it experientially through writing practice, can help us to develop as writers.

We have also suggested, in our opening chapter, that in order to make sense of this reflexivity in the writing process we need to re-consider current and dominant thinking in the humanities about subjectivity. This book was motivated in part by our dissatisfaction with the dominant view in postmodern theory that writing is an impersonal process, and that the self is a fiction no longer relevant to discussions of writing. Whilst agreeing that the old essentialist notion of self was not satisfactory, we felt that the notion of the 'subject' constructed by language which came to replace it was insufficient to account for the lived experience of the practising writer; in particular that it didn't have a place for the felt, bodily experience that so many writers speak about. As will be clear from what we have said, we believe that there needs to be a thorough re-thinking of the concept of self and its role in the writing process from the point of view of the practising writer.

We have made a start on this project here, by drawing together, and where appropriate reinterpreting, a range of thinking about subjectivity and writing, in an attempt to look at, and think differently about, the connection between them. Clearly there is much more thinking to be done, and we hope that others will take up some of the ideas we have presented and explore them further. We believe that reinstating a notion of self, thought of as a process rather than as an entity, and taking into account both a bodily felt self and the self in language, will not only make conceptual thinking about writing more relevant and appealing to the practising writer, but will also stimulate new avenues to explore within current theoretical debates.

Our focus on the self does not mean, however, that we are suggesting that all writing is simply expressive of the self. Self-expression may be a consequence of writing for some people and, particularly in the early stages of a writing apprenticeship, we may find that using autobiographical material as a starting point, and reflecting on our writing process in the way we have suggested, helps us to access personal material and to express it. But as we develop as writers and learn to distance ourselves from our personal material, self-expression is likely to give way to other concerns, such as the desire to create writing that embodies experience and ideas in ways that have a broader appeal than the purely personal.

Nor are we suggesting that all writing necessarily *originates* in the self. There is no doubt that we imbibe unconsciously or acquire consciously techniques and genres of writing that are dominant in our cultures; there is no doubt that the things we write about are often common themes in our cultures. Rather, what we have been exploring here is the extent to which the self is *implicated* in our writing, and how important it is for us, as developing writers, to be able to draw on it freely, in its many manifestations. After all, whatever comes from outside is inevitably filtered through our individual conscious and unconscious processes. If it is the case, as suggested by current thinking in the cognitive and neuro-sciences, that most of our mental processes are unconscious and that each of us has a unique mental make-up as a result of our different bodies and different life experience, then that filtering is going to be crucial to the way we work and re-work ideas into a final product.

No matter how finite or communal the material coming to us from the outside world, we have the opportunity of making our own unique contribution as writers, our own particular ways of speaking to others via the page. To repeat Mikhail Bakhtin: 'No-one else can do what we can do, ever'.

Notes

Chapter 1   The Self

1. Descartes' understanding of thinking seems to embrace feeling also, but he associates this feeling capacity with the mind rather than with the body (Flew, 1971, pp. 281–2). See Chapter 7.
2. Some contemporary feminist thinkers, such as Hélène Cixous and Luce Irigaray, have sought to reintroduce an element of essentialism into our understanding of male and female identity. Similarly, Gayatri Spivak reintroduces essentialist thinking into postcolonial studies. See Chapter 10.
3. The discussion of social constructionism draws on McCall (1977).
4. Eugenics was a system of thought devised by Francis Galton in the nineteenth century. He believed that differences between people, such as intelligence, were due to genetic inheritance rather than environmental factors. This led to the view that some races or classes of people were superior to others, which resulted in racist policies and enforced sterilisation (Laland and Brown 2002, pp. 37–39).
5. Although Kristeva is not of course saying that what the infant experiences is *undifferentiated*, but rather that the infant doesn't have a conception of a *boundedness* that 'comes between' itself and the differentiation it reaches for. Differentiation here functions more like graduations (in our own experience we might think of graduations of colour or heat) on a plane rather than the interplay between entities.

Chapter 2   Voice

1. The 'utterance' in Bakhtin's thinking is 'a unit of speech communication', whether a word or a collection of words (or even an oral gesture) written or spoken by an individual to one or more others in a particular social context (Morson and Emerson, 1990, pp. 125–6).
2. Traditional meanings of 'discourse' are a conversation, a speech or treatise, or 'text above the level of the sentence', but the term has come to be associated with the way interest groups exercise power in society through particular 'communicative practices' (Pope, 1995).
3. Bakhtin uses the term 'ideological' not so much with its political connotation but as an adjective derived from 'ideas' (Morson and Emerson, 1990).
4. 'Phatic utterance' means words or sounds in language which don't convey information but are there for social or emotive purposes, e.g. 'well-well'; phatic utterances comes closest to the idea of bodily gesture in language.

5. For an interpretation of the poem in terms of Hopkins' struggle with his religious vocation, see Gardner (1961), pp. 180–84; cf. Sprinker (1980), pp. 3–15, for an understanding of this poem as the poet's process of 'selving'.
6. 'Deconstruction' has been defined as a way of looking at traditional concepts such as 'Being' or 'Self' and revealing their internal contradictions and metaphysical assumptions (OED).

Chapter 3 Authorship

1. Cixous uses the term 'ego' in the Freudian sense to denote the dominant 'I-self', which is both conscious and unconscious.

Chapter 4 Creativity

1. Modernism in the literary sense denotes the move away from nineteenth century realism by writers around the turn of the twentieth century and the conjuring up of the 'inner reality' of individual characters through techniques such as stream of consciousness and free indirect discourse (see Stevenson, 1998).
2. Caliban is a character in Shakespeare's play *The Tempest* (1611); there are many echoes of this play in Coover's story.
3. 'Metafiction' denotes fiction that reflects and comments on its own fictional status.

Chapter 5 The Reader

1. We are grateful to the author, who wishes to remain anonymous, for permission to reproduce this poem.

Chapter 7 Memory and History

1. Though Berkeley and Hume took up the challenge of earlier work by John Locke; whose *An Essay Concerning Human Understanding*, published in 1689, explores both material and immaterial aspects of human nature in the light of each other (Locke, 1975; Berkeley, 1988; Hume, 1990).
2. As would Gerard Manley Hopkins, in his Terrible Sonnets, and, in the twentieth century, Herbert Lomas in *Letters in the Dark*. (Hopkins 1979, pp. 61–3, Lomas, 1986). The sonnet form works out a conceit, an idea or theme extended through the poem and hence *through time*. This working out, a formalised struggle with its own poetic matter, is one expression of the ambivalence – the risk of conflict – inherent in any bringing-together of hitherto dissociated ideas. It's as foundational to the genre, and perhaps as

cathartic, as the misunderstandings which must precede the happy ending of romantic fiction. Paradox, which stages the oscillations of ambivalence, is peculiarly suited to the working out of such a conceit. It can also represent that oscillation between presence and absence which the loved one who is unattained or unattainable embodies.

3. This formal association is doubled by paradoxical imagery through which (the paradox of) release through dedication is worked out. The poet appropriates not merely romantic but sinful *sexual* love ('ravish'/'chast') and adultery ('engaged'/'divorce') to his Christian iconography. He also 'abases' himself into the female role ('Take mee'...'Ravish').

4. Medieval Christian poetry had continued the Biblical tradition of Church or believer as the 'bride of Christ', but did not use secular *forms* to do so.

5. A trope is a discrete figure in a text, either an idea or a rhetorical form.

6. Sigmund Freud's *The Interpretation of Dreams* was not published till 1900, but his correspondence with Fleiss and work with Breuer – which developed the views, notably on the unconscious, he formulates there – both started around 1887/8 (Freud, 1976).

7. St Teresa (1515–1577) was born Teresa Sánchez de Cepeda y Ahumada. Her foundation, the Discalced Carmelite Order, was secured by the co-foundation of an order of friars in 1568 by her pupil, Juan de Yepes, St John of the Cross (1542–1591).

8. This model of a continuum between what we write and a writing process going on beyond the page is part of contemporary thinking about literacy as a collective practice. Jane Mace's work on scribing shows how translation, transliteration and social negotiation (asking questions) are all actions being carried out in a shared social space beyond, but helping to constitute, the text (Mace, 2002).

9. 'I live without living in myself/and in such a manner hope/to die in order not to die.// I don't live in myself/and cannot live without God.' Own translation.

10. Doctrine holds that there is only one Way, or process, for all Christians: 'I am the Way, the Truth and the Light. No man cometh unto the Father except by me' (St John, XIV, 6–7).

11. Other holocaust testimony may be archived but virtually unknown. Several interviewees in the Archive of Refugee Clinicians' Testimony at Oxford Brookes University refer to memoirs which they have published or would like to publish. Some suggest that the memoir contains a fuller account of what they're telling their interviewer, others that it is more authoritative because it has been fully reflected upon. None says that they feel their oral account is more authoritative; and yet, because they are unknown *as writers*, it is this oral testimony which is given authority *by the archive* in which it is collected. The Archive of Refugee Clinicians' Testimony at Oxford Brookes University includes taped interviews with doctors, nurses and dentists, the majority of whom left Central Europe for Britain between 1936 and 1938. Copies of these tapes are also preserved in the National Life History Archive at the British Library.

12. For a more detailed way of thinking about the different relationships between personal development and literary benefits from the writing process, see Hunt and Sampson, 1998, pp. 199–203.

13. Oates's monumental *Blonde*, retelling the life of Marilyn Monroe, was sold and reviewed as fiction though based more or less closely on factual information in the public domain (Oates, 2001).

Chapter 8   Geography and Culture

1. Transference is the technical psychoanalytic term for the way we repeat emotional experiences by projecting onto some other object – classically, the analyst – the emotions originally generated in an earlier formative relationship, often with a parent (Laplanche and Pontalis, 1988, pp. 455–462).

2. Plato says that he will ban poetry from *The Republic*, because, in reading it, citizens re-enact the emotions it records (Plato, 1965, pp. 383–6). Kearney 'prefer[s] to translate *mimesis*[…] as a kind of creative retelling, thereby avoiding the connotations of servile representation mistakenly associated with the traditional term "imitation"' (Kearney, 2002, p. 133). In doing so he excludes from his very interesting account of the importance for human lives of story-telling the kinds of texts in which nothing new is going on. As he also makes clear, the idea of 'creative retelling' as something which differentiates itself from what went before also respects the integrity of experience:
   The bottom line, as the judge in the New York court ruling on Joyce's *Ulysses* said, is that 'no one was ever raped by a book'. To suggest otherwise is not only to underestimate ordinary people's intelligence, but grossly to insult those who experience *real* violence in the *real* world. (*op. cit.* p. 134)

3. 'Ce n'est pas qu l'incurieux refuse de s'intéresser à l'éxterieur pour ne plus s'intéresser qu'à soi. À soi il n'est pas capable de s'intéresser non plus. Il est simplement devenu incapable de se séparer de soi; ou plutot: il crois que s'intéresser, ce serait se perdre, se séparer de soi. Et plus que tout, dans ces périodes-là, il est enchainé à cette coïncidence avec soi: un soi vide, douloureux, inassouvi, impérieux.'
   'It's not that someone who's incurious refuses to be interested in the outside world in order to be no longer interested in anything except himself. He's no longer capable of being interested in himself. He's simply become incapable of separating from himself: or, more accurately, he believes that to take an interest would be to lose himself, to become separated from himself. And more than anything, during such periods, he is trapped in this coincidence with a self which is empty, sad, unassuaged and imperious' (own translation) (Pachet, 1993, p. 27).
   Pachet's vision of incuriosity as a kind of hapless terror is echoed in the psychoanalytic idea of abjection.

4. 'Il faut naitre, il faut grandir, il faut en savoir le maximun. Puis il faudra mourir.'
   'We have to be born, we have to grow up, we have to know ourselves as much as possible. Then we will have to die' (own translation) (Jean Brugeilles q. Yhuel, 1993, p. 49).

5. As we have seen in Lacan's account of the relationship between different cultural viewpoints, this repressed material acquires what Julia Kristeva calls 'the power of horror' (*Pouvoirs de l'horreur*) (Kristeva, 1980).

6. *Nacionalnost*, an abstract noun and a more recent coinage, has quasi-administrative connotations.

Chapter 9   Embodied Selves

1. Anna Akhmatova, Nikolay Gumilev and Osip Mandelstam were the core of the group of Acmeists, founded in 1913. Gumilev was shot in 1921.

Mandelstam, first arrested in 1934, died in a Siberian transit camp in 1938; his sometime lover Marina Tsvetayeva killed herself in 1941 after a life of poverty and state persecution. Akhmatova, who survived until 1966, also helped preserve Mandelstam's prison-camp writing, the Voronezh poems.

2. Butoh was founded in 1959 by two dancers trained in Neue Tanz, Tatzumi Hijikata and Kazuo Ohno. It is a practice in which the dancer experiences *through* the body rather than imposing shape or action *on* the body. Elsewhere in the same passage, Nakamura, who belongs to the Hijikata school of Butoh, writes that:
'Dance is the body in crisis, and the dancer is the artist who claims his right to the crisis, or demands it for his body and through his body. What is 'the body in crisis?' It means that the balance of the body is in crisis' (Nakamura, 1999 p. 61).

3. In periphrasis a longer descriptive phrase, such as 'the protector of heroes', does the work of naming 'the chief'. Where this phrase is metaphorical – 'the whale's land' for 'the sea' – it's known as a kenning.

4. Rachel Bromwich points out that many elements of *roman cortois*, including 'the continental attitude of extreme abasement in love', are 'only slightly and sporadically discernable in the work of any Welsh poet before Dafydd ap Gwilym' (Bromwich, 1967, pp. 22–23).

5. 'It's a dream: how swiftly life passes!'. There are four patterns of alliteration and matching stresses in *cynghanedd*: *Groes* (Criss-Cross); *Draws* (Across), *Sain* (Sounded) and *Llusg* (Dragged). For more on formal *cynghanedd*, see Conran 1992; Hopwood 2004.

6. Some of the origins of Hopkins' 'Sprung Rhythm' are in the rhythmical complexity of *cynghanedd*. 'Vowelling off', his own term for an arrangement of consecutive vowels in order of increasing openness of their sound – a soundscape he uses to mimic spiritual transcendence, for example in 'The Windhover' – is also, in its attention to the patterning and meaning of vowel sounds, indebted to *cynghanedd* (Hopkins, 1979, p. 30).

7. Charlotte Brontë's line has a trace of complicity about it: a suggestion of 'Wouldn't you?' It's as if the reader, like the best friend/bridesmaid, assists in everything about the marriage – and yet does not. This oscillation between invited participation and *de facto* separation from Jane as bride is what sexualises the 'bedroom door'. It makes it clear that *there is something beyond it* (Brontë, C., 2003).

8. The doctrine of revealed religion holds that faith cannot be achieved by mere human effort: God comes to the believer, not the believer to God.

9. Language, unlike numbers or figures, refers to extra-linguistic things, like objects, actions and relations between them. These are its referents.

10 The codification of logic may in some senses respond to the contemporary invention of democracy, a form of authority no longer embodied in one particular individual but available to all citizens. The pre-Socratic *demos*, however, had an exclusively aristocratic and male body. Today we could ask questions about this sentence which would not have occurred to someone doing logic in that earlier context: were no women mentioned simply because there were none in the household? Is it specifically the men *themselves* who vote or are these proxy votes? Or are household votes distributed on the basis of number of males acquired – a form of wealth analogous to slaves or head of cattle – in a matriarchal society?

11. Perhaps it's worth noting that much theoretical debate on human rights focuses on the puzzle of social disparity, in other words on what is apparently *not* inalienable (Rawls, 1976).

12. Two well-known epistolary novels, Richardson's *Clarissa* and, in French, Laclos' *Les Liasons Dangereuses*, both deal with deceit and betrayal (Laclos, 2005; Richardson 1986). Their epistolary form stages the significance of partial knowledge, unreliable narrators and textual manipulation.

13. Morrison's later book about his mother, which concentrates largely on her relationship with his father, is less reflexive: as if the author has been to some degree freed into the position of omniscient narrator (Morrison, 2003).

14. If reflexive forms destabilise the authority of the author, other fictions problematise the ideal of the disembodied thinker. As we've seen elsewhere, in *Middlemarch* Dorothea falls for Casaubon's 'fine mind' but finds it is not finally enough to make a relationship with (Eliot, 1971). In *Cyrano de Bergerac*, Rostand's heroine falls in love with the poet's mind as it is expressed in verse, but assumes it to be embodied in the young man whose beauty seems to match it, rather than in her ugly – and notorious – cousin who in fact wrote the poems (De Rostand, 2000). In *Keep the Aspidistra Flying*, Gordon Comstock, Orwell's young idealist who has turned his back on careerism and financial reward, finds lack of money is an even more defining prison of the intellect (Orwell, 2000).

15. In earlier Western medicine, 'humours' – liquids found in particular parts of the body – were associated with certain moods or temperaments. Several of these 'bodily' temperaments – choleric, sanguine, bilious – remain in contemporary English usage.

16. In the Republic of Ireland writers and artists do not pay income tax; the Irish government funds the *aiosdana*, an association of distinguished writers and artists who receive an annual stipend for life.

Chapter 10   An Essential Self?

1. Although essentialism, which as Rob Pope points out has as its root the Latin *esse* – to be – names a way of being, other approaches to gendered identities may also identify ways of being without identifying them as *productive of* being a woman (Pope, 2005). For example, traditional distributions of domestic labour may be seen as external, although determining, conditions of what it means to be a woman in a particular culture: rather than as *produced by* her nature.

2. 'Midway life's journey I was made aware/That I had strayed into a dark forest,/ And the right path appeared not anywhere' Dante, trans. Housman, L. *The Divine Comedy* Canto I (Dante, 1977, p. 3).

3. Duncker returns to the theme of gender ambiguity elsewhere in her fiction. *James Miranda Barry*, her second novel, uses the scale and diction of the mainstream historical novel in a fictionalised account of the Army Surgeon who, on his death, was discovered to be a woman (Duncker, 2000).

4. Because it is nostalgic for the meaning of being in each of its particular identities (in the Heideggerian sense of *Being* as the inseparability of identity from existence) Aristotle's is also a very essentialist view. It was no coincidence that,

as we saw in Chapter 9, Aristotle formulated ideas about the essential identities of women on the basis of their contemporary roles (Aristotle, 1990, pp. 4–20) One of the problems with this view is that it makes the leap from the necessary link between existence and identity – nothing can exist without existing *as* – to the assumption that this link is fixed. Heidegger does not look forwards, towards modifications in identity, but backwards, to origins, with his belief in the importance of authenticity to pre-existing identities, his use of (sometimes spurious) etymology and his attachment to place. Heidegger's successor and sometime exegete (in *Of Spirit: Heidegger and the question*) Derrida responded, at least in part, to this metaphysical anchoring of identity in a particular given form when he developed the idea that identity is deferred to boundaries to the encounter with the other (*différence*) (Derrida, 1989).

5. Angela Carter explored the capacity of folktale for staging the unconscious of gendered experience not only in her book-length exploration of Bluebeard and other stories, *The Bloody Chamber and other stories* (Carter, 1995) but in novels including *The Magic Toyshop* (Carter, 1992). *Nights at the Circus*, a novel about twins, takes the theme of Shakespearean doubling as one of its starting points (Carter, 1994). However, asides also form part of her contemporary, feminist novelist Fay Weldon's rhetorical apparatus. Although a realist, Weldon often uses hard-pressed women narrators whose personae dominate the stories they tell (Weldon, 1993).

6. For example, Charlotte Bunch's discussion of the ways 'the particular material reality of lesbian life [made] political consciousness more likely' in the 1970s when lesbians were the only middle-class women who would 'have to support ourselves for the rest of our lives' not only shows how times have changed for all women, but gives some insight into the close associations between feminism and gay politics at the time (Bunch, 1991, pp. 324, 323).

7. 'Cauldron logic' is a particular kind of 'protesting too much' in which the elements of the protest contradict each other: it takes its name from the metaphor of the neighbour who lends a cauldron and gets it back with a hole in it. The borrower comes up with a series of mutually contradictory excuses. The cauldron's proverbial hole also stands for the 'hole' in such arguments.

8. As Sartre points out, this is finally a narcissistic relationship, since the only reader equipped to read a text with full comprehension is the writer himself (Sartre, 1948). As such it is latently tyrannical. The writer acts out this infantile stage of development, not only on his characters but on his reader. In the shared textual world, the reader must think the writer's thought: although under pressure the boundaries of the text prove to be porous, and a reader is able to read critically, observing technical flaws and successes and refusing the seduction of thinking the text *as* the writer has it.

Even in the case of technological interventions into texts – such as interactive e-narratives or audience-elected endings to radio pieces – the text, though fragmented into a plurality of non-linear or mutually-contradictory accounts, remains intact *in itself*: the reader choosing from among alternative pieces of text in the same way that she chooses among the texts available in a bookshop or in the 'virtual library' of every available text. Every text can be said to locate itself in contradistinction to all other texts, as Harold Bloom notes, taking the example of the mutual resistances of successive literary generations (Bloom, 1997). And in this virtual world of all-texts, the reader also locates the text by *foregrounding* it (in an area marked 'interesting' or 'accessible'). Since the writer knows this, the ideal reader makes a Kleinian return, introjected as an angry, absent or good, loving figure whom the writer obeys while defining herself against him.

Meanwhile, in the family romance of peri-textual power relations, it's perhaps not surprising that literary critics, those 'ideal' readers in the paradigmatic Platonic sense, have thought through the role of the reader in completing a text through interpretation. In this view, texts are passive objects radically open to the readerly process, which reinserts the actions of subjectivity (Fish, 1980).

References

Abrams, M.H. *The Mirror and the Lamp: Romantic Theory and the Critical Tradition* (Oxford: Oxford University Press, 1953)

Adorno, T. *The Jargon of Authenticity*, trans. K. Tarkowski and F. Will (London: Routledge & Kegan Paul, 1973)

D'Aguiar, F. *Feeding the Ghosts* (London: Chatto and Windus, 1997)

Allen, G. *Intertextuality* (London and New York: Routledge, 2000)

Alvarez, A. *The Writer's Voice* (London: Bloomsbury, 2005)

Amichai, Y. *Selected Poems*, T. Hughes and D. Weissbort (eds) (London: Faber, 2000)

Angelou, M. *I Know Why the Caged Bird Sings* (London: Virago, 1993)

Applebaum, D. *Voice* (Albany: State University of New York Press, 1990)

Aquinas, T. *Summa Theologica*, Vol. 1, D.J. Sullivan (ed.) (Encyclopedia Brittanica, 1952)

Arberry, A.J. trans. *The Koran Interpreted* (London: Allen and Unwin, 1964)

Aristotle. *The Politics*, S. Everson (ed.) (Cambridge: Cambridge University Press, 1988)

Aristotle. *The Politics* Book I, 3–13, S. Emerson (ed.) (Cambridge: Cambridge University Press, 1990, 4–20)

Attridge, D. *The Singularity of Literature* (London: Routledge, 2004)

Atwood, M. *Cat's Eye* (London: Bloomsbury, 1989)

Atwood, M. *Negotiating with the Dead* (Cambridge: Cambridge University Press, 2002)

Aull, C.D. *Reflexive Ethnography* (London: Routledge, 1999)

Austen, J. *Pride and Prejudice* (London: Wordsworth Classics, 1992)

Bakhtin, M. 'Discourse in the Novel', trans. C. Emerson and M. Holquist in Michael Holquist (ed.) *The Dialogic Imagination: Four Essays by M.M. Bakhtin* (Austin, Texas: University of Texas Press, 1981, 259–422)

Bakhtin M. *Problems of Dosteovsky's Poetics*, trans. C. Emerson (ed.) (Minneapolis and London: University of Minnesota Press, 1984)

Bakhtin, M. *Speech Genres and Other Late Essays*, trans. V.W. McGee (Austin: University of Texas Press, 1986)

Bakhtin, M. *Art and Answerability*, trans. V. Liapunov (Austin: University of Texas Press, 1990)

Bakhtin, M. *Towards a Philosophy of the Act*, trans. V. Liapunov in M. Holquist (ed.), (Austin: University of Texas Press, 1993)

Bakhtin, M. *Carnival and other subjects*, D. Shepherd (ed.) (Amsterdam and New York: Rodopi B.V.Editions, 1993)

Banville, J. 'Making Little Monsters Walk' in C. Boylan (ed.) *The Agony and the Ego: The Art and Strategy of Fiction Writing Explored* (London: Penguin Books, 1993, 105–12)

Barth, J. 'Life Story' in his *Lost in the Funhouse* (London: Secker and Warburg, 1969)

Barthes, R. 'Écrivains et écrivants' in his *Essais critiques* (Paris: Seuil, 1964)

Barthes, R. 'An introduction to the structural analysis of narrative', *New Literary History* 6, 1966, 237–272.

Barthes, R. 'Death of the Author' in his *Image-Music-Text*, trans. R. Heath (London: Fontana, 1977a, 142–148)

Barthes, R. 'The Grain of the Voice' in his *Image-Music-Text*, trans. S. Heath (ed.) (London: Fontana, 1977b, 179–189)

Barthes, R. 'The Writer on Holiday' in his *Mythologies*, trans. A. Lavers (London: Granada, 1981, 29–31)

Barthes, R. 'From Work to Text' in his *The Rustle of Language*, trans. R. Howard (London: Blackwell, 1986, 56–64)

Barthes, R. *Roland Barthes by Roland Barthes*, trans. R. Howard (Berkeley, California: University of California Press, 1994)

Bauby, J-D. *The Butterfly and the Diving Bell*, trans. J. Leggat (London: Fourth Estate, 1998)

Bayley, J. *Iris: A memoir* (London: Abacus, 1999)

de Beauvoir, S. *The Second Sex*, trans. H.M. Parshley (ed.) (London: Picador, 1988)

Beckett, S. *Waiting for Godot* (London: Faber, 1970)

Benjamin, W. 'What is Epic Theatre' in his *Illuminations*, trans. H. Zohn (London: Fontana, 1973, 149–156)

Benjamin, W. *Illuminations*, trans. H. Zohn (London: Fontana Press, 1992)

Bennett, A. (ed.) *Readers and Reading* (London and New York: Longman, 1995)

Benveniste, E. *Problems in General Linguistics*, trans. M.E. Meek (Miami: University of Miami Press, 1971)

Berkeley, G. *Principles of Human Knowledge*, R. Woolhouse (ed.) (Harmondsworth: Penguin, 1988)

Berlin, I. 'The Counter-Enlightenment' in his *Against the Current: Essays in the History of Ideas* (London: Pimlico, 1997)

Berry, J. *Lucy's Letters* (London: New Beacon Books, 1982)

Berryman, J. *Dream Songs* (New York: Farrar, Strauss, Giroux, 1969)

Bhatt, S. *Brunizem* (Manchester: Carcanet, 1988)

Blanchot, M. *The Space of Literature*, trans. A. Smock (Lincoln: University of Nebraska Press, 1982)

Bloom, H. *The Anxiety of Influence* (New York: Oxford University Press, 1973)

Bloom, H. *A Map of Misreading* (New York: Oxford University Press, 1975)

Bloom, H. *The Anxiety of Influence: A Theory of Poetry* (New York: Oxford University Press, 1997)

Boden, M.A. *The Creative Mind: Myths and Mechanisms* (London and New York: Routledge, 2nd ed. 2004)

Bollas, C. *Being a Character: Psychoanalysis and Self Experience* (London: Routledge, 1993)

Bollas, C. *Cracking Up* (London: Routledge, 1997)

Bollas, C. *Free Association* (Cambridge: Icon Books, 2002)

Booth, W. *The Rhetoric of Fiction* (Harmondsworth: Penguin, 2nd ed. 1991; 1st ed. 1961)

Borges, J.L. 'Borges and I' in his *Labyrinths* (Harmondsworth: Penguin, 1981a, 282–3)

Borges, J.L. 'The Argentine Writer and Tradition' in his *Labyrinths* (Harmondsworth: Penguin, 1981b, 211–220)

Bowra, M. *The Romantic Imagination* (London: Oxford University Press, 1966)

Brande, D. *Becoming a Writer* (London: Macmillan, 1992)

Brecht, B. 'Short Description of a New Technique of Acting Which Produces an Alienation Effect' trans. J. Willett (ed.) In *Brecht on Theatre: the Development of an Aesthetic* (New York: Hill and Wang, 1964, 136–147)

Bromwich, R. *Tradition and Innovation in the Poetry of Dafydd ap Gwilym* (Cardiff: University of Wales Press, 1967)

Brontë, C. *Jane Eyre* (Harmondsworth: Penguin, 2003)

Brontë, E. *Wuthering Heights*, D. Daitches (ed.) (Harmondsworth: Penguin, 1965)

Brown, C. *My Left Foot* (London: Minerva, 1990)

Bunch, C. 'Not for Lesbians Only' in S. Gunew (ed.) *A Reader in Feminist Knowledge* (London: Routledge, 1991, 319–325)

Burke, S. (ed.) *Authorship from Plato to the Postmodern: A Reader* (Edinburgh: Edinburgh University Press, 1995)

Burke, S. *The Death and Return of the Author* (Edinburgh: Edinburgh University Press, 2nd edition, 1998)

Burroway, J. *Writing Fiction: a guide to narrative craft* (London: Addison Wesley, 2002)

Butler, J. 'Performative Acts and Gender Constitution: An Essay in Phenomenology and Feminist Theory' in S.E. Case (ed.) *Performing Feminisms: Feminist Critical Theory and Theatre* (Baltimore: Johns Hopkins University, 1990, 270–282)

Butler, J. and Scott, J.W. (eds) *Feminists Theorise the Political* (London: Routledge, 1992)

Butler, M. *Romantics, Rebels and Reactionaries: English Literature and its Background 1760–1830* (Oxford: Oxford University Press, 1981)

Butterworth, G. 'An Ecological Perspective on the Origins of Self' in J.L. Bermúdez et al (eds) *The Body and the Self* (Cambridge, Mass.: MIT Press, 1998, 87–106)

Byatt, A. S. *Possession* (London: Vintage, 1991)

Cadava, E., Connor, P. and Nancy, J.-L. (eds) *Who Comes After the Subject* (New York and London: Routledge, 1991)

Caesar, A.H. *Characters and Authors in Luigi Pirandello* (Oxford: Clarendon Press, 1998)

Calvino, I., Queneau, R. and Fournel, P. *Oulipo Laboratory*, trans. H. Mathews and I. White (New York: Atlas Press, 1995)

Canetti, E. *Kafka's Other Trial: The Letters to Felice* (Harmondsworth: Penguin, 1982)

Carper, T. and Attridge, D. *Meter and Meaning: An Introduction to Rhythm in Poetry* (London: Routledge, 2003)

Chaitin, G.D. 'Desire and Culture: Transference and the Other' in *Rhetoric and Culture in Lacan* (Cambridge: Cambridge University Press, 1996, 150–194)

Carter, A. *The Magic Toyshop* (London: Virago, 1992)

Carter, A. *Nights at the Circus* (London: Vintage, 1994)

Carter, A. *The Bloody Chamber and Other Stories* (London: Vintage, 1995)

dir. Chadha, G. *Bend it Like Beckham* (Twentieth Century Fox, 2002)

Chatman, S. *Story and Discourse: Narrative Structure in Fiction and Film* (Ithaca and London: Cornell University Press, 1978)

Chatwin, B. *The Song Lines* (London: Picador, 1994)

Cixous, H. 'The Laugh of the Medusa' in E. Marks and I. de Courtivron (eds) *New French Feminisms* (Hemel Hempstead: Harvester Wheatsheaf, 1981)

Cixous, H. 'From the Scene of the Unconscious to the Scene of History' in *The Future of Literary Theory*, R. Cohen (ed.) (New York and London: Routledge, 1989, 1–18)

Cixous, H. *The Book of Promethea*, trans. B. Wing (Lincoln: University of Nebraska Press, 1991)

Cixous, H. 'Bathsheba or the interior Bible', trans. C.A.F. MacGillivray, in her *Stigmata: Escaping Texts* (London and New York: Routledge, 1998, 3–19)

Cixous, H. and Calle-Gruber, M. *Rootprints: Memory and Life Writing* (London: Routledge, 1997)

Clare, J. 'I am' in H. Gardner (ed.) *The New Oxford Book of English Verse* (Oxford: Oxford University Press, 1972, 601)

Clark, T. *The Theory of Inspiration* (Manchester: Manchester University Press, 1997)

Coleridge, S.T. *Biographia Literaria* (1817)

Collins, W. *The Woman in White* (Harmondsworth: Penguin, 2004)

Conley, V. *Hélène Cixous* (Hemel Hempstead: Wheatsheaf, 1992)

Conrad, J. *Lord Jim* (London: Dent, 1900)

Conrad, J. *Heart of Darkness* (Harmondsworth: Penguin, 1995)

Conrad, J. *The Heart of Darkness* (Harmondsworth: Penguin, 2004)

Conran, T. 'Appendix on Metre' in his *Welsh Verse* (Bridgend: Seren, 1992, 310–339)

Cooley, C.H. *Human Nature and the Social Order* (New York: Scribner's, 1902)

Coover, R. 'The Magic Poker' in his *Pricksongs and Descants* (London: Picador, 1973, 14–35)

Corradi Fiumara, G. *The Other Side of Language: A Philosophy of Listening*, trans. C. Lambert (London and New York: Routledge, 1990)

Culler, J. 'Reading as a Woman' in his *On Deconstruction* (London: Routledge and Kegan Paul, 1983, 43–63)

Cunningham, M. *The Hours* (London: Fourth Estate, 1999)

van Daalen, M. 'ik zal een grafschrift voor je maken dat iedereen van buiten kent' in *Poetry Route, Comité Stenen Strofen* (Committee of the Stone Stanzas) (Bergen Op: Zoom, 2000)

Dalrymple, W. *In Xanadu* (London: Flamingo, 1990)

Damasio, A. *The Feeling of What Happens: Body, Emotion and the Making of Consciousness* (London: Vintage, 2000)

Damasio, A. 'Some Notes on Brain, Imagination and Creativity' in K.H. Pfenninger and V.R. Shubik (eds) *The Origins of Creativity* (Oxford: Oxford University Press, 2001)

Dangor, A. *Bitter Fruit* (London: Atlantic Books, 2004)

Dante Alighieri in P. Milano (ed.) *The Portable Dante* (Harmondsworth: Penguin, 1977)

Darwish, M. 'The State of Siege', trans. S. Maguire in *Modern Poetry in Translation Series 4: 1*

Davies, I. *Writers in Prison* (Oxford: Basil Blackwell, 1990)

Davies, T. *Humanism* (London and New York: Routledge, 1997)

Delillo, D. *White Noise* (New York: Viking, 1984)

Dennett, D.C. *Kinds of Minds: Towards an Understanding of Consciousness* (London: Wiedenfeld and Nicholson, 1996)

De Quincey, T. *Confessions of an English Opium-Eater and Other Writings* (Oxford: Oxford University Press, 1985)

Derrida, J. *Of Grammatology* trans. G. Spivak (Baltimore and London: Johns Hopkins University Press, 1976)

Derrida, J. *Writing and Difference*, trans. A. Bass (Chicago: Chicago University Press, 1978)

Derrida, J. 'Qual Quelle: Valéry's Sources', in his *Margins of Philosophy*, trans. A. Bass (Chicago: Chicago University Press and Hemel Hempstead: Harvester Wheatsheaf, 1982)

Derrida, J. *Truth in Painting*, trans. G. Bennington and I. Mcleod (Chicago and London: University of Chicago Press, 1987)

Derrida, J. *Of Spirit: Heidegger and the question*, trans. G. Bennington and R. Bowlby (Chicago: University of Chicago Press, 1989)

Derrida, J. *Given Time: Vol. 1. Counterfeit Money*, trans. P. Kamuf (Chicago: Chicago University Press, 1992)

Derrida, J. *Points...Interviews, 1974–1994*, trans. P. Kamuf et al in E. Weber (ed.) (Stanford: Stanford University Press, 1995)

Derrida, J. *Monolingualism of the Other; or, The Prosthesis of Origin*, trans. P. Mensah (Stanford: Stanford University Press, 1998)

Descartes, R. 'Discourse on the Method' in *Philosophical Writings*, trans. E. Anscombe and P.T. Geach. (London: Open University Press, 1970)

Descartes, R. 'Meditations on First Philosophy' in *The Philosophical Writings of Descartes Vol II*, trans. J. Cottingham, R. Stoothoff, and D. Murdoch (Cambridge: Cambridge University Press, 1984, 3–62)

Descartes, R. *The Philosophical Writings Volume II*, trans. J. Cottingham, R. Stoothoff and D. Murdoch (Cambridge: Cambridge University Press, 1989)

Diderot, D. trans. J. Barzun, and R.H. Bowen, *Rameau's nephew and other works* (New York: Hackett, 2003)

Diski, J. *Don't* (London: Granta Books, 1998)

Docherty, T. *Reading (Absent) Character: Towards a Theory of Characterization in Fiction* (Oxford: Clarendon Press, 1983)

Donald, M. *Origins of the Modern Mind* (Cambridge: Harvard University Press, [1991])

Donne, J. *Poems*, J. Hayward (ed.) (Harmondsworth: Penguin, 1969)

Downie, R. 'Writing, Education and Therapy: Literature in the Training of Clinicians' in F. Sampson (ed.) *Creative Writing in Health and Social Care* (London: Jessica Kingsley, 2004, 124–137)

Drakulić, S. *Café Europa* (London: Abacus, 1996)

Duncker, P. *Hallucinating Foucault* (London: Picador, 1997)

Duncker, P. *James Miranda Barry* (London: Picador, 2000)

Durrell, L. *The Alexandria Quartet* (London: Faber, 1986)

Eakin, P.J. *Fictions in Autobiography* (Princeton: Princeton University Press, 1985)

Elbow, P. *Writing Without Teachers* (Oxford: Oxford University Press, 1973)

Elbow, P. *Everyone Can Write* (Oxford: Oxford University Press, 2000)

Elfyn, M. *Cell Angel* (Newcastle upon Tyne: Bloodaxe Books, 1996)

Eliot, G. *Middlemarch* (Harmondsworth: Penguin Books, 1971)

Eliot, T.S. 'Tradition and the Individual Talent' in his *Selected Essays* (London: Faber and Faber, 1951)

Eliot, T.S. 'The Three Voices of Poetry' in his *On Poetry and Poets* (London: Faber, 1957, 89–102)

Eliot, T.S. 'East Coker' in *Collected Poems 1909–62* (London: Faber, 1985, 196–204)

Ewen, J. 'The theory of character in narrative fiction' (in Hebrew) in *Hasifrut*, 3, 1971, 1–30

Ewen, J. *Character in Narrative* (in Hebrew) (Tel Aviv: Sifri'at Po'alim, 1980)

Fabb, N. *Linguistics and Literature: An Introduction* (Oxford: Basil Blackwell, 1997)

Fanthorpe, U.A. *A Watching Brief* (Calstock, Cornwall: Peterloo Poets, 1987)

Fanthorpe, U.A. *Safe as Houses* (Calstock, Cornwall: Peterloo Poets, 1995)

Faulkner, W. *As I Lay Dying* (London: Chatto, 1958)

Fetterley, J. *The Resisting Reader: A Feminist Approach to American Fiction* (Bloomington: Indiana University Press, 1978)

Fielding, H. *Bridget Jones's Diary* (London: Picador, 2001)

Fish, S. *Is there a text in this class? The Authority of Interpretive Communities* (Cambridge, MA: Harvard University Press, 1980)

Flew, A. *An Introduction to Western Philosophy* (London: Thames and Hudson, 1971)

Flint, R. 'Fragile Space: Therapeutic Relationship and the Word' in F. Sampson (ed.) *Creative Writing in Health and Social Care* (London: Jessica Kingsley, 2004, 138–153)

Safran Foer, J. *Everything is Illuminated* (Harmondsworth: Penguin, 2003)

Safran Foer, J. *I'm Okay* (London: Hamish Hamilton, 2005)

Forster, E.M. *Aspects of the Novel* (Harmondsworth: Penguin Books, 1979)

dir. Forsyth, B. *Gregory's Girl* (1980)

Foucault, M. 'What is an Author?' in his *Language, Counter-Memory, Practice* (Ithaca: Cornell University Press, 1977)

Foucault, M. *Technologies of the Self*, L.H. Martin et al (eds) (London: Tavistock, 1988)

Foucault, M. *History of Sexuality, Vol. 1*, trans. R. Hurley (London: Penguin Books, 1990)

Frank, A. *Anne Frank's Diary*, trans. F. Goodrich and A. Hackett (New York: Josef Weinberger Plays, 1996)

Franzen, J. *The Corrections* (London: Fourth Estate, 2002)

Freud, S. *Introductory Lectures on Psycho-Analysis*, trans. J. Riviere (London: George Allen and Unwin, 1949)

Freud, S. *The Interpretation of Dreams: Pelican Freud Library Vol 4*, trans. J. Strachey in A. Richards (ed.), (Harmondsworth: Penguin, 1976)

Freud, S. 'Little Hans' in *Case Histories I: Pelican Freud Library Vol 8*, trans. J. Strachey A. Richards (ed.), (Harmondsworth: Penguin, 1977, 169–305)

Freud, S. 'Creative Writers and Daydreaming' in his *Art and Literature*, trans. J. Strachey (Harmondsworth: Penguin, 1985, 129–141)

Freud, S. *The Essentials of Psycho-analysis*, trans. J. Strachey A. Freud (ed.) (Harmondsworth: Penguin Books, 1991)

Friel McGowin, D. *Living in the Labyrinth: A Personal Journey Through the Maze of Alzheimer's* (Cambridge: Main Sail, 1993)

Furness, T. and Bath, M. *Reading Poetry* (Harlow: Prentice Hall, 1996)

Gallagher, S. and Shear, J. (eds) *Models of the Self* (Exeter: Imprint Academic, 1999)

Gardner, W.H. *Gerard Manley Hopkins* (London: Oxford University Press, Vol. 1, 1961)

Gates, H.L. Jr. 'The Master's Pieces: On Canon Formation and the African-American Tradition' in his *Loose Canons* (Oxford: Oxford University Press, 1992)

Gergen, K. *The Saturated Self* (New York: Basic Books, 1991)

Gibbons, S. *Cold Comfort Farm* (Harmondsworth: Penguin, 2003)

Gibson, W. *Tough, Sweet, and Stuffy* (Bloomington and London: Indiana University Press, 1966)

Gibson, W. 'Authors, Speakers, Readers, and Mock Readers' in J.P. Tompkins (ed.) *Reader-Response Criticism* (Baltimore and London: Johns Hopkins University Press, 1980, 1–6)

Giddens, A. *The Consequences of Modernity* (Cambridge: Polity Press, 1991)

Gilbert, S.M. and Gubar, S. *The Madwoman in the Attic: The Woman Writer and the Nineteenth Century Literary Imagination* (New Haven, Connecticut: Yale University Press, 1979)

Goerke, N. *Farewells to Plasma*, trans. W. Martin (Prague: Twisted Spoon Press, 2001)

Goffman, E. *The Presentation of Self in Everyday Life* (Garden City, N.Y.: Doubleday, 1957)

Goldberg, N. *Writing Down the Bones* (Boston and London: Shambhala Publications, 1986)

Golding, W. *The Hot Gates* (London: Faber, 1965)

Goody, J. *The Interface Between Writing and the Oral* (Cambridge: Cambridge University Press, 1987)

Grant, L. *Remind Me Who I Am, Again* (London: Granta, 1999)

Greer, G. *Daddy We Hardly Knew You* (London: Random House, 1990)

Grimble, A. *A Pattern of Islands* (London: John Murray, 1952)

Gunew, S. (ed.) *A Reader in Feminist Knowledge* (London: Routledge, 1991)

ap Gwilym, D. *Poems*, R. Bromwich (ed.) (Llandysul: Gomer Press, 1982)

Harnad, S. 'Quote/Commentary – Journals in Hypertext Space' in Gàcs, A. (ed.) *Dissolving and Emerging Communities: The Culture of Periodicals from the Perspective of the Electronic Age* (Budapest: Budapest University of Technology and Economics, 2004)

Hartill, G. *Creative Writing: Towards a framework for evaluation* Occasional Papers No. 4 (Edinburgh: University of Edinburgh, undated)

Hartman, G. *The Unmediated Vision* (New York: Harcourt, 1966)

Hartman, G. *Saving the Text* (Baltimore and London: Johns Hopkins University Press, 1981)

Hasek, J. *The Stories of the Good Soldier Svejk* (Harmondsworth: Penguin, 1990)

Heaney, S. *Death of a Naturalist* (London: Faber, 1966)

Heaney, S. *Wintering Out* (London: Faber, 1972)

Heaney, S. 'Feeling into Words' in his *Preoccupations: Selected Prose 1968–1978* (London: Faber, 1980, 41–60)

Heaney, S. *The Government of the Tongue* (London: Faber, 1988)

Heidegger, M. *Being and Time*, trans. J. Macquarrie and E. Robinson (Oxford: Basil Blackwell, 1990)

Hemingway, E. *A Farewell to Arms* (London: Penguin Books, 1964)

Herbert, G. *Poems*, D. J. Enright (ed.) (London: Everyman, 1997)

Hillis Miller, J. 'Wallace Stevens' Poetry of Being' in R.H. Pearce and J. Hillis Miller (eds) *The Act of the Mind: Essays on the poetry of Wallace Stevens* (Baltimore: Johns Hopkins Press, 1965)

Hirsch, E.D. Jr. *Validity in Interpretation* (New Haven, Connecticut: Yale University Press, 1967)

hooks, b. *Yearning: Race, Gender, and Cultural Politics* (Boston: South End Press, 1990)

Hopkins, G. M. *Poems*, R. Bridges (ed.) (London: Oxford University Press, 1938)

Hopkins, G.M. *The Notebooks and Papers* H. House (ed.) (London and New York: Oxford University Press, 1937)

Hopkins, G.M. *Poems and Prose*, H. Gardner (ed.) (Harmondsworth: Penguin, 1979)

Hopwood, M. *Singing in Chains: Listening to Welsh Verse* (Llandysul: Gomer, 2004)

Hughes, T. *Moortown* (London: Faber, 1979)

Hughes, T. *River* (London: Faber, 1983)

Hume, D. *Enquiries Concerning Human Understanding and Concerning the Principles of Morals* (Oxford: Clarendon Press, 1989)

Hume, D. *A Treatise of Human Nature* (Oxford: Clarendon, 1990)

Hunt, C. *Therapeutic Dimensions of Autobiography in Creative Writing* (London: Jessica Kingsley, 2000)

Hunt, C. 'Reading Ourselves: Imagining the Reader in the Writing Process' in G. Bolton et al (eds) *Writing Cures* (London: Brunner-Routledge, 2004a)

Hunt, C. 'Writing and Reflexivity: Training to Facilitate Creative Writing for Personal Development' in F. Sampson (ed.) *Creative Writing in Health and Social Care* (London: Jessica Kingsley, 2004b)

Hunt, C. and Sampson, F. *The Self on the Page: Theory and Practice of Creative Writing in Personal Development* (London: Jessica Kingsley, 1998)

Huxley, M. and Witts, N. (eds) *The Twentieth Century Performance Reader* (London: Routledge, 2002)

Irigaray, L. *Ce sexe qui n'en est pas un* (Paris: Minuit, 1977)

Irigaray, L. *Speculum of the Other Woman*, trans. G.C. Gill (New York: Cornell, Ithaca, 1985)

Irigaray, L. 'Questions to Emmanual Levinas'. trans. M. Whitford in M. Whitford (ed.) *The Irigaray Reader* (Oxford: Basil Blackwell, 1991, 178–189)

Irigaray, L. *The Irigaray Reader*, M. Whitford (ed.) (Oxford: Basil Blackwell, 1991)

Iser, W. *The Act of Reading* (Baltimore and London: Johns Hopkins University Press, 1978)

Iser, W. *The Implied Reader* (Baltimore and London: Johns Hopkins University Press, 1980)

Jacobus, M. *Psychoanalysis and the Scene of Reading* (Oxford: Oxford University Press, 1999)

Jack, I. 'Introduction' in *Granta: The First Twenty-one Years* (London: Granta, 2001, vii–ix)

Jones, A.R. (1981) 'Writing the Body: Toward an Understanding of *l'Écriture Feminine*' in R.R. Warhol and D.P. Herndl (eds) *Feminisms* (New Brunswick, N.J.: Rutgers University Press, 1991)

Jones, B.T. 'A Conversation with Bill T. Jones' in *Ballet Review* 18(4) 73–5.

Josipovici, G. *On Trust* (New York: Yale University Press, [1999])

Jung, C.G. (1916) 'The Transcendent Function' in J. Chodorow (ed.) *Jung on Active Imagination* (Princeton, N.J.: Princeton University Press, 1997)

Kafka, F. 'Metamorphosis' in *Metamorphosis and Other Stories* (Harmondsworth: Penguin, 1974)

Kafka, F. *The Trial* (London: Gollancz, 1935)

Kafka, F. *The Castle* (London: Secker and Warburg, 1953)

Kafka, F. *The Diaries of Franz Kafka 1910–23* (Harmondsworth: Penguin, 1978)

Kaplinski, J. *Evening Brings Everything Back*, trans. the author with F. Sampson, (Newcastle upon Tyne: Bloodaxe, 2004)

Kavaler-Adler, S. *The Compulsion to Create: A Psychoanalytic study of Women Artists* (New York and London, Routledge, 1993)

Kearney, R. *Dialogues with Contemporary Continental Thinkers* (Manchester: Manchester University Press, 1984)

Kearney, R. *On Stories* (London: Routledge, 2002)

Keats, J. (1947) *The Letters of John Keats*, M.B. Forman (ed.) (London and New York: Oxford University Press)

Kelman, J. *How Late it Was, How Late* (London: Secker and Warburg, 1994)

King, B. *Derek Walcott: A Caribbean Life* (Oxford: Oxford University Press, 2000)

Klein, M. *The Selected Melanie Klein*, J. Mitchell (ed.) (Harmondsworth: Penguin, 1986)

Kocsther, A. *The Act of Creation* (London: Pan 1977)

Kosinski, J. 'Notes of the Author on *The Painted Bird*' in *Passing By: Selected Essays 1960–1991* (New York: Random House, 1992)

Kristeva, J. *Pouvoirs de l'horreur* (Paris: Éditions de Seuil, 1980)

Kristeva, J. 'The Bounded Text' in her *Desire in Language*, trans. T. Gora et al (London: Blackwell, 1984a)

Kristeva, J. *Revolution in Poetic Language*, trans. L.S. Roudiez (New York: Columbia University Press, 1984b)

Kundera, M. *The Unbearable Lightness of Being*, trans. M.H. Heim (London and Boston: Faber and Faber, 1985)

Kundera, M. *The Art of the Novel* (London and Boston: Faber and Faber, 1990)

Lacan, J. *Les quatre concepts fondamentaux de psychanalyse 1964*, J-A. Miller (ed.) (Paris: Éditions de Seuil, 1973, vol. xi)

Lacan, J. *Ecrits: a Selection*, trans. A. Sheridan (London: Routledge, 1977)

Laclos. *Les Liasons Dangereuses*, trans. Helen Constantine (ed.) (Harmondsworth: Penguin, 2005)

Lakoff, G. and Johnson, M. *Philosophy in the Flesh* (New York: Basic Books, 1999)

Laland, K.N. and Brown, G.R. *Sense and Nonsense: Evolutionary Perspectives on Human Behaviour* (Oxford: Oxford University Press, 2002)

dir. Langton, S. *Pride and Prejudice* (London: BBC Worldwide, 1995)

Laplanche, J. and Pontalis, J-B. *The Language of Psychoanalysis*, trans. D. Nicholson-Smith (London: Karnac Books & The Institute of Psychoanalysis, 1988)

Lappin, E. 'The Man With Two Heads' in *Granta 66: Truth and Lies* (London: Granta, 1999)

Lecoq, J. in collaboration with Carasso, J-G. and Lallias, J-C. *The Moving Body: Teaching Creative Theatre*, trans. D. Bradby (London: Methuen, 2000)

Lee, L. *Cider with Rosie* (London: The Hogarth Press, 1959)

Lee, L. *As I Walked Out One Midsummer Morning* (London: Deutsch, 1969)

Lejune, P. *On Autobiography* (Minneapolis: University of Minnesota Press, 1989)

Lessing, D. *The Golden Notebook* (London: Flamingo, 2002)

Lessing, D. *The Grass is Singing* (London: Flamingo, 2002)

Levi, P. *If This is a Man*, trans. S. Woolf (London/New York: Orion Press, 1959)

Levi, P. *The Periodic Table*, trans. M. Rosenthal (London: Michael Joseph, 1985)

Levin, J.D. *Theories of the Self* (Washington: Hemisphere Publishing Corporation, 1992)

Levinas, E 'Reality and its Shadow' in Lingis (ed.) *Collected Philosophical Papers* (Dordrecht: Martinus Nijhoff, 1987, 1–13)

Levinas, E. *The Levinas Reader*, S. Hand (ed.) (Oxford: Basil Blackwell, 1989)

Levine, G. (ed.) *Constructions of the Self* (New Brunswick, New Jersey: Rutgers University Press, 1992)

Lewis, G. *Parables and Faxes* (Newcastle upon Tyne: Bloodaxe, 1995)

Litt, T. *Finding Myself* (London: Hamish Hamilton, 2003)

Locke, J. *An Essay Concerning Human Understanding* (Oxford: Oxford University Press, 1975)

Lodge, D. *After Bakhtin* (London: Routledge, 1990)

Lodge, D. *Consciousness and the Novel* (London: Secker and Warburg, 2002)

Lomas, H. *Letters in the Dark* (Oxford: Oxford University Press, 1986)

Lyons, P. (1999) 'Who is the I in this poem?' *Auto/Biography* 7, Nos. 1 and 2, 77–82.

Lyotard, J-J. 'Answering the Question: What is Postmodernism' in I. Hassan and S. Hassan (eds) *Innovation/Renovation* (Madison WI: University of Wisconsin Press, 1983, 71–82)

Lyotard, J-J. trans. G. Bennington and B. Masumi *The Postmodern Condition* (Manchester: Manchester University Press, 2001)

Mace, J. *The Give and Take of Writing: Scribes, Literacy and Everyday Life* (Leicester: Niace, 2002)

dir. Maguire, S. *Bridget Jones* (Los Angeles: Columbia Tristar, 2001)

MacIntyre, A. *After Virtue: A Study in Moral Theory* (Notre Dame: University of Notre Dame, 1984)

Marangou, N. 'St Catherine' in F. Sampson (ed.) *Orient Express 4: Where are we going?* (Oxford 2003, 198)

Marks, E. and de Courtivron, I. *New French Feminisms: An Anthology* (Hemel Hempstead: Harvester Wheatsheaf, 1981)

Mayle, P. *Toujours Provence* (Harmondsworth: Penguin, 2001)

Mazza, N. *Poetry Therapy: Interface of the arts and psychology* (New York: CRC Press, 1999)

McCall, G.J. 'The Social Looking-Glass: a sociological perspective on self-development' in T. Mischel (ed.) *The Self: Psychological and Philosophical Issues* (Oxford: Blackwell, 1977)

McHale, B. *Postmodernist Fiction* (London and New York: Routledge, 1987)

Mead, G.H. *Mind, Self and Society* (Chicago: Chicago University Press, 1934)

Merleau-Ponty, *Phenomenology of Perception*, trans. C. Smith (London: Routledge and Kegan Paul, 1962)

Middlebrook, D. *Her Husband: Ted Hughes and Sylvia Plath – A Marriage* (Harmondsworth: Penguin, 2004)

Miller, N. 'Changing the Subject: authorship, writing and the reader' in M. Biriotti and N. Miller (eds) *What is an Author?* (Manchester: Manchester University Press, 1993)

Milner, M. *A Life of One's Own* (Harmondsworth: Penguin, 1952)

Milner, M. *On Not Being Able to Paint* (Oxford: Heinemann, 1971)

Milner, M. 'The Framed Gap' in her *The Suppressed Madness of Sane Men* (London: Tavistock, 1987, 79–82)

Modell, A. *Imagination and the Meaningful Brain* (Cambridge, Mass, and London: MIT Press, 2003)

Moggach, D. 'Fleshing My Characters' in C. Boylan (ed.) *The Agony and the Ego: The Art and Strategy of Fiction Writing Explored* (London: Penguin Books, 1993, 131–40)

Morrison, B. *And When Did You Last See Your Father?* (London: Granta, 1993)

Morrison, T. *Beloved* (New York: Vintage, 1997)

Morrison, B. *As If* (London: Granta, 1998)

Morrison, B. *Things My Mother Never Told Me* (London: Vintage, 2003)

Morson, G.S. *Hidden in Plain View: Narrative and creative potentials in 'War and Peace'* (Aldershot: Scholar Press, 1987)

Morson, G.S. and Emerson, C. *Mikhail Bakhtin: Creation of a Prosaics* (Stanford: Stanford University Press, 1990)

Müller, H. *The Land of Green Plums* (London: Granta, 1998)

Murdoch, I. *The Sea, The Sea* (Harmondsworth: Penguin, 1989)

Murdoch, I. *Jackson's Dilemma* (London: Chatto and Windus, 1995)

Murphy, R. *The Body Silent* (New York: Norton, 1990)

Murray, L. *Fredy Neptune* (Manchester: Carcanet, 1998)

Nabokov, V. 'Problems of Translation: *Onegin* in English', *Partisan Review* 22, 1955, 496–512.

Nabokov, V. *Pnin* (New York: Vintage, 1989)

Nakamura, F. extracts from *Yameru Mahima* (*The Bald Primadonna*) (Tokyo 1997) trans. A. Or in *Helicon Magazine* Vol 29, 1999: *The Body*, 60–2

Neisser, U. 'Five Kinds of Self-knowledge' *Philosophical Psychology* 1, No. 1, 1988, 33–58.

Nelles, W. 'Historical and Implied Authors and Readers' *Comparative Literature* 45, 1993 22–46.

Nettle, D. *Strong Imagination: Madness, Creativity and Human Nature* (Oxford: Oxford University Press, 2001)

Nichols, G. *The Fat Black Woman's Poems* (London: Virago, 1984)

Nicholls, S. *Writing the Body: Ways in which creative writing can facilitate the expression of a bodily felt sense of self*, unpublished DPhil thesis (University of Sussex, in preparation)

Nietzsche, F. *Ecce Homo*, trans. R.J. Hollingdale (Harmondsworth: Penguin, 1979)

Nolan, C. *Under the Eye of the Clock* (London: Weidenfeld and Nicolson, 1987)

Nye, A. *Words of Power: A Feminist Reading of the History of Logic* (London: Routledge, 1990)

Oates, J.C. *Black Water* (London: Picador, 1994)

Oates, J.C. *Blonde* (New York: Ecco Press, 2001)

O'Brien, J. 'A Simple Question: Why are there so few literary translations published each year in the United States, and what can be done about this cultural travesty?' in *Context: A forum for literary arts and culture* (Normal, Illinois: Center for Book Culture, 2003, 47)

O'Hanlon, A. *The Talk of the Town* (London: Sceptre, 1999)

Okri, B. *Famished Road* (London: Vintage, 1992)

Olshen, B. 'The Self' *In Encyelopedia of Life History*, (ed.) M. Jolly (London and Chicago: Fitzroy Dearbom Publishers, 2001, pp. 799–801)

Ong, W. 'The Writer's Audience is Always a Fiction', in his *Interfaces of the Word: Studies in the Evolution of Consciousness and Culture* (Ithaca and London: Cornell University Press, 1977, pp. 53–81)

Ortega y Gasset, J. 'The Misery and Splendour of Translation', trans. E. Gamble Miller in R. Schulte and J. Biguenet (eds) *Theories of Translation: An Anthology of Essays from Dryden to Derrida* (Chicago: University of Chicago Press, 1992, 93–112)

Orwell, G. *Keep the Aspidistra Flying* (Harmondsworth: Penguin 2000)

Oswald, A. *Dart* (London: Faber, 2002)

Oz, A. *The Same Sea*, trans. N. de Lange (London: Chatto and Windus, 2001a)

Oz, A. 'Amos Oz in Interview with Melvyn Bragg' (London: ITV, The South Bank Show, 4th March 2001b)

Pachet, P. 'Le temps qui reste' in N. Czehowski (ed.) *La curiosité* (Paris: Éditions Autrement, 1993, 17–32)

Palmer, A. *Fictional Minds* (London and Lincoln, Nebraska: University of Nebraska Press, 2004)

Palmieri, G. '"The Author" according to Bakhtin, and Bakhtin the Author' in D. Shepherd (ed.) *The Contexts of Bakhtin.* (Amsterdam: Harwood, 45–56)

Paris, B.J. *Experiments in Life: George Eliot's Quest for Values* (Detroit: Wayne State University Press, 1965)

Paris, B.J. *Character as Subversive Force in Shakespeare: The History and Roman Plays* (Rutherford, NJ: Fairleigh Dickinson University Press, 1991a)

Paris, B.J. *Bargains with Fate: Psychological Crises and Conflicts in Shakespeare and his Plays* (New York: Plenum Press, 1991b)

Paris, B.J. *Imagined Human Beings: A Psychological Approach to Character and Conflict in Literature* (New York: New York University Press, 1997)

Paris, B.J. *Re-reading George Eliot: Changing Responses to her Experiments in Life* (New York: State University of New York Press, 2003)

Passmore, J. *The Perfectibility of Man* (London: Duckworth, 1970)

Peever, A. and Sampson, F. *Riddle* (Wycombe Borough Council, 1997)

Perec, G. *A Void*, trans. G. Adair (London: Harvill, 1996)

Pfenninger, K.H. and Shubik, V.R. (eds) *The Origins of Creativity* (Oxford: Oxford University Press, 2001)

Phillips, C. *The Final Passage* (London: Picador, 1995)

Pirandello, L. *Six Characters in Search of an Author and Other Plays*, trans. M. Musa (London: Penguin Books, 1995)

Pirandello, L. 'Sincerità e arte', *Il Marzocco*, 1897.

Plato, *The Republic*, trans. H.D.P. Lee (Harmondsworth: Penguin, 1965)

Plato, trans. Grube, G.M.A. *Five Dialogues: Euthyphro, Apology, Crito, Meno, Phaedo* (New York: Hackett, 2002)

Poe, E.A. 'The Philosophy of Composition' in *Selected Writings of Edgar Allan Poe*, D. Galloway (ed.) (Harmondsworth: Penguin, 1967, 480–492)

Polo, M. *The Travels of Marco Polo* (London: Wordsworth Classics, 1997)

Pope, R. *Textual Intervention* (London: Routledge, 1995)

Pope, R. *Creativity: History, Theory, Practice* (London and New York: Routledge, 2005)

van der Post, L. *Testament to the Bushmen* (Harmondsworth: Penguin, 1985)

Poulet, G. 'Criticism and the Experience of Interiority' in *The Structuralist Controversy*, R.A. Macksey and E. Donato (eds) (Baltimore: Johns Hopkins University Press, 1972, 56–72)

Powell, A. *To Keep the Ball Rolling* (Chicago: University of Chicago Press, 2001)

Powell, A. *A Dance to the Music of Time* (12 volumes: Chicago: University of Chicago Press, 1995)

Prince, G. 'Introduction to the Study of the Narratee' in J.P. Tompkins (ed.) *Reader-Response Criticism* (Baltimore and London: Johns Hopkins University Press, 1980, 7–25)

Prokopiev, A. 'Aunts', 'Three Oxfordshire Gardens' and 'Ethica Anthropofagon', trans. the author with F. Sampson in *Orient Express* 1–2, Autumn 2002, 51–9.

Proust, M. *In Search of Lost Time, Time Regained and Guide*, trans. C. K. Scott Moncrieff, T. Kilmartin & D. J. Enright (eds) (6 volumes: London: Vintage, 1996)

Qualley, D. *Turns of Thought: Teaching Composition as Reflexive Inquiry* (London: Heinemann, 1997)

Rabinowitz, P. J. 'Whirl Without End: Audience-Oriented Criticism' in G.D. Atkins and L. Morrow (eds) *Contemporary literary Theory* (London: Macmillan, 1989, 81–100)

Rabinowitz, P. J. (1977) 'Truth in Fiction: A Reexamination of Audiences' *Critical Inquiry* 4, 1, 121–142.

Ratushinskaya, I. 'No, I'm Not Afraid' in *No, I'm Not Afraid*, trans. D. McDuff (Newcastle upon Tyne: Bloodaxe, 1986, 137)

Rawls, J. *A Theory of Justice* (Oxford: Oxford University Press, 1976)

Reitman, dir, 1994 *Junior*

Rhys, J. *Wide Sargasso Sea* (Harmondsworth: Penguin, 1980)

Rich, A. *Adrienne Rich's Poetry and Prose*, B. Charlesworth Gelpi and A. Gelpi (eds) (New York and London: W.W. Norton & Co, 1975)

Richardson *Clarissa*, A. Ross (ed.) (Harmondsworth: Penguin, 1986)

Riding, L. 'Because of Clothes' in *The Poems of Laura Riding* (Manchester: Carcanet, 1980, 285)

Riley, D. 'A Short History of Some Preoccupations' in J. Butler and J.W. Scott (eds) *Feminists Theorise the Political* (London: Routledge, 1992, 121–129)

Rimmon-Kenan, S. *Narrative Fiction: Contemporary Poetics* (London and New York: Routledge, 1996)

Roe, S. 'Shelving the Self' in S. Roe et al, *The Semi-Transparent Envelope* (London and New York: Marion Boyars, 1994, 47–92)

Rose, G. *The Broken Middle* (Oxford: Basil Blackwell, 1992)

Rose, J. *The Haunting of Sylvia Plath* (London: Virago 1991)

Rose, J. *Albertine* (London: Vintage, 2002)

Rostand, De E. *Cyrano de Bergerac*, trans. C. Fry in N. Cronk (ed.) (London: Dover, 2000)

Rousseau, J. *The Social Contract and Discourses*, trans. G.D.H. Cole, revised and augmented J. H. Brumfitt & J. C. Hall (London: J. M. Dent, 1986)

Rousseau, J. *The Confessions*, trans. J. M. Cohen (Harmondsworth: Penguin, 1988)

Roy, A. *The God of Small Things* (London: Flamingo, 1998)

Royle, N. *Derrida* (London: Routledge, 2003)

Ruskin, J. from *Modern Painters* in C. Wilmer (ed.) *Unto this Last and other writings* (Harmondsworth: Penguin, 1985, 141–154)

Ruthven, M. *A Satanic Affair: Salman Rushdie and the Wrath of Islam* (London: Hogarth Press, 1991)

El-Sadaawi, N. *God Dies by the Nile* (London: Zed Books, 1985)

Said, E. *Orientalism: Western Concepts of the Orient* (Harmondsworth: Penguin, 2003)

St Augustine. *Confessions* (London: Dover, 2002)

St. John of the Cross. *Poems*, trans. R. Campbell (Harmondsworth: Penguin, 1960)

St Teresa. *The Life of St Teresa of Ávila by Herself*, trans. J.M. Cohen (Harmondsworth: Penguin, 1958)

Salinger, J.D. *Catcher in the Rye* (London: Hamish Hamilton, 1951)

Sampson, F. 'Thinking About Language As a Way Through the Would: Some Sources for a Model' in Hunt and Sampson 1998, pp. 129–141

Sampson, F. *The Healing Word* (London: Poetry Society, 1999)

Sampson, F. 'North/South: A Poetic Palimpsest of the Mediterranean?' in *Symposium Proceedings: 'East/West: The Poetic Palimpsest of the Mediterranean'* (Macedonia: Struga International Poetry Nights, 2003)

Sampson, F. *Creative Writing in Health and Social Care* (London: Jessica Kingsley, 2004)

Sampson, F. 'A topical and urgent matter: David and Helen Constantine on the new *Modern Poetry in Translation*' in *Poetry London*, Autumn, 2004b.

Sand, G., Flaubert, G. and Eyre, R. *Chère Maitre*, trans. F. Steegmuller (London: Absolute Classics, 2003)

Sansom, P. *Writing Poems* (Newcastle upon Tyne: Bloodaxe, 1994)

Sartre, J-P. *Qui est-ce que la literature?* (Paris: Gallimard, 1948)

Sartre, J-P. *Words*, trans. I. Clephane (Harmondsworth: Penguin, 1967)

Saussure, F. de *Cours de linguistique générale* (Paris: Payot, 1973)

Scarry, E. *Dreaming by the Book* (New York: Farrar, Straus, Giroux, 1999)

Schama, S. *Landscape and Memory* (London: Harper Collins, 1996)

Schaverein, J. *The Revealing Image: Analytical Art Psychotherapy in Theory and Practice* (London: Jessica Kingsley, 1999)

Schlemmer, O. 'Man and Art Figure' in W. Gropius and A. Weisinger (eds) *The Theater of the Bauhaus* (Middletown, Connecticut: Wesleyan University Press, 1961, 17–32)

Scholes. R. and Kellogg, R. *The Nature of Narrative* (New York: Oxford University Press, 1966)

Sebald, W.G. *Austerlitz*, trans. A. Bell (Harmondsworth: Penguin, 2001)

Shakespeare, W. *The Tempest* (1611)

Shakespeare, W. 'Sonnet 18' in P. Alexander (ed.) *Complete Works* (London and Glasgow: Collins, 1971, 1311)

Shelley, P.B. 'A Defence of Poetry' in *The Major Works*, Z. Leader and M. O'Neill (eds) (Oxford: Oxford University Press, 2003)

Shields, C. *Unless* (London: Fourth Estate, 2003)

Simmonds, P. 'Paradise' *The Guardian Review* 29/05/04, 3.

Simpson, R. *The Feeling of Colour and Sound: a study in the light of the works of J.M.W. Turner and G.M. Hopkins* (unpublished MA thesis, University of Sussex, 2003)

Smith, A. *The Wealth of Nations* (London: Bantam Classics, 2003)

Solomon, N. *Judaism: A very short introduction* (Oxford: Oxford University Press, 2000)

Sommer, D. 'Textual Conquests: on readerly competence and minority literature' in *Modern Language Quarterly* 54, 1, 1994, 523–51.

Spivak, G.C. 'The Politics of Translation' in L. Venuti (ed.) *The Translation Studies Reader* (London: Routledge, 2000, 397–416)

Sprinker, M. *A Counterpoint of Dissonance: The aesthetics and poetry of Gerard Manley Hopkins* (Baltimore and London: Johns Hopkins University Press, 1980)

Stern, D. *The Interpersonal World of the Infant* (London: Karnac Books, 1998)

Stevens, R. (ed.) *Understanding the Self* (London: Sage, 1996)

Stevens, W. *Selected Poems* (London: Faber and Faber, 1965)

Stevenson, R. *Modernist Fiction* (London: Prentice Hall, 2nd ed. 1998)

Stockwell, P. *Cognitive Poetics: An Introduction* (London: Routledge 2002)

Strand, M. *Selected Poems* (Manchester: Carcanet, 1995)

Swift, G. *Last Orders* (London: Picador, 1997)

Tar, S. *A mi utcánk* (Our Street) (Budapest: Magvéto, 1995)

Taylor, C. *Sources of the Self* (Cambridge: Cambridge University Press, 1992)

Terkel, S. *Hope Dies Last* (London: Granta, 2004)

Tighe, C. *Writing and Responsibility* (London: Routledge, 2005)

Tolstoy. L. *Anna Karenina*, trans. R. Pevear and L. Volokhonsky (eds) (Harmondsworth: Penguin, 2001)

Tolstoy, L. *The Kingdom of God is Within You: Christianity not as a Mystic Religion but as a New Theory of Life*, trans. C. Garnett (Lincoln, Neb.: University of Nebraska Press, 1984)

Turner, R.H. 'The Real Self: from institution to impulse' *American Journal of Sociology* 81, 1976, 989–1016.

Tusa, J. *On Creativity: Interviews Exploring the Process* (London: Methuen, 2003)

Ugresic, D. *Thank You for Not Reading*, trans. C. Hawkesworth (Normal, Illinois: Dalkey Archive Press, 2003)

Vaughan, H. *Complete Poetry* (New York: W.W. Norton, 1969)

Venuti, L. (ed.) *The Translation Studies Reader* (London: Routledge, 2003)

Voloshinov, V.N. *Marxism and the Philosophy of Language*, trans. L. Matejka and I.R. Titunik (Cambridge, Mass.: Harvard University Press, 1973)

Voltaire, F.M.A. *Philosophical Dictionary*, trans. T. Besterman (ed.) (Harmondsworth: Penguin, 1972)

Walcott, D. *Omeros* (London: Faber, 1990)

Walker, A. *In Search of our Mothers' Gardens* (London: Virago, 1984)

Walker, C. 'Feminist Literary Criticism and the Author' *Critical Inquiry* 16, Spring 1990, 551–71.

Weldon, F. *The Life and Loves of a She-Devil* (London: Sceptre, 1993)

Welsh, I. *Filth* (London: Jonathan Cape, 1998)

Welsh, I. *Trainspotting* (London: Vintage, 1999)

Wesling, D. and Slawek, T. *Literary Voice* (Albany: State University of New York Press, 1995)

White, P. *The Tree of Man* (Harmondsworth: Penguin, 1965)

Wilkomirski, B. *Fragments* (New York: Random House, 1998)

Will and Grace (Contender Entertainment, 2001)

Willey, B. *Nineteenth Century Studies* (London: Chatto and Windus, 1950)

Williams, R. 'Argument: Text and performance' in *Drama in Performance* (Harmondsworth: Penguin, 1972, 170–188)

Williams, R. *The Country and the City* (London: The Hogarth Press, 1993)

Wimsatt, W.K. Jr. and Beardsley, M.C. 'The Intentional Fallacy' in *The Verbal Icon: Studies in the Meaning of Poetry* (Lexington, Kentucky: University of Kentucky Press, 1954)

Winnicott, D.W. 'The Capacity to be alone' (1958) in his *Maturational Processes and the Facilitating Environment* (New York: International Universities Press, 1965)

Winnicott, D.W. 'Ego Distortions in Terms of True and False Self' (1960) in his *Maturational Processes and the Facilitating Environment* (New York: International Universities Press, 1965)

Winnicott, D.W. *Playing and Reality* (London: Tavistock Publications, 1971)

Winterson, J. *The Passion* (Harmondsworth: Penguin, 1987)

Winterson, J. *Sexing the Cherry* (London: Vintage, 1990)

Winterson, J. *The PowerBook* (London: Vintage, 2001)

Wollheim, R. 'Minimal Art' in his *On Art and the Mind* (Cambridge, Mass.: Harvard University Press, 1974, 101–111)

Wolosky, S. 'Samuel Beckett's Figural Evasions' in S. Budick and W. Iser (eds) *Languages of the Unsayable: The Play of Negativity in Literature and Literary Theory* (Stanford CA: Stanford University Press, 1987, 165–186)

Woolf, V. *A Room of One's Own* (London: Grafton, 1985)

Woolf, V. 'Women and Fiction' in D. Cameron (ed.) *The Feminist Critique of Language* (London: Routledge, 1990, 33–40)

Woolf, V. *Mrs Dalloway* (Oxford: Oxford University Press, 1992)

Woolf, V. 'A Mark on the Wall' in her *Selected Short Stories* (Harmondsworth: Penguin, 1993, 53–60)

Woolf, V. *The Hours: The Full British Museum Manuscript of Mrs Dalloway* (Lanham, MD: University Press of America, 1996)

Wordsworth, W. 'Preface to Lyrical Ballads' in F. Kermode, J. Hollander, H. Bloom & L. Trilling (eds) *The Oxford Anthology of English Literature Volume II* (Oxford: Oxford University Press, 1973, 592–611)

Yashin, M. (ed.) *Step-Mothertongue: From Nationalism to Multiculturalism: Literatures of Cyprus, Greece and Turkey* (London: Middlesex University Press, 2000)

Yhuel, I. 'En pays de connaissance' in N. Czehowski (ed.) *La curiosité: les veriges du savoir* (Paris: Éditions Autrement, 1993, 34–49)

Young, I.M. '"Throwing like a Girl": A Phenomenology of Feminine Body Comportment, Motility and Spatiality' in J. Allen and I.M. Young (eds) *The Thinking Muse: Feminism and Modern French Philosophy* (Bloomington and Indianapolis: Indiana University Press, 1989 51–70)

Zadura, B. 'I'm Withdrawing from Life', trans. T. Pióro in F. Sampson (ed.) *Orient Express Vol 6, Autumn 2004*, 132–157.

Index